THE STREETS OF POMPEII

Henry Reed

The Streets of Pompeii

and other plays for radio

British Broadcasting Corporation

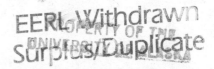

Published by the
British Broadcasting Corporation
35 Marylebone High Street
London WIM 4AA
SBN 563 10164 4
First published 1971
© Henry Reed 1970
Printed in England by
Adlard and Son Ltd, Bartholomew Press, Dorking

Contents

Foreword

These scripts were all written a long time ago. They were not, for the most part, written with any idea that they might appear in print. When it was suggested that they should, I was naturally delighted: it seemed to be implied that they had not entirely gone in one ear and out of the other. And though I am in no way a perfectionist, I was glad of what seemed to be a fresh opportunity of emendation, revision and improvement of the texts themselves. After all, I had seemed to manage such alterations, sometimes to the extent of large-scale rewriting, whenever the things had been given, as most of them had, completely new productions. But now, alas, at this late date, even when I have been disconsolate at what I have seen on the pages in front of me, I have found that apart from an occasional correction, deletion, restoration, or removal of thoughtless anachronism, I have not been able to do much to make them better.

It is not simply a question of distance in time; it is not that it is impossible to recapture an earlier style, for after all it *is* possible to do so. It is at once altogether cruder and subtler than this. Any form of dramatic writing, however magical his initial solitude may be for the dramatist, is written with the ultimate idea of collaboration; and it is perhaps most pleasant when he has clear hopes of who his eventual collaborators may be. But in radio, once the script has been acted, it is no longer entirely one's own. The actors have departed, and unconsciously taken away odd, unfinished bits of the author's self with them, in a way that can never be so in the theatre. *Real* plays (as I still think of plays for the theatre) are never the sole property of their original company of players: if they have in themselves any power of survival, they will be done by many other companies, and perhaps done in many different ways. With radio, however seriously one has worked on the script itself, however delightful the experience of rehearsals and presentation may have been, the thing has, as a rule, been done once for all. I am myself lucky in having been given many chances for second, or even third, thoughts. But this is by no means the same as what is offered to a play during its comparatively prolonged rehearsals, and its possible 'run', in the theatre: through these, a 'definitive' text may eventually be attained, and attained within a reasonable time. It is, for me at any rate, difficult to conceive that any work of the kind proffered here can ever achieve this. The things are neither plays nor poems (and I have never accepted the word 'features') but I am reminded of what Valéry is said to have said of a poem: it can never be finished, it can only be relinquished. These are things I have, not always easily, and without the stimulus of my splendid casts at my side (to say nothing of the exemplary talent and patience of Douglas Cleverdon), at last come to relinquish.

As for the pieces themselves: all of them are about Italy, in one way or another, and that is why they have been grouped together. For what they are worth, they must constitute memorials, however ephemeral, to the love I have always felt for her. This has not excluded moments of irony: but what real and enduring love ever has? *Return to Naples* is wholly autobiographical; so are certain parts of *The Streets of Pompeii*. The other scripts, which all involve actual historical characters, may appear on the surface rather more learned: but the learning is, inevitably, the learning of others, which I have stolen, adapted, malformed, sometimes inverted, and almost invariably fantasised over. But the pieces are not offered as works of scholarship, and I have therefore not listed my 'sources'; for this might sometimes cause anger where I feel only gratitude. Readers who know my sources will be able to blame or pardon me accordingly.

H.R.

Leopardi
Part one: The Unblest

To Marius Goring

An early version of *The Unblest* was broadcast on 9 May 1949 in a production by Rayner Heppenstall. The version given here was first broadcast on 15 October 1950. The production was by Douglas Cleverdon and the cast was as follows:

GIACOMO LEOPARDI
  (as a boy)   *David Page*
  (as a man)   *Marius Goring*
PAOLINA, his sister
  (as a girl)   *Denise Bryer*
  (as a woman)   *Barbara Lott*
CARLO, his brother (as a boy) *Jeremy Spenser*
                   (as a man) *Derek Hart*
COUNT MONALDO LEOPARDI,
  his father   *Carleton Hobbs*
COUNTESS ADELAIDE
  LEOPARDI, his mother   *Gladys Young*
LUIGI, his brother   *Timothy Harley*
PIERFRANCESCO ('Pietruccio'),
  his youngest brother   *Sheila Moloney*
MARCHESA VIRGINIA MOSCA,
  his grandmother   *Susan Richmond*
COUNT GIACOMO LAZZARI   *Ronald Simpson*
COUNTESS GELTRUDE
  LAZZARI   *Jacqueline Thompson*
COUNT CARLO ANTICI,
  Adelaide's brother   *Malcolm Graeme*
VITTORIA LAZZARI   *Sheila Moloney*
PIETRO GIORDANI   *James McKechnie*
CATERINA   *Beryl Calder*

The date: 1808 to 1822.

(A summer morning in 1808. The watch-tower clock of Recanati is striking six. As it does so, a shutter creaks open)

Giacomo Morning, oh morning! Morning at last, oh morning,
Oh morning, morning, and it is morning again!
Soft glance across the town; long look across the watch-tower;
Bright eye on the belfry. I am ten, at last:
Ten, ten, ten. Soft glance across the town,
Do not look back; look, look, look, look at me,
The only unshuttered window in the city,
The Palazzo Leopardi: and I, the cleverest leopard,
With the softest footfall, and the sharpest ears,
Have pounced upon you, you unsuspecting morning.
I am ten at last. My birthday has come again.
Carlo is sleeping, half-way back in the night;
In her cold room Paolina is dreaming still;
Tiny Luigi lies in his feverish bed;
And my parents have not begun the day's first quarrel.
I will be Pompey, I will be Caligula . . .
Oh morning, morning, across the twittering rooftops,
Oh slumbering, umbered city, oh Recanati,
Wake! You may celebrate. I have set you free.
You may do today as you please, I shall not rebuke you.
Only do not brawl and quarrel in the morning light,
And treat your children kindly. Peace, gentle city.
In a summer morning, of thirty thousand windows,
My window alone is open. I am ten today,
And I will not think of anything but sunlight,
And I will not think of night, or the creaking wainscot,
And I will not think of masks, or of dead people,
And I will not think of monks, or my mother's anger,
And I will not think of the changes in my body,
And I will not think.
                    Bright eye on the belfry . . .
Soft glance upon me . . . I will close the shutters.
And now there are once more thirty thousand shutters,
All closed, in Recanati . . . But see, my morning lies
In honeyed ladders across the marble floor:

Ingannatore . . . I will go and wake Paolina.
   (*half-fade*)

Paolina (*fade in*) Six hundred and sixty-six, six hundred and sixty-seven,
   Six hundred and sixty-eight, six hundred and sixty-nine,
   Six hundred and seventy.
    (*door*)
                         Six hundred and seventy-one,
   Six hundred and seventy-two.

Giacomo   Paolina!

Paolina   Go away.
   Six hundred and seventy-three, six hundred and seventy-four.

Giacomo Paolina! What are you doing?

Paolina   I am counting up to a thousand.
   Six hundred and seventy-five, six hundred and seventy-six.
   And after that I shall say my prayers twice over,
   Six hundred and seventy-seven.

Giacomo   How stupid!

Paolina Six hundred and seventy-eight, six hundred and seventy-nine.

Giacomo Do stop, Paolina, don't you know what day it is?

Paolina No, and I don't care. Six hundred and eighty,
   Six hundred and eighty-one.

Giacomo   Paolina!

Paolina   Six hundred and eighty-two.

Giacomo Paolina, I will put the pillow across your mouth,
   And sit on you till you stop!

Paolina   . . . eighty-three . . . dred . . . ty-four,
   Six hundr . . .

Giacomo   You are impossible!

Paolina (*in rapid anger*)   And so are you.
   Don't be so rude. What have you come here for,
   If only to be rude? Why don't you go back to bed?

Giacomo (*in tears*) You are insufferable!

Paolina (*as before*)   So are you!
   And at your age you ought to be more courteous;
   You are two years older than . . . (*her anger collapses*)
               Why, Giacomo, it's your birthday!
   You are ten! Oh, darling, I am so sorry.
   Come and sit on my bed. I didn't forget,
   I didn't, really, I thought of it all night.

Please, please forgive me and kiss me . . .
Many happy returns of the day.

Giacomo (*wiping his eyes*)   Thank you.
I am in double numbers now.

Paolina   Where's Carlo?

Giacomo Carlo is still asleep. I didn't wake him.
There is plenty of time before mass for the council of war.

Paolina You see I have mended the drum?
(*three taps on drum*)
Carlo must try not to beat it so loudly in future.

Giacomo He is a very impetuous child.

Paolina   Giacomo . . .

Giacomo   Yes?

Paolina Giacomo: I want you to pray with me for poor Luigi.

Giacomo But we shall all pray for him at mass.

Paolina I want a special prayer from *us*. When we pray with mother,
We seem to be praying for something different.
We do not seem to be praying that he shall get well,
But only that he shall be made worthy of heaven.

Giacomo Yes.

Paolina   I love him; and I want him for *us*.
I want him only for here, for us, for ever . . .
Kneel down.

Giacomo   Mother would say that this was a selfish prayer.

Paolina I have thought how to pray.

Giacomo (*after a pause*)   I will say it after you.
(*he repeats her words in the background faintly*)

Paolina Dear Mary, Mother of God, dear Mother of Jesus,
We pray that out dear brother, Count Luigi Leopardi,
May soon get well and be restored to us,
For though eternal heaven may be better than this small earth,
Earth may be good for Luigi, who is only six.
Intercede for us, oh dear Mother of Jesus,
And make this prayer that we pray an unselfish one . . .

Giacomo And make this prayer that we pray an unselfish one.

Both Amen.

Giacomo (*thoughtfully*) Yes. I should think that might do.

Paolina Now we must wait and hope.

Giacomo You don't love Luigi more than me, do you?

Paolina You are my favourite person in all the world . . .

13

Giacomo And now I suppose I must go and wake up Carlo.

Carlo (entering) Carlo is not asleep, as a matter of fact.
It is not very easy to sleep when one's brother rises
At six o'clock to apostropofe the morning.

Giacomo I must have apostropofed it pretty loudly,
If I woke up *you*.

Carlo   As a matter of fact,
I am a very light sleeper, as a matter of fact.

Giacomo On any other day than the Royal Birthday,
Such statements would be rewarded as they deserve:
Simply, but amply.

Paolina (hastily)   But today is a day of peace.

Carlo Permit me to wish you many happy returns of the day.

Giacomo We thank you, one and all. We thank you also,
For the divers birthday presents we have received:
The embroidered handkerchief given me by Queen Paolina
Four days ago, and General Carlo's pencils,
Bestowed upon me a generous week in advance.

Carlo Better early than never, dear monarch.
They might have got rather *worn*, had I waited much longer.

Giacomo Rather *more* worn is what we suppose you to mean?

Carlo (indignantly) If you don't like . . . (stops abruptly)

Giacomo (coolly)   You were about to remark . . .?

Carlo Nothing, dear monarch, just a touch of the wind.
I *suffer* from the wind a little in the early morning,
As a matter of fact.

Paolina   So we have often noticed.

Giacomo It is time, my friends, to proceed to affairs of state.

Paolina Ah yes, yes, yes. Carlo, let us all be seated.

Giacomo Today I must reveal such new preparations
As we have decided upon against the French,
To relieve the sufferings of our bitterly oppressed province.

Carlo Death to the French! Death . . .!

Giacomo   Death to the French, you say?
And what of Austria, who would replace the French?

Carlo &
Paolina Hear, hear! Yes, death to Austria! Death to them both!

(drum)

Giacomo We speak under correction, but I think we speak for all,
When I say that a city is not made only of walls,

But is also made of men. And our city, Recanati,
Is made, I think, of that especial type of men
That do not toady to a despicable conqueror.

Carlo & ⎱
Paolina ⎰ Hear, hear!

Giacomo (*emotionally*) You will pardon me if I speak impetuously,
From a patriot's full heart, gentlemen . . .

Carlo   Go on, sir!

Giacomo Thank you. But the rulers we will bow to
Are not the rulers we are wont to see here:
The infamous scum, the degraded foreign dregs
Conscribed by an upstart Corsican!

Carlo   By God, sir!
I wish I were ten years younger, I do, sir, by God!

Paolina Carlo, dear, you must not use that expression!

Carlo I was carried away by my feelings, I promise you, madam,
As a matter of fact . . .

Giacomo There is a time, gentlemen, there is a time for words.
And there is also a time when the time for words is past.
And, that time come, it is another time!
It is a time for . . .?

Carlo   For what?

Giacomo For *deeds*, you silly bumpkin!

Carlo Deeds! Yes, I forgot deeds! Deeds! Deeds!

Paolina Deeds! Deeds! . . .

Carlo Down with the French!

Giacomo Down with the Corsican!

Paolina Down with the foreign invaders!

Carlo And a time for deeds is also the time for song!
(*sings*, nobilmente, *with drum*)

> Our fair land lay wrapt in slumber,
> Caring naught for grief and strife,

All   Till a coward braggart foeman
> Tried to change our way of life . . .

(*crescendo molto*)

> But he did not know we were ready,
> He did not know we were ready,
> He di–hid not know. He di–hid not know . . .

(*door*)

Paolina (*terrified*) Giacomo! Carlo! Stop!

(their noise dies suddenly away. There is a pause)

Adelaide Is it to disturb the priests at their morning devotions,
        Or is it to establish yourself on the level of the servants,
        That you choose to shout and sing in the early morning?
        Or is it some other device of impudence you have thought of?
Paolina It is Giacomo's birthday, mother.
Carlo   Giacomo is ten today.
Adelaide All night long your father and I have watched
        At the side of your dying brother.
Monaldo   Adelaide!
Paolina No, no, no! Father, it's not true, is it?
Adelaide Am I to speak?
Monaldo   It seems so.
Adelaide All night long your brother Luigi has lain
        At the threshold of death.
Paolina   That means he will recover!
Adelaide Through the whole of the night your father and I have prayed,
        Through the whole of the night the doctor has fidgeted and
                                fussed,
        And at the moment of God's great decision,
        We rise from our prayers to *this*!
Paolina   He will recover!
Adelaide He will recover.
Paolina *(rapturously)*   Then why don't you sing too?
        In a year he too will sing. He will be strong again.
        We shall have another brother in the palace.
        Giacomo! Carlo!
Adelaide   Is it a cause for pride,
        Is it a cause for disreputable revelry,
        That God, who drew so near to that little soul,
        Should turn His back upon him? Even today
        He might have been already one of God's angels.
Monaldo You must not talk like that in front of the children!
Adelaide The worthy doctor did what he called his best.
        'I am doing my best,' he said, 'I am doing my best.'
        But will God call it so?
Paolina   He will recover.
Adelaide God's hand, so easy to recoil, always turns back,
        Defeated by a meddling physician.

Monaldo My dear, you are overwrought; and I beg you . . .
Adelaide God's hand turns from the house; and I am again frustrated.
   I have never known that greatest blessing of mothers,
   The giving-back, the returning of the clean small soul,
   All uncontaminated into the hand of God.
Monaldo Adelaide . . .
Adelaide   Women throughout the city
   Have stillborn children, or children whom God's heart
   Cannot bear to see set to the ways of vanity,
   Degraded to the stupid postures of lust,
   Inveigled into the shifts of politicians;
   The commonest footman's wife can yield her children
   To the blessed arms of eternity, while I
   Must be forced to the dutiful administration
   Of the quackeries of doctors. I must give hourly medicines,
   Must shelter my infants from the winds of heaven
   God sends to reach for them, must nurse them back to health,
   Must help them back to a life they will havoc with sin,
   Where they will ruin family fortunes, let money go
   Squandered on emptiness and undowered marriages. Well!
   If they must come to that, if that must be
   My curious task, then I would do it; my only hope
   Would be that they should be spared the snares
   Which you call cleverness, and wit, and beauty,
   That they should not find the roads to vanity easy.
   Sooner than that, I would have them . . .
Giacomo (*shouts*)   Deaf and blind!
   (*a horrified silence. Then he cries at the top of his voice*)
   You talk so loud to keep yourself from thinking!
   You would have us deaf and blind!
   (*pandemonium*)
Monaldo⎱ Giacomo! I forbid you to speak like that!
Paolina⎰ Giacomo darling, what have you said?
 Carlo What do you mean?
Giacomo (*hysterically*) She would have us deaf and blind!
   I will say it again, I will say it to the end:
   She talks so loud to keep herself from thinking.
   (*he collapses into sobs*)
Adelaide You filthiest of children, how do you dare
   To address me in such tones and in such language?

17

Monaldo! Have you no more to do than stupidly gape,
While your wicked children trample upon their mother?

Monaldo Come, they are not trampling upon you, my dear.
Giacomo is a wicked boy and will be punished,
But I expect he was overwrought.
I think we are all a little overwrought;
Even you, I think, my dear, are a little overwrought.

Giacomo Mother, I am sorry . . .

Adelaide (*withdrawing*)   You can say so to your father.

Monaldo Go, my dear, go. I shall deal with him as he deserves.
Giacomo, you will dress and come down to the library.

Giacomo (*a whisper*) Yes, father.

Paolina Oh father, please remember it is Giacomo's birthday.

Carlo We are all to blame, father. Don't punish Giacomo, father.
I would have said the same in his position,
As a matter of fact . . . I . . . I mean . . .

Monaldo   Carlo, go to your room and dress.

Carlo Yes, father. I didn't know what I was saying. I was overwrought.

Monaldo You will dress too, Paolina.

Paolina   Yes, father.

(*pause*)

Monaldo And if we sin we must be punished, Giacomo.
Separately punished for each separate sin,
As I have always been.

Giacomo   Did you ever sin, father?

Monaldo No man is without sin, Giacomo. When I was your age,
My sins were much as yours are, almost as frequent,
And as unpardonable.

Giacomo   What were they, father?

Monaldo I was disobedient, like you.

Giacomo   To whom, father?

Monaldo To my mother, Giacomo.

Giacomo   And all the time, father?

Monaldo Not always, no.

Giacomo   But when especially, father?

Monaldo Once in my youth, Giacomo, I defied my mother.
There she sat, over there, in the chair by the window.
She filled the chair, and then in a terrible moment
The chair was empty. She had flung herself at my feet.

Whenever I look at that empty chair today,
I still expect to find her, here at my feet.
I can never blot out her tearful, imploring face.

Giacomo Imploring for what, father?

Monaldo That . . . I should not marry.

Giacomo You disobeyed her, father.

Monaldo Yes, Giacomo . . .
God's arsenals are full of recondite weapons,
And His anger is inexhaustible.

Giacomo Have you known His mercy also?

Monaldo No, Giacomo, not yet . . .

Giacomo I see, father . . .

Monaldo Your mother, my dear, is perfect.
We may not like or understand her ways,
But God will love her for them.

Giacomo So I have heard her suggest.

Monaldo It might seem better to you or to Paolina,
If we had fewer footmen, and a little more food.

Giacomo Yes, father.

Monaldo You may think it is idle to keep three coaches,
When all we use them for is to go to mass,
A distance we could very easily walk . . .

Giacomo Yes, father.

Monaldo With far less trouble than those who, in any case, have to.
And even *I* have been sometimes tempted to wonder
Why for the last three years not a single penny
Of the Leopardi exchequer has passed through my hands.
Such thoughts are sinful. The bright day dissipates them.

Giacomo I hope so, father.

Monaldo Your mother, Giacomo.
Came like a blessing into the family,
Revived us, and here we are.

Giacomo (*almost a whisper*) Yes, father, here we are.

Monaldo And we must help her in her tasks, Giacomo,

Giacomo (*sighing*) Yes, father. How is Luigi?

Monaldo (*after a pause*) Luigi will not die.
We watched all night. Suddenly in the early morning,
I looked up from my prayers, as I thought,
Until I realised I had been lightly sleeping.
And then I saw Luigi was also sleeping.

The others neither moved nor saw me. Quietly,
I stretched my hand towards his forehead; knew
That his veins once more were the veins of those who have learnt
The way, thank God, to return. And then we heard
Singing and shouting at your end of the house.

Giacomo Oh, father, how wrong and thoughtless of us.

Monaldo And when we do wrong, we must be punished, Giacomo.
You see that, now, I think?

Giacomo (*softly*)   I see that, father.

Monaldo And do you see one other thing?

Giacomo   Yes, father . . .
I see that today you do not intend to punish me.

Monaldo No, I do not. And can you imagine why?

Giacomo   No, father.

Monaldo No. The reason does not matter. I shall leave you now
To get yourself ready for mass. And I wish you a happy birthday.

Giacomo Thank you, father.
                    (*door*) Oh, father, father . . .

          (*pause*)

Carlo Giacomo.

Giacomo   Yes?

Carlo   Have you finished your lesson?

Giacomo   Yes.

Carlo Giacomo.

Giacomo   Yes?

Carlo   Are you lost in thought?

Giacomo   Yes.

Carlo   Oh . . .
          Giacomo.

Giacomo   Yes?

Carlo   Isn't it hot?

Giacomo   Yes.

Carlo Let's go up to the bedroom and open the shutters.
Perhaps 'they' will be there again.

Giacomo   You know they will.
They are always there in the afternoon at this time;
They will be sewing.

Carlo   Well, I always love to see them,
Especially the little fair one. I could watch her for ever.

Giacomo Carlo, you are getting to be a most improper boy.
If mother heard you she would say you were lecherous:
And so you are. Still, you're at a peculiar age.
Carlo Who is?
Giacomo You.
Carlo What, at *eight?* Eight isn't a peculiar age!
Eleven's the peculiar age.
Giacomo Indeed . . . ? We will go upstairs.
Don't make a noise.
(*half-fade. Pause*)

Carlo Help me, Giacomo. I can't reach the handle.
Come on. Why are you standing there?
Giacomo I don't know that I want to, after all.
Carlo Why?
Giacomo I think that I am frightened of what I feel.
Carlo Very well, then, just help me with the catch.
And then stand back from the window, will you, please?
I am quite satisfied with the way *I* feel.
Giacomo You are abominably precocious. Very well.
But I shan't stay with you.
(*catch*)
You can open the shutters yourself.
Carlo Of course I can.
(*shutters*)
Oh, what lovely heat!
I could take off all my clothes . . .
Giacomo (*from a distance*) Are they both there? . . . Carlo!
Carlo Yes, both of them. They are sewing a big green cloth.
It is half-way out of the window. Do come and see them.
Giacomo No . . . What are they wearing?
Carlo Oh, just the same black dresses.
They have slipped them down over their shoulders,
Because of the heat, I suppose. Do come and see.
Giacomo No.
Carlo Why not? Now one of them has looked up,
My one, the little fair one. She's waving to me.
Now she's bent over her work again. Now they're both looking.
Your one as well, the dark one. They are both waving.
Do you think I dare call out to them?

Giacomo (*no longer distant*)   No, never.
It would be the end of everything . . . Oh, God!
How beautiful they are . . .
(*softly*) Distant, imprisoned loves. The ancient windows.
The green cloth on the sunlit wall. Golden head, his.
Dark head, not ever mine . . . Help me, oh heaven . . .
Carlo Giacomo, you are almost crying.
Giacomo (*thickly*)   Be quiet.
Carlo Isn't it kind of them to show us their shoulders?
I wish I had shoulders like that to show to people.
Shall I show them my stomach? Yes, I will get a chair to stand on.
Giacomo Don't be ridiculous, Carlo. Put that chair *back*.
What do you think you are doing?
                    I am being perfectly reasonable:
I wish to show them my stomach.
Giacomo Put that chair back by the wall, I tell you!
I have never known anyone so stupid as you!
Carlo But, Giacomo, why shouldn't I? Let me go, Giacomo.
You never let me do anything I want. *LET ME GO!*
(*the heavy chair falls onto the marble floor. Silence. Footsteps approaching*)
Giacomo (*in a horrified whisper*) There's somebody coming!
Carlo   It will be mother.
Giacomo Hush! Oh God, not now! Don't let her find us again.
Not twice . . .
Carlo   Sh . . . !
(*door*)
Giacomo Paolina!
(*Carlo bursts into laughter*)
Giacomo (*angrily*) Carlo, be quiet!
Paolina   What is the matter?
Giacomo (*unsteadily*) Pick up that chair, Carlo; put it back by the wall.
(*to Paolina*) We thought you were mother.
Carlo   Pooh, I was not frightened.
Giacomo I daresay not. It is not your birthday.
Carlo What have birthdays to do with it?
Giacomo   Everything.
It was to have been a day for once unsacrileged.
I was to have been a king.
Paolina   You are still a king, Giacomo.

Giacomo   Now
     I want neither to be a king nor to act as one.
 Paolina Why are your wrists so hot?
Giacomo   The nerves in them are burning,
     As I see the shapeless waste slowly develop
     Of a day that was to have been a triumphal march.
     It is almost the longest day: it was made for me,
     And is being taken from me. The honouring crowds of hours
     Are scattering and dispersing about the streets;
     The cavalcade can no longer hold together.
 Paolina You will still be king tomorrow.
Giacomo (*slowly*)   I want
     Neither to be a king nor to act as one.
     I have another way of winning.
 Paolina   Winning what?
Giacomo (*calmly*) Paolina; you, I, and Carlo, and little sick Luigi,
     And our other brothers and sisters, if we have any others,
     And they are sinful enough to survive, shall any of us
     Ever be other than servile priests in a desert,
     With mother and father like two great ruined statues,
     At nightfall, at Memphis?
 Paolina   Where is Memphis?
Giacomo   In Egypt . . .
     Shall we, do you think?
 Paolina (*almost in tears*) I don't know.
Giacomo   Shall we spend our lives
     With attentive footsteps, a menace at our back,
     And inaccessible light in front of us?
     And all ways *desert*? *I* will not, Paolina.
     No, Carlo: *I* will not. I have a way of winning.
 Paolina   What way?
Giacomo The library.
  Carlo   That old place?
Giacomo (*inspired*)   I am going to know
     All the books in the world and all the languages!
     They shall know my plan; but not know where it shall lead me.
 Paolina It will need a very great deal of work.
Giacomo I am prepared for that. I am ten years old.
     I am old enough to make a decision and keep it.
     In future you and Carlo will have to find

23

Another king to lead you against the French.
I have other things to do. I shall work underground,
And rich in knowledge I shall emerge again:
Omnipotent and great.

Paolina   But, Giacomo ...

Giacomo   Yes?

Paolina Won't you ... *play* with us any more?

Giacomo   That goes, I'm afraid, without question.

Carlo Giacomo!

Giacomo (*kindly*) I shall always take the liveliest interest
In everything you do and ... (*very unsteadily*) and tell me of.
Don't ... don't let old Carlo capitulate to the French ...

Carlo Of course I shan't!

Giacomo   I might even ... if you have trouble ...
I might ... (*then, pulling himself together*)
No, Paolina and Carlo, I shan't be playing again.
This is an abdication.

Paolina   No, Giacomo, not yet.

Giacomo   It is a vow.

Paolina No, no, no!

Giacomo   It is a vow, Paolina. I had made it
Before you came into the room. I shall not break it ...
I shall see you at supper. Good-bye.

Paolina   Giacomo!

(*door. Pause*)

Carlo (*sleepily*) Giacomo ... Giacomo.

Giacomo   What?

Carlo   Why don't you come to bed?
You will go blind if you read there any longer ...
Giacomo.

Giacomo   What?

Carlo   That candle will be burnt right out in a minute.

Giacomo Well, when it is, I will come to bed. You go to sleep.
I never need sleep.

Carlo   What are you learning?

Giacomo A Greek vocabulary.

Carlo   Wouldn't it wait till tomorrow?

Giacomo Of course it would. It would wait till next week if I let it.
It is better learnt now. At this time of night

You forget the words the minute you have learnt them,
But they dance all night in your head . . . and tomorrow
The dance comes clear.

Carlo (sleepier still)   I don't believe it.

Giacomo Nevertheless it is so.

Carlo   Don't believe . . .

Giacomo The light is going . . . One last word and I . . .
I can just see the letters close to the flame.
Hypharpazo . . .

Carlo   Mean?

Giacomo (very sleepy)   I snatch away from . . .

Carlo (a whisper) Believe . . . (he sleeps)

Giacomo   Away from, snatch . . .
Hyphar . . . sleep; and in sleep am sleeping.
Dia ti hypharpasthes emou? Snatched from me, you,
Why were you snatched from me? Why are you going?
My birthdays are going, that will not come again,
And heavy lids close over the bright eye;
Snatched from me, my birthdays are all snatched from me . . .
  (pause . . . cross to echo)

Leopardi And after a few of them I shall be here to meet you

Giacomo I know you will I do not want to meet you

Leopardi I am only you

Giacomo   I know you are I do not want to meet you
I do not want to go on

Leopardi   You are going on now

Giacomo I do not want

Leopardi   I do not want to come on

Giacomo I want to stay here

Leopardi   I want to come back to you

Giacomo I want you to come back

Leopardi   I cannot come back again

Giacomo I must come on to meet you

Leopardi   You must come on again

Both   Yes

Giacomo In you for ever

Both   Yes

Leopardi   You are only and always me

Both   Yes

25

Leopardi I love you Giacomo I shall always love you
Giacomo I hate you Giacomo I shall always hate you
Leopardi You are changing Giacomo
Giacomo   Giacomo you are changing
Leopardi I do not want to come on
Giacomo   I shall always hate you
Leopardi You will hate me more than you know
Giacomo   I will try to love you
Leopardi I do not want you to love me
Giacomo   Once I did not expect you
Leopardi I always expected you
Giacomo   And I am here Giacomo
Leopardi I have always known you would come
   Both   Yes
Giacomo I must be silent Giacomo
Leopardi   Now you are here
Giacomo Now I am here Giacomo
   Both   Yes
Leopardi   You must be silent now
Giacomo I must be silent and always silent and always
Leopardi   Yes.
          (*long pause*)

          Yes, it is I. You were snatched from me away.
          I am Giacomo Leopardi; and for ever.
          Why have you gone? Why were you snatched from me?
          Dia ti hypharpasthes emou? Why *were* you?
          Sleep; and in sleep am sleeping. Hypharpazo.
            (*he is awake, and suddenly speaks bitterly and clearly*)
          Why were you snatched from me in the early morning?
          Could you not stay with me, straight and clear-eyed,
          With me for always, and not this thing I am?
          Or when you went, could you not take your fears?
   Carlo (*now a young man*) What is the matter, Giacomo?
Leopardi   What?
   Carlo   Why are you awake?
Leopardi For nothing. I am sorry. Go back to sleep.
   Carlo What time is it?
Leopardi   It is hardly morning. Go back to sleep again.
          I shall get up.

26

Carlo   Do you want me to get up with you?

Leopardi No, my dear boy. Go back to sleep.

Carlo   What is the matter, Giacomo?
Didn't you sleep well?

Leopardi   Heavily, at all events.

Carlo Don't wander about the room like that, Giacomo.
It is icy in here; and I suppose it is raining again?

Leopardi Where is the looking glass?

Carlo   Get back into bed . . .
    (*brief pause*)

Leopardi How pleased she must be with her handiwork!
If that hard heart is ever touched to delight,
How she must feel it at the sight of her eldest son!
How she must love me! And how she must hate you, Carlo,
Who have survived so far as to be tall and strong,
And who, even here, can live.

Carlo   Dear Giacomo,
Why do you torture yourself? In a blink of your eye,
There is more wisdom than there is in my whole brain,
What should the rest matter?

Leopardi   When I entered that library,
I was still a child. Those eight years might be forty,
To judge by the result. Look at me, Carlo.
Could they not break my rebellious childish vow,
And cry to me, 'Here is the sun, Giacomo, dance in it, sing!
It will only be yours for a time, enjoy it now!'

Carlo We *did* call, Giacomo: I and Paolina.

Leopardi   I heard your call.
And shooed you out of doors; across my pages
Flickered your laughter from the courtyard and the garden,
And I was never tempted.

Carlo   Never at all?

Leopardi   Not once.

Carlo No. You were never there. And Paolina,
Rebuked by your absence, at last deserted me;
Luigi was too young. You cannot pretend
I have used my solitude well.

Leopardi   You don't feel guilty, Carlo?

Carlo No, I don't think so. But you don't imagine
My escapades have anything *noble* about them?

27

Leopardi They must sometimes have rapture . . .
  Carlo   Very little.
     Would you like me to tell you about them?
Leopardi   No.
  Carlo Why do you never let me?
Leopardi   There is such a thing as envy.
  Carlo Envy! Good God! You should come with me and learn.
     I have asked you often enough.
Leopardi (*in intense anger*)   Carlo!
  Carlo Don't, Giacomo; I'm sorry. Please let me go.
Leopardi I thought you loved me, Carlo.
  Carlo   I do love you.
     More than anyone in the world, more even than Paolina.
Leopardi There is no need then that family affection,
     So rare a passion in this house, should blind you
     To what I am and what I look like. You and she
     Are all I have and hope for. There is no place *there* for deceit.
  Carlo I must go and get ready for mass. So must you.
     I will go and wake Luigi. (*fade*)

Leopardi (*after a pause*)   There in the library
     In the sound of their brave voices, I became as I am.
     Their voices stopped, I did not observe the silence,
     Till I looked up from the page and saw myself.
     The blackened hungry mouth in the yellowed face,
     The bent bone in the breast.
     (*shortly and sharply: the word can no longer be suppressed*)
           Hunchback . . .
     And that was I. And is, and will be always.

Paolina (*off*) Giacomo . . .
Leopardi   Oh, come in, Paolina. You see how vain I'm getting:
     Admiring myself in a mirror . . . Is that what you thought I was
                   doing?
Paolina Giacomo, darling, I thought nothing at all.
     Or rather, I always think of you, or most of the time,
     But not to anatomise your actions.
Leopardi Do you know what I was thinking?
Paolina   No.
Leopardi   Do you want to know?

28

Paolina *(uncertainly)* Yes . . .

Leopardi   I was wondering, Paolina,
How many people live as I do, far from their kind.

Paolina Oh, many, many people, Giacomo.

Leopardi   That was my answer too.
Does that surprise you?

Paolina   No.

Leopardi   Many, I told myself.
There are many people who live apart from their kind.
Then I went on from there. How many people, I asked,
Who spend their lives sending letters to distant friends
Whom they have never seen, come to a point
Where they have to describe more than their thoughts
                             and ambitions:
Where they have to describe *themselves?*

Paolina *(a whisper)*   Giacomo!

Leopardi And thirdly: how many of *them*
Have to describe a thing such as *I* must describe?

Paolina Giacomo, please, my darling . . .

Leopardi   Paolina!
It is *this*: this creature here you see and pity,
Whom I have to describe in my letters to Pietro Giordani.

Paolina *(tentatively)* Have you heard from Giordani lately?

Leopardi   Lately? Good God,
I have had no answer to my last three letters.
I feel utterly alone again: it is as if
The window in a tower from which I had watched
The sunlit reaches of a life I burn and crave for
Had slowly been bricked up.

Paolina   It has not been.
You will hear again from him and when you do,
In a single hour the landscape will be wider still,
Until one day there will be no tower or window:
You will be free to wander there, and leave us.

Leopardi You will come too, Paolina.

Paolina   Do you think so?

Leopardi   Yes.

Paolina You think so. Here are the others. Good morning, Carlo.
Good morning, Luigi.
    (good mornings)

Carlo (*mockingly censorious, in the accents of his mother*) Paolina!
Since when has it been becoming to a well-bred young woman
(Or rather one whom we have tried to make well-bred,
And it has been, God knows, an uphill battle)
To wander casually into gentlemen's apartments?
Luigi (*aged about thirteen*) Trying to see, no doubt, what is much better
hidden.

Paolina It *would* be much better hidden if only it were.
Let me fasten your awful cassock, you stupid baby.
Luigi It is the latest *fashion* in cassocks, didn't you know?
'Seductive model for the well-groomed novice.
And in size eighteen for cardinals and archbishops.'
I expect Giacomo's old Giordani wears his like this.
Carlo It is odd to think that Giordani is a priest.
Leopardi I never remember it. And he is hardly *old* Giordani.
He is only forty-four.
Luigi   The bloom of youth. of course.
Shall we have to wear these things tomorrow?
Paolina Why not?
Luigi   Visitors, darling.
Leopardi   What visitors?
Luigi Can you have forgotten? The Lazzaris are coming.
Carlo God, so they are.
Luigi   And today we have Grannie for dinner.
Carlo What an eviscerating round of gaiety we move in, don't we?
Luigi I have never seen the Lazzaris, have I?
Paolina None of us have, I think.
Carlo   I have seen Uncle Lazzari.
He was enormously fat.
Paolina   Have you seen them, Giacomo?
Leopardi No. And I shall not see them now.
Luigi   Why not?
Leopardi I shall stay up here. I shall stay up here and work.
I have no wish to see any visitors except Giordani.
Carlo And he may never come.
Leopardi (*firmly*)   I shall stay up here, and work.
          (*half-fade. Pause*)

          (*fade in coffee-cups and Monaldo quietly clearing his throat*)
Adelaide I never know why you are so discontented.

If it is fame you want – though the best lives
Have carefully sheltered themselves from such a disaster –
You have fame in Recanati; and even if its cause
Is scarcely reputable, *you* should be pleased with that,
With your peculiar views.

Leopardi   My views are perfectly normal.

Adelaide Whatever they are, you do not get them from me;
Or from your father, I will say that for him.

Pierfrancesco (*aged four*) Perhaps he gets them from Grannie.

Monaldo   Pietruccio,
Either eat your apple, or leave it. And do not talk.

Pierfrancesco Yes, father. I would much rather eat it than leave it.

Monaldo Then do so.

Marchesa   I hardly think Giacomo gets his views from me,
Though it is an interesting suggestion on Pietruccio's part.

Leopardi I wish to be *free:* to come and go as I choose,
And where I choose. That is all.

Adelaide   Then turn to Truth,
And the Truth shall make you free. And the Truth is,
That here you are perfectly circumstanced and cared for.
No one was ever surrounded with so much love.
Your foolish brothers and sisters dote on you.
Your father even admires your so-called writings.
While I – did ever a mother care for her children as I have?
I have sheltered you from childhood, in the face
Of every wicked treachery that children can think of.
It has been an uphill battle, I can assure you.
And have I ever faltered?

Leopardi   No, mother, you have never faltered.

Adelaide Paolina, would you say that I have ever faltered?

Paolina No, mother.

Adelaide   Luigi?

Luigi   No, mother.

Adelaide   Carlo?
            (*pause*)

Carlo (*disconcertingly*) I am so little a judge of faltering, mother.
I would rather you said than I.

Pierfrancesco   Giacomo:
What is faltering?

Leopardi (*rapidly and savagely*) Faltering, my sweet Pietruccio,

31

Is lapsing, in a moment of aberration,
To indulge for a moment, for a single moment,
The desires of someone else. I hope you will do it often.

Monaldo Giacomo, I have told you repeatedly
Not to take your mother's words and falsify them!

Leopardi I am sorry, father. I am very sorry, mother.
Perhaps it was Truth that made me free for a moment.

Monaldo Giacomo, will you curb your impudent tongue,
Or else go back to your books?

Leopardi   I will go back to my books,
If you will all excuse me.

Adelaide   You will stay where you are.
I do not know why, but whenever your father's mother
Comes down to dine with us, one of you precipitates
Some brutish family quarrel.

Marchesa (*placidly*)   Oh no, my dear.
Please don't mind me. In Monaldo's father's day,
When Monaldo was a boy, there were never any quarrels:
There was really never anything to quarrel about,
The children were so contented, though I'm sure I can't think
                                                                                    why,
For I'm afraid I never looked after them in the way that you do.
No, Adelaide, *I* never mind hearing you quarrel;
I never have done, and I never shall:
It's nice to hear so much liveliness in the house.
    (*pause*)
Do go on, my dear, with whatever it was you were saying.

Adelaide There has been so much outrageous interruption,
I have forgotten what I was saying.

Marchesa (*after an infinitesimal pause*)   What a pity . . .
Pietruccio, your hair needs cutting.

Pierfrancesco I'm faltering, Grannie, I'm faltering.

Paolina⎱ Pietruccio!
Luigi⎰ Hush, Piero!
    (*Leopardi and Carlo giggle. Coffee-cups*)

Marchesa Well, some would approve of that, and others less so.
You had better accompany me to my room, Pietruccio,
And we will discuss the political situation.
Thank you, Adelaide, for a pleasant dinner;
No, thank you, Giacomo, I can get up by myself.

(*scrape of chair*)
Your mother's quite right, dear boy; she probably thinks
That if she gave you money, you would only spend it.
I gave your father money, and *he* always spent it.
Didn't you, Monaldo?

Monaldo   Yes, mother.

Marchesa   Yes, mother.
He always spent every penny he could lay his hands on;
I sometimes think he thought that was what it was for.
Good night, Monaldo, Paolina, Giacomo, Carlo, Luigi.
And good night to *you*, Adelaide.

Adelaide Good night, dear, and God bless you.

Marchesa (*politely*)   What did you say?

Adelaide I said God bless you.

Marchesa   Ah, yes. Well, thank you, my dear.
And God bless you, too. Come, Pietruccio.
(*there is a pause as they depart*)

Monaldo I am afraid she was in rather a difficult mood to-night.
I am very sorry, my dear.

Adelaide   It is not for me to forgive her.
Forgiveness can only come from the hand of God.
And I have grown used to her jealousy in all its forms.

Monaldo I think, my dear, whatever my mother's faults,
You cannot call her jealous.

Adelaide   Her faults are not my concern.
Those of my children are, and I will curb them.
I trust that when the Lazzaris come tomorrow,
And your Uncle Antici comes in to dinner,
There will be no similar demonstrations.

Leopardi I cannot speak for the self-control of the others.
But you need not fear for me. I shall not come down from the
                                          library.

Adelaide And why not, may I ask? . . . Giacomo, answer me!

Monaldo What do you mean by this nonsense, Giacomo?
Answer your mother.

Leopardi   No, father, or I may be tempted
To speak in words she may not care to hear.

Adelaide I am quite indifferent to the words you speak in,
Whichever of your filthy books you have culled them from.

Leopardi For once, mother, they would be from yours, not mine.

33   B

Adelaide I am not prepared to listen to your blasphemous insults.
I have asked you a question, and you will answer it:
Why should you not come down to meet the Lazzaris?

Leopardi Very well, since you insist, I will tell you.
My reason is this, mother: (*quietly*) behold your son.

Monaldo Giacomo!

Adelaide　　　　　No, Monaldo, let him say what he wants to.

Monaldo It is ridiculous nonsense. The boy's hysterical.

Leopardi I am not hysterical. I have said all I had to say.

Adelaide I have beheld you with equanimity for eighteen years.
I can continue to do so.

Leopardi　　　　　　　　　With equanimity!
With perverted joy, with hideous mounting triumph,
As you saw me blinding and crippling myself at my books;
With consciousness that whatever I gained from study
I should lose in health and wholesomeness and grace;
With the sure knowledge that I could be left to myself,
Safely, till I should come at last to such a plight
That the cheapest, easiest slut in Recanati
Would recoil from touching me. Well, you have won, mother.
And I say it to you again: behold your son!

Adelaide So at last it is out. At last you see, Monaldo,
What the son you are so proud of carries in his heart;
That that precocious brain you admire so much
Shares the language and thoughts of the commonest tradesman's son,
And if it were not for me he would share their habits.
It was not *I* who set these thoughts in him.

Monaldo　　　　　　　　　　　Adelaide:
I may have been lax and indulgent in many ways,
But I have never given the boy any book or writing,
Or uttered a word that could have perverted his thoughts.

Adelaide No. The perversion comes from a more distant quarter.
We all know whence.

Leopardi (*passionately*)　　　And I know whom you mean!
And it is not true! Not true, and never could be!
My mind may be as foul as even you can believe it,
But I swear before God that none of the worst of me
Comes from Pietro Giordani: the worst is all myself.

Monaldo Father Giordani's advanced ways of thinking
Are not the same as mine. But I cannot say

          That his letters have been either blasphemous or indecent.
          We must blame you alone for your thoughts, Giacomo.
Leopardi Yes, me alone . . . (*painfully*) And I am sorry for them.
Monaldo But I may as well tell you at once, Giacomo,
          That if there are further outbursts of this nature,
          Or if your mother's deepest feelings are again insulted,
          Giordani will never come here; nor will you see him.
Adelaide I am not aware that he will come here in any case.
Monaldo I have promised Giacomo that if his friend
          Is ever in the neighbourhood, he may receive him here.
          Perhaps I should have told you, my dear.
Adelaide   Have told me?
Monaldo I mean that perhaps I should have asked for your approval.
Adelaide Which would certainly have been withheld.
Monaldo   I am sorry for that.
          But Giordani is a distinguished scholar and a priest,
          And I have made the boy that promise. In any case
          I think it unlikely Giordani will venture here.
Leopardi But if he does, you will not break your promise?
          You *will* not, father?
Monaldo   I shall consider myself
          Released from any obligation to keep my promise,
          If you behave again as you have this evening.
Leopardi I will not, father. And I am sorry for what I said.
Adelaide It is contemptible to barter thus with your children,
          Who should in any case have no such promises made them.
Monaldo When the Lazzaris come to see us tomorrow,
          You will go down to the courtyard with the others to meet them.
          They are gentle people and exceedingly well-bred.
          You will see that they do not out-do you in politeness.
          The Countess herself is an extremely well-bred woman.
          They are *all* well-bred . . .
            (*pause*)

Geltrude Ah, what bliss to get free from that beastly carriage:
          It has given me the worst indigestion I have ever had.
          And my husband is convinced it has given him bedsores.
          Countess Leopardi, how fine and well you are looking!
          And Count Monaldo *always* looks well. But you really shouldn't
          Have all come to meet us in this bitter weather.

35

Adelaide It is our privilege.

Geltrude   And my pleasure, my dear.
I am bound to say I always *like* to be greeted.
I always feel if there's no one in the courtyard
A spasm of apprehension: suppose they have forgotten!
Will it shock anyone if I yawn and stretch in public?
A-a-aah! How beautiful your house looks from here.
Where is my husband?

Adelaide   Monaldo has gone to help him out of the carriage.

Geltrude Which becomes increasingly difficult as the years go on.
How lucky you are to have so slim a husband.
Don't you ever go down on your knees at night, Contessa,
And say 'Thank you, dear Lord, for my beautiful *slim* husband'?

Adelaide No. I do not.

Geltrude   Then you should, my dear, you should.

Adelaide My husband's size is a matter of indifference to me.
I have other things to think of.

Geltrude You would think of little else if you were married to my husband.
Lazzari! Don't stay there dawdling, come along.
Contessa Leopardi and I were admiring your heroic figure.

Lazzari Yes, there's more of it to admire than there used to be.
Geltrude never gives me a moment's peace about it.
If you ask me, my wife thinks of nothing but the senses.

Adelaide (*abruptly*) You must allow me to introduce my children.

Geltrude We feel we know them very well already.
This is Paolina. Paolina, my dear, kiss me.

Paolina (*shyly*)   Welcome to Recanati.

Geltrude Thank you, my dear. This is my little Vittoria.
You must look after her for me while we are here.
Well, go on, kiss each other, don't stand gaping.
    (*laughter and a double kiss*)

Lazzari I expect it's the boys Vittoria wants to kiss.
She takes after her mother, Monaldo.

Monaldo   I . . . suppose so.

Adelaide My boys are, I am glad to say, rather reserved.
We are not much given to kissing in our family.

Geltrude I see we shall have to effect a substantial change
While we are here. Why, what a handsome young man!
You are that brilliant Giacomo I have heard of.

Adelaide No, this is Carlo.

Carlo   Welcome, Contessa.
I hope you have had a comfortable journey.

Adelaide Luigi, and Pierfrancesco, my youngest children.

Geltrude My darlings . . .

Luigi   Could Vittoria kiss *me*, perhaps.
I am only fifteen years of age.

Pierfrancesco   No, *me*, Contessa:
Please let Vittoria kiss *me*.
      (*laughter, though not from everyone*)

Adelaide Children: do you realise you are talking to visitors?

Luigi I am very sorry, mother.

Pierfrancesco   I am rather sorry, too.

Luigi I *should* have said, you are welcome to Recanati.

Geltrude Thank you; I am sure I am, my sweetheart.
And where is this handsome Giacomo I have heard of?

Adelaide (*incisively*) I hardly think you will find him very . . .

Monaldo (*interposing*) This is my eldest son, Contessa Lazzari,
Count Giacomo Leopardi. I am very proud of him.
Well, reasonably proud, I mean.

Geltrude   I am sure you are right to be.

Leopardi (*barely audible*) How do you do?

Adelaide   And now shall we all go in?

Paolina Mother, may I take Vittoria to see her room?

Adelaide The servants will do that. Run along now, back to your books.

Geltrude Good-bye, my dears, we shall meet again very soon.

Children (*except Leoarpdi*) Good-bye, Contessa, good-bye.

Carlo (*receding*) Giacomo, wait for me.

Luigi (*receding*) Pietruccio, isn't she lovely?

Pierfrancesco (*receding*) She kissed *me* on the mouth . . .

Geltrude How proud you must be of such a family!
And Paolina is so charming. She will be pretty, I think.

Adelaide Pretty?

Geltrude   Of course she will. You must let me do her hair.

Adelaide So long as her hair is clean, that is all that matters.
I do not want the child to grow up like a harlot.

Geltrude I am sure she will not do that!

Lazzari   Tell me, Monaldo.
Why are the four boys all dressed up like priests?
Is it a game, or something?

Monaldo   Well . . . not exactly; no.

37

Adelaide How else should they be dressed?
　　　　Like children who flaunt their limbs about the streets?
　　　　And shout indelicacies to one another?
Geltrude (*receding*) I have never *seen* a child do what you say.
　　　　You must lead very gay lives here in Recanati.

　　　　(*the music of an amateur string band in background. Laughter of
　　　　Geltrude, Antici, Lazzari, distant. Carlo and Leopardi are playing
　　　　chess, with ironical courtesy*)
Carlo Pawn to king's fifth, I think?
Leopardi 　　　　　　　　　　　　You move into danger, Carlo.
Carlo I know what I am doing.
Leopardi 　　　　　　　　　Do you, dear Carlo? Check.
Carlo A trivial gesture, sir, easily avoided.
　　　What do you think of la Lazzari, eh?
Leopardi Check to the queen.
Carlo 　　　　　　　　　Didn't you hear my question?
Leopardi (*deliberately*) My main preoccupation, as you know,
　　　　Is never to be seen. Why should I bother to notice
　　　　People I am bent on avoiding. (*pause*) Well?
Carlo (*drily*) Why are your hands trembling?

　　　　(*laughter in the background, Geltrude's ringing above the rest*)
Geltrude Trionfo! Trionfo! Trionfo!
Lazzari (*distant*) 　　　　　　Good! I warned you of her, Marchesa.
Leopardi Check to the queen, I said.
　　　　(*lose music*)

Carlo 　　　　　　　　　　　Why are your lips quivering?
Leopardi They are not. Check, I tell you.
Carlo 　　　　　　　　　　My castle protects her, *caro*.
Leopardi I can sacrifice a knight.
Carlo 　　　　　　　　I can sacrifice a queen.
　　　Look out, dear Giacomo, another queen is approaching.
Leopardi Thank you. Your side of the board looks rather thin.
Carlo Still, I can take your knight.
Leopardi 　　　　　　　　A pathetic diversion, even if you could;
　　　　And you cannot.
Carlo 　　　　　Why?
Leopardi 　　　　　　　You discover a check to your king.

Geltrude Why, my poor Carlino, whatever is happening?
         You seem to have no pieces left at all.
  Carlo Then perhaps you'll allow me to advance this last little pawn?
         Believe me, Contessa, you see here a brother
         Without remorse or kindness to the young,
         Who gives us no encouragement, tyrannises . . .
Leopardi   Check.
Geltrude I wish I understood what it all meant.
  Carlo Giacomo will teach you.
Leopardi   And mate in three moves.
  Carlo Damnation, how? I beg your pardon, Contessa.
Leopardi There, there, and there.
         (creep in music)
Paolina   Oh, Giacomo, no!
Vittoria How cunning of him. Oh, my poor little Carluccio.
Geltrude No, no, explain to me; I don't understand.
  Carlo My usual congratulations, Giacomo.
         (music up and down)

Antici If you ask me, Lazzari, Adelaide sells all Monaldo's wine,
         And gets this stuff made up at the chemist's. Isn't that so, Monaldo?
Monaldo Come, come, Antici . . . I am afraid, Lazzari,
         My brother-in-law is rather critical of this household.
Lazzari I expect he claims a brother-in-law's privilege, what?
  Antici I was brought up with Adelaide for eighteen years.
         I would recognise her hand in anything. She treats the cellars
         Just as she treats Monaldo and the children,
         She won't let 'em mature.
Lazzari   H'm! What does Monaldo say?
Monaldo I am not in the habit of criticising my wife, Lazzari.
  Antici What you can't say of your wife, I may at least be permitted
         To say of my sister. Look at young Giacomo, there . . .
Lazzari He seems to be getting on very well with my wife . . .
         (music up and down)

Geltrude Now this, I know, is the king and this is the queen.
 Vittoria And the kings and queens always start facing each other.
Geltrude Vittoria, I do not want two teachers, thank you.
         You have my leave to go and make love to Carlo.
         Comfort the poor boy for his defeat. Now, Giacomo.

Leopardi The castles go at the end and the knights go next to them.
Geltrude The castles go at the end and the knights go next to them.
    (*music up and down*)

Monaldo But this is his *home*, Antici, I want him here.
    God help me, he is the only friend I have.
    Yes, the only friend. I should . . .
Antici   I have said beware.
    Those powers of his are still in their infancy;
    When they mature, he will blame you and his mother
    In words so remorseless they will tear your . . .
Monaldo   I have said he shall stay here.
    Oh! excuse me a moment, my wife is beckoning me . . .
    (*he recedes. Antici groans softly*)
Lazzari A curious family, this, Antici, wouldn't you say?
Antici That boy, Lazzari, though you will scarcely believe it
    Of a brilliant boy who is very nearly twenty,
    Has never once been out of this house alone.
Lazzari Good God! Poor boy! What does he do for . . . hmhm?
Antici   Exactly.
Lazzari That's bad, Antici, that is. Very bad indeed.
    (*music up and down*)

Geltrude You mean you will let me have my bishop back? How kind of you
    To let me change my mind. Don't you sometimes feel angry
    At an irretrievably lost opportunity?
Leopardi We do not have opportunities in Recanati.
Geltrude You will do one day. And surely you know already
    How angry it can make you when a person
    Has made a rude remark, and you can only think
    Of the appropriate retort after they have gone?
Leopardi That situation never arises in our family:
    The same remarks recur so frequently
    You can always get your retort in sooner or later.
    (*Geltrude laughs*)
    (*music up and down*)

Monaldo I would not call the room disorderly, my dear.
    Everything seems to be just where it was before.
Marchesa Spiritually disorderly, I think she means, Monaldo;
    I think that is what you mean, isn't it, my dear?

40

Adelaide Why have Vittoria and Carlo left the room?

Monaldo Have they, my dear? I am afraid I never noticed.

Adelaide You notice nothing. Send one of the servants to find them.

Monaldo Of course, my dear. In fact I will go myself.

Marchesa I do not suppose anything sordid will happen between them;
Or if it does, it will probably have happened already.
They went out nine minutes ago by my watch.

Adelaide I am not the victim of such thoughts, my dear.

Marchesa I only thought that my thoughts were following yours;
But there you are: thoughts are peculiar things.
And we can never know each other's, can we?
I expect there are some times when you can't even guess mine . . .
Giacomo seems unusually contented this evening.
I wonder what *he's* thinking.

Adelaide   Giacomo, at least, is safe.

Marchesa There now, my dear, we do sometimes think alike:
I was just thinking, Giacomo, at least, is safe.
(*music up and down. Geltrude's and Leopardi's tones have become
intimately bantering*)

Geltrude   I think you had better
Abandon Recanati, and come back with us to Pesaro.
Then I would have a true *cavaliere servente*.

Leopardi That would be heaven. You would find me very devoted.

Geltrude You say that *now*, of course. But you would soon neglect me.
There are many beautiful women in Pesaro.

Leopardi You must surpass them all. Like the moon
Dimming the radiance of the stars about her.

Geltrude   Who said that?

Leopardi *I* said it, Contessa.

Geltrude   Giacomo, you are blushing,
And I do not wonder. Who wrote those lines? Tell me.

Leopardi Sappho.

Geltrude   Aha! I knew, you see! I know you scholars,
You get your pretty speeches out of books.
And you have no feelings at all.

Leopardi   Oh, Contessa,
A little fervour does occasionally animate us;
Though only under the most powerful stimulus.

Geltrude Yes, and I expect that Socrates said *that* first.

41   B*

Leopardi Contessa, I swear by Mercury Trismegistus . . .
Geltrude   There!
    (both laugh)
Adelaide I think you must have had enough of chess for tonight, Contessa.
    You will be very tired for your journey tomorrow.
Leopardi Tomorrow!
Geltrude   Yes, Giacomo, we are leaving a day early.
Leopardi Mother, you did not tell me!
Adelaide   I was unaware
    That every arrangement had to be communicated to you.
    I will remember in future.
    (music coming up)
Geltrude   Now, Giacomo,
    Do not pretend you are sorry. Tomorrow evening,
    You will be making the same amorous protestations
    To someone else. Contessa Adelaide,
    I am very shocked at you. You allow your sons to dress
    Like priests only as a naughty decoy.
    I shall warn everybody about what you have done . . .
    (the music drowns their voices)

    (no fade in: but softly)
Leopardi I do not want to recover . . . If I recover,
    It is only the window again, and the view from the window. . .
    Innocent passers-by, you do not know
    How you companion my waking nights, how you are forced
    To meet my shut eyes' gaze, when I wake in the morning.
    Clod-hopping youth, hold your arms tight round that girl.
    In the waning day, draw her into the shadows;
    Let the shadows embrace you both as you embrace.
    You cannot escape me; while your mouth
    Lies upon hers, she has been also mine.
    Dark-eyed girl at the fountain, vainly, vainly,
    You hide your bending breasts with that brown hand:
    You also have been mine, mouth, breast and thigh . . .
    And other, special pleasures I have known:
    When the town palpitates under the sultry heat,
    I have come, after dinner, to your shuttered rooms,
    Where the slit sun lies thinly on the floor;
    The esoteric lusts of the afternoon

Have all been ours; you have expected them,
Matronly, naked, sweating; the open kiss
On the unwashed mouth, the delaying slow caress,
The fat experience, the expert groin. Satiety ...
Help me, incredible God! unmake my fever,
Give me my unhorizoned innocence,
Or send me him who shall restore me to it,
And it to me. Send me Giordani. Send him ...
April, and May, and June, and July, passing.
And only this small town twitching in the twilight.
In glowing alley and square, around the fountain,
The fiddles murmuring, the orchestras of evening
Tuning for the evening's passion: nothing but this! ...
    (*pause. Door*)

Paolina (*off*) Giacomo! Where are you?
Leopardi   I am here.
Paolina (*approaching*)   I could not see you
    In that dark corner. Come and sit in the sun.
Leopardi I prefer it here. Is he still talking to father and mother?
Paolina Yes. Aren't you coming to meet him?
Carlo (*approaching excitedly*) Giacomo, he's here!
Leopardi I know, I know. He will come up here. I shall not come down.
    I cannot meet him in front of father and mother
    While they are angry with me. He will understand.
    Is he still talking to them?
Carlo   Yes. And I think they are rather impressed.
Paolina He is quiet and courteous.
Carlo   Giacomo, is it true
    He will ask them if he may take you to Macerata?
Leopardi Yes. It is equally true that they will refuse.
    How could they bear to have one of us out of their sight,
    Fifteen miles away, and for a whole ten hours?
Paolina Still, he will ask them.
Carlo   And mother will reply
    With one of her passionate non-sequiturs
    That smack one's brain into a kind of stupor.
Paolina (*from the doorway*) Giacomo, he's in the hall ... He's coming up.
Carlo Shall we stay, Giacomo?
Paolina   Of course not, Carlo. Come along.

Leopardi Please, Carlo: just this once.

   Carlo (*banteringly*)   I know, I know.

       Old friends forgotten. No use. Finished, done with.

       Incipit vita nova. See you in a fortnight's time.

Leopardi You will see me in half an hour.

  Paolina (*off*)   Come on, Carlo.

    Carlo (*off*) You will find him in there, Father Giordani.

  Paolina (*off*) He's hiding in the corner.

Giordani (*off*) Thank you.

Leopardi Help me, oh God, help me to be brilliant,

       And not to disappoint him.

        (*silence. Then Giordani speaks, ardently and forcefully*)

Giordani Giacomino! So there you are at last. And here am I.

       And let me tell you at once that I have discovered

       That Giacomo Leopardi, whose every word I trusted,

       Turns out to be the most unprincipled liar

       Who has ever written to me. You cunningly build up

       A picture of a tumbledown provincial hovel,

       Extremely dark, almost completely bookless,

       Without any servants, and overrun by priests.

       And what does the disconcerted visitor find?

       An entrance-hall like a paradise of marble,

       The largest library outside of Bologna,

       A dozen footmen, no sign of a *sottana*,

       Punctilious and courteous parents and brothers,

       And I do not know what other treasures besides!

       I do not wonder that you hide your head with shame!

       This is a writer's paradise!

       (*pause*)

       I know why you are sitting there in the dark.

       It is only to give substance to the worst lie of all:

       Which was, that you never smiled. I observe a grin

       Which threatens you with imminent decapitation

       If it grows any larger. Come out from that chair!

       Here is a perfectly excellent patch of sunlight:

       Come: stand in it! And tell me you are sorry. There.

       (*pause*)

Leopardi Oh, good Giordani, you have come at last: a day I have prayed

                                     for.

       You cannot imagine how much ... And now you are here,

Forgive me if for a moment I am suddenly so weary
I can scarcely bear to talk.

Giordani   Of course, Giacomino.
It is a great day for me as well.

Leopardi   Something has happened
Of which you are unaware.

Giordani   What?

Leopardi   This morning
I broke a sacred rule of this priestly household:
I came out alone to meet you. I did not find you,
But today I walked in a street for the first time alone,
At the age of nearly twenty. At last I experienced
Freedom. I know how people feel
Everywhere, daily. Oh, dear Giordani, their lives!
They are so full of unnoticed ecstasy!

Giordani Why, yes, it would certainly be unnoticed.

Leopardi They move in cities, greet each other, sit
In inns and cafés. Hurry through streets about their busy
                                        mornings.

They lay their hands on friendly parapets,
Loll against the windy stone. Their skin
Darkens with the deepening year. While I . . .
(*he breaks down*)
For God's sake, Giordani, take me away from here.

Giordani (*gently*) I have no powers to take you away, Giacomino.
And without disrespect to your parents, I hardly think
That either would respond very well to that suggestion.

Leopardi Must I die where I was born?

Giordani   Hush, Giacomino.
We must do what we can, break them in very gently:
I have asked them to let me take you to Macerata.
They answered yes.

Leopardi (*overwhelmed*)   What?

Giordani   They told me I might take you there:
Though only of course for the day.

Leopardi   Only!
Giordani, you cannot know what you are saying.
If the gates of heaven had opened in front of me,
Their trumpets could make no greater sound in my ears.

Giordani Macerata is a very small place to get excited about.

45

Leopardi If it were Athens, Jerusalem or Byzantium,
          It could mean no more to me at such a moment.
          It is as well that I broke out this morning,
          Or Macerata, suddenly sprung upon me,
          Would be more than I could bear. Oh, Giordani,
          I am forgetting my manners. You have made this journey
          Especially to see me, and all I can do is talk
          Of another journey. It will not tire you, will it?
          Say it will not!
Giordani   I am never tired, Giacomino.
          And being with you, the time will pass very quickly!
Leopardi But no, Giordani, the time must *not* pass quickly!
          No, it must *not* pass quickly.
               (*half-fade. Pause*)

Paolina So you *are* going with him to Macerata, Giacomo?
Leopardi Yes. Almost, I think, for the first time in his life,
          Father asserted his own will against mother's.
Paolina How wonderful for you, darling; oh, my darling.
Leopardi I feel as anxious as if I were a child again:
          Do you remember how terror mixed with delight
          At the thought of a party? We seemed incapable
          Of joy in a present moment.
Paolina   We always knew
          How soon the end would come.
Leopardi   Perhaps that was why it came,
          So often, so much sooner than it should.
Paolina   Yes. There always seemed
          Some sort of trouble; I always remember
          The upturned chair, the broken wineglass,
Leopardi The games unplayed, the weeping children.
Paolina It will not be like that today, Giacomo.
          Carlo and I and Luigi will *wish out to you*, from here,
          All the happiness in the world.
Leopardi (*pleased*)   And when will you do it?
Paolina At seven o'clock this evening.
Leopardi   I shall remember.
          I feel as if I were going away for a month.

          (*hooves and carriage wheels. Hold*)

Giordani   Someone waved to us from an upper window,
      As we came away.

Leopardi   That would be Paolina.
      Dear child, she is almost as happy at this as I am.

Giordani   You are lucky in your brothers and sister, Giacomo.

Leopardi   Transcendently, Giordani . . . Well?

Giordani   Well?

Leopardi   'But your mother and father', you were going to say.

Giordani   Was I? . . . Perhaps. But it is no matter.

Leopardi   I am not disloyal, believe me, Giordani. But today,
      Let us forget them . . . What a heavenly sound!

Giordani   What sound?

Leopardi   The horses' hooves.

Giordani   You will soon get tired of those.

Leopardi   Never, Giordani . . . (*suddenly*) Giordani, I have known a mother,
      Impeccable in all her faith and observances,
      Yet drained of every sense of compassion or love;
      Who has envied the poor the frequent deaths of their children,
      And when her own infants died, gave thanks to heaven;
        (*the sound of hooves dies down*)
      We did not die. I need not recount our story.
      You can see how glad she is that I am deformed,
      Paolina plain and sallow. Why should I avoid a word
      For a feeling which our household has never hidden?
      It is hate we feel.

Giordani   So I supposed. But hate is a mystery.
      I have sometimes wondered during these last few days,
      If the hate you feel is not the other side of a love
      Which also exists somewhere, if you could find it.

Leopardi   Yes, I have thought of that; it could easily be believed,
      But I am sure it is not so. Do you think I have not seen
      In others the thing you refer to?

Giordani   Indeed?

Leopardi   Indeed.
      I know the families of the Marches. I have observed them
      On their rare, chilling visits. I know those mothers,
      Who hold the purse-strings tightly – though never so tightly as ours;
      I know those elder, mother-haunted sons,
      And I know I am not of them. I wish I were.
      In their sort of prison there are such shafts of light

47

That they do not see the nature of the place at all.
Ours is a simpler place. And we know we are there.
    (*hooves in faintly*)

Giordani I see. I am sorry for my naïve suggestion.

Leopardi (*gently*) You will never understand me, if you think
That hate can never be simple: an impressed coin
With a blank on the other side. And so, I think, could love be,
If I could ever find it. Listen to the horses' hooves.
And I almost think I could find it anywhere:
Among those yellowing trees on Monte Tabor,
In the village ahead, in the inn we passed just now,
In Macerata, Pisa . . . anywhere . . .
Oh blest, blest world, oh trees of autumn, oh people!
These horses have wings on their hooves, I think, Giordani!
    (*the horses' hooves grow faster, and then fade slowly out*)

Paolina Carlo. Luigi.

Both (*promptly*) Paolina?

Paolina   Put your books away. It's two minutes to seven.

Luigi Magic. Hurrah. Good night, little books, good night.

Carlo Sleep well, milord Byron and Guglielmo Shek-spir.
Good night.

Paolina   Come to the window, both of you, quickly.

Carlo Et me voici, ma chère.

Luigi   What are we to do?

Paolina Put one hand on the window-sill.

Luigi (*gravely*)   A pleasure.

Paolina And one in mine.

Carlo   An even greater pleasure.

Paolina Now wait.
    (*pause. The watch-tower begins to strike seven*)
    Now think of him, and wish.

Paolina Giacomo, dear brother, we wish you well and happy.

The three We wish you well and happy.

    (*the Recanati bell cross-fades to the louder one of Macerata: Leopardi
    is laughing uncontrollably. Pouring. Clink of glasses. Both he and
    Giordani are very slightly drunk*)

Giordani It is perfectly clear what I mean. I mean that you cannot tell,
In a time like ours, what any man may mean. I mean,

In a world lying sideways, lying, as it were, on its *side*,
People who nod may appear to be shaking their heads.
I say this a little obscurely because, as often happens,
I feel suddenly rather drunk.

Leopardi   I am rather drunk myself.

Giordani *(politely)* Not in the slightest. Above all, Giacomino:
Don't be seduced, *ever*, by the praise of your elders.
It will come thick and fast, and as you get older,
It will come faster still, and possibly thicker.
Ignore it, Giacomo. Your elder applauders
Will have a natural interest in pretending
You are still young, and they are not too old
To appreciate the young. Do I make myself clear?

Leopardi Not altogether, perhaps.

Giordani   Oh yes, I do.
A poet does not write for his elders, Giacomo.
The praise of one's elders is as valueless as their censure.
Praise or blame are never of much importance,
Whoever they come from, but it is better if they come from
                                        the young.

Leopardi Yes, that is curious. I have sometimes felt
That however kindly father's contemporaries
Have spoken of me, and however greedy for praise
The moment has found me, I have sometimes felt
That they do not know what they are talking about.

Giordani *(loudly)* Quite right quite right! And the young who praise
Don't often know either; but they have the advantage
That they may live to learn. Above all, Giacomo,
When you move out to the worlds of Milan and Bologna,
Don't be misled by the damned bluestocking women
Who will be waiting for you.

Leopardi   But I long for the praise of women!

Giordani Of course you do. *(darkly)* And it's the worst of all.

Leopardi How?

Giordani *(after a moment's thought, obscurely)* They *get* at you.

Leopardi *(laughing)* I am willing to be got.

Giordani Get *at*, I said, not get . . . Get *at*; not get.
Once let a woman set eyes upon your work,
And *oh*, what helpful suggestions she will have to offer!
What you can say and what you can't say: I *know*.

Leopardi But . . .

Giordani   You'll live to regret it, if you ignore what I say.
          Once alter a word at the suggestion of a woman,
          And she'll come to believe she wrote the whole damned book.
          You hear them at it everywhere . . . Pisa . . . Florence . . .
                                                              Bologna.

          And oh the *crossness* if somebody else has praised you!
          If they see you getting a bit above yourself.
          And why in God's name shouldn't you get above yourself?
          (*luminously*) It's the only way up.
              (*Macerata bell strikes the quarter*)

Leopardi Another quarter of an hour and we must go.
              (*Recanati watch-tower strikes the quarter*)

Paolina How quickly these hours must have gone for him, Carlo.

Carlo Poor Giacomo, yes. Will he ever get free, I wonder?

Luigi Will any of us ever get free?

Paolina   We live like chidden infants.
          What difference is there between now and childhood?
          The chairs and tables remain erect, the wine unspilt;
          We weep a little less. But I see no difference.

Carlo How curious that you should say that. I was just thinking
          Of those dreadful children's parties.

Paolina   I have thought of them all day.
          I wonder how many . . .
              (*door*)
                                  Oh, did you want me, mother?

Adelaide What are you all doing at that open window?
              (*pause*)

Giordani What is the matter, Giacomo, why do you look so pained?

Leopardi I am sorry, Giordani. My thoughts wandered for a moment
          Back to Paolina, Carlo and Luigi. And the joy I always feel
          In thinking of them was suddenly blurred and twisted.
          My family again, Giordani. I am sorry.

Giordani There is another family.

Leopardi   Another?

Giordani   Disunited,
          Ridiculed, and its name forgotten, whose touching image
          I have grown to love and pray for.

50

        (*pause*)
      I think you pray for it too.
Leopardi (*just audible*)   *Oh, Italy!*
Giordani Italy: that lost name for a lost possession,
      Torn by the robbers like the garments of Jesus:
      As once by Sforza, Visconti, Medici, Este:
      And now by France and Austria and the popes . . .
      Whose are we now?
Leopardi   Not whose we shall be tomorrow.
Giordani The washing-women look up from the fountain daily
      And can scarcely remember who is their latest possessor,
      And worse, can scarcely care.
Leopardi   On foreign cannon
      The shadows of *our* leaves and flowers fall.
Giordani We have come from Recanati to Macerata,
      Which once was another country.
Leopardi   And may be again.
Giordani Giacomo: for God's sake do not let your home
      (And do not think you will always be pent in it)
      Don't let that home imprison all your thoughts;
      Nor think that freedom when it comes will be
      Simply the avenue to pleasure and fame.
      You will learn that pleasure quickly vanishes.
Leopardi That I have learnt already.
Giordani   And fame more quickly blackens
      In the hands of those who win it.
Leopardi   I will try to believe that too.
      Perhaps you are right. Perhaps the world
      Will seem to be no larger than Recanati,
      Its praise as quickly valueless . . .
           (*suddenly*) No, no, Giordani, no!
      I cannot bear to forgo the thought of that world:
      Let me believe in it a little longer . . .
Giordani   If I could,
      Instead of taking you back to Recanati,
      I would begin to take you to that world tonight.
      And whatever I have said, it is still a world you must have.
Leopardi I know it has streets and houses. And I know that I shall find them.
      And that they will find me also.
      (*long pause*)

Adelaide I will not be fobbed off with these foolish excuses.
　　　　　 Since that man came and went, he has not been the same child.
　　　　　 Everyone I meet remarks on the difference.
Monaldo They do not all disapprove of the difference.
Adelaide I am not in the habit of regulating my conscience,
　　　　　 By the comments of others. That man Giordani
　　　　　 Has wrecked all discipline and decent feeling in him.
　　　　　 I am surprised you can let your family name be debased
　　　　　 By allowing your eldest son to wander the streets alone.
Monaldo I think his solitude means a great deal to him.
Adelaide He can be perfectly solitary in his own room.
　　　　　 It was half past ten when he came in this evening.
　　　　　 For three months now he has come and gone as he pleases.
　　　　　 If you cannot think what such a thing means to a mother,
　　　　　 Your humanity must have shrunk to a very low point.
　　　　　 I do not intend to submit any longer
　　　　　 To what appears to me to be a conspiracy
　　　　　 Between you and him to set my feelings at nothing.
Monaldo There has been no conspiracy, my dear.
　　　　　 He asked me for what he called his freedom. I gave it.
Adelaide Then either you will withdraw his freedom, or I shall.
Monaldo I will speak to him tomorrow.
Adelaide 　　　　　　　　　　　　 Then I shall speak tonight.
Monaldo Very well. I will tell him tonight. Paolina:
　　　　　 Will you ask Giacomo to come down here for a moment?
Paolina Father . . .
Adelaide 　　　　 Yes?
Paolina 　　　　　　　 Giacomo is . . . not in.
Adelaide I heard him come in half an hour ago.
Paolina Yes, mother. But I am afraid he has gone out again.
　　　　　 He has been rather restless today; as you know,
　　　　　 His eyesight is bad once more: the daylight distresses him.
　　　　　 He prefers the darkness . . .
Monaldo 　　　　　　　　　　　 I will wait up till he comes in.
　　　　　 But I do not know how to re-impose an inhibition,
　　　　　 Having once relaxed it: it is very hard on Giacomo.
Adelaide It is for his own good. Either you will tell him, or I.
Monaldo It is I who will tell him. If you will all leave me,
　　　　　 I will wait for him here.
Adelaide 　　　　　　　　　　 You will tell him

52

How gravely offended his poor mother is
That her eldest son . . .

Monaldo   I shall know what to tell him, my dear.
It will not be the first time I have had to rebuke him . . .
  (*pause*)

  (*it is out of doors, at night*)

Leopardi Oh, good Giordani, what have you done with me?
I thought that with you I had learnt so much.
And had achieved my freedom. Freedom meant
This that I have, and cannot value now.
For look, I pace the streets I wanted and find no comfort.
The moon fails, and the city, and the night.
Inside the walls the barely murmurous houses
Sink to an utter silence; the last syllables of talk
End, and I am excluded from even the silence.
Outside the city gates there lies, or does not lie,
What you call Italy. Under the dust the untrod theatre,
The blurred forgotten steps under the pine;
The singing bird over the stone arch,
The stone arch broken over nothing, reaching out
Into nothing: the doorway welcoming nothing.
Oh, lost, lost country under the dust,
Be my father. You would find me a dutiful son.
  (*footsteps approaching. Wooden heels*)
Who walks behind me on those clicking heels
What step accompanies my step? Is it murder? Or theft?
  (*footsteps nearer*)
These clicking footsteps have a meaning, meant for me.
Ask? And not fear? Not fear, oh God, not fear.
Ask. Wait, now, wait. Ask . . . Good evening.
  (*two final footsteps*)

A girl (*brightly*) Good evening.
Leopardi   What time is it, do you know?
  Girl (*amused*) Midnight, perhaps. It is not very late.
Leopardi Where . . . are you going?
  Girl   Oh, down below.
Leopardi You live near here?
  Girl   Yes, down in via Fabrizi; where do you?

53

Leopardi In the piazzetta ...

Girl But that is here, only a few steps away.

Leopardi Yes, it is here.

(*pause*)

How old are you?

Girl (*vivaciously*) How old do you think I am?

Leopardi About eighteen.

Girl Good! I am nearly eighteen and a half.

Leopardi What do you do?

Girl Do?

Leopardi Do for a living.

Girl (*brightly: pouting*) Nothing.

Leopardi You are lucky.

Girl Yes; I am rather lucky ...

Leopardi Well, it is getting late.

Girl No, it is not yet late, it is only midnight.

Leopardi Would you like me to walk a little way with you?

Girl Certainly. Where shall we go?

Leopardi One way is as good as another. Downwards?

Girl No. Let us go upwards, there, the way we have come.

Leopardi Upwards then ...

(*her heels begin again*)

What do you do all day, if you work at nothing?

Girl There are the fields. There are walks about the streets.
Oh, there are things to do ... And what do *you* do?

Leopardi I ... I write.

Girl A poet?

Leopardi Yes.

Girl Good.

Leopardi (*simply*) Shall we sit down here, on this little low wall?

Girl No, let us go up there; it is quieter and darker.

Leopardi It is quiet everywhere. But, yes, it is darker there.

Girl Give me your hand, and then you will not stumble.

Leopardi (*barely audible*) Thank you.

(*pause*)

Girl There.

Leopardi It is so dark I cannot see your face.
Or anything of you.

Girl You will soon get used to the dark.

(*pause*)

Why do you keep your lips closed when you kiss me?

Leopardi (*whispers*)   I am sorry.
(*pause*)

Girl Do you like me?

Leopardi (*simply*) Of course I like you. I love you.

Girl Eeeh! *Caro* . . .

Leopardi   What is your name?

Girl (*mockingly*)   What does my name matter?

Leopardi What can I call you?

Girl   They call me by all sorts of names.
You could call me Caterina, if you wished to.
Why not be quiet, and make love properly?
What is the matter, are you tired?
Perhaps you have already made love tonight?

Leopardi No, I am tired, that is all . . . (*wretchedly*) And I cannot
Make love in a street.

Girl (*suddenly brisk*)   No: it is ugly.
You are quite right: it is not nice: *è brutto, brutto.*

Leopardi   Kiss me.
Kiss me again, and I must go . . . Caterina.
(*pause*)
I am dreadfully sorry,
To have wasted your time for you . . . I want
To go away from Recanati.

Girl (*charmingly*)   To go away?
And where will you go?

Leopardi   I want to go to Rome.
Or Florence perhaps.

Girl   Ah, Rome is beautiful;
And Florence is beautiful too.

Leopardi   Have you been there?

Girl   No.
But Florence and Rome must be very beautiful.
And Venice is beautiful too. I have been to Ascoli,
And once to Sinigaglia . . . Be careful not to stumble.
(*heels again*)
There are loose stones in the street.

Leopardi (*in despair*)   This is your life, Caterina?

Girl (*cheerfully*) This is my life, yes.

Leopardi   My name is . . .

55

Girl   No. Do not tell me.
Don't let us bother with names.
Leopardi (*bitterly*)   No, let us not.
What should my name be worth to anyone?
  Girl I only tell you that for your own good.
It is better to have no names.
Leopardi   Like butterflies. . . .
Caterina: (*almost frightened*) I have nothing to give you.
  Girl   Hush, *caro*: that was nothing.
Leopardi No, it was nothing . . . Good night, Caterina.
  Girl Good night, *caro*.
       (*clicking fades. Pause. The town clock, and then a clock in the
       palazzo strikes half past midnight. Leopardi's steps are heard
       crossing the marble floor*)

Monaldo (*at some distance*) Giacomo . . .
Leopardi   Oh . . . You shouldn't have waited up for me, father.
Monaldo (*approaching*) It is very late, Giacomo.
Leopardi   It is half past twelve.
Monaldo I waited up because I have something to say to you.
Leopardi A message, I expect, father?
Monaldo   What do you mean?
Leopardi I believe you have to say that mother
Is extremely displeased at the way I am behaving.
Monaldo We are both of us distressed, Giacomo,
At the way things appear to be going with you.
Leopardi Was mother's word: distressed?
Monaldo   It does not matter.
Leopardi No, it has ceased to matter. But I expect
She was either extremely displeased, or gravely offended.
Her children can inspire no other emotions in her.
Monaldo I don't know what emotions you expect to inspire
Other than those you do.
Leopardi   None, father, none.
Only extreme displeasure and grave offence.
Our remarkable gift as a family is that we can still
Distinguish between the two. But at least there are no other
                                                              variants.
There are no such things as ordinary beings are touched by:
As shame or pity, remorse, penitence or guilt.

Monaldo Why should your mother feel such things?

Leopardi   Why do you?

Monaldo Are you being impertinent, Giacomo?

Leopardi   I think not, father, no.

Monaldo We all have things in life that we regret;
But if we strive for goodness our sins are forgiven.

Leopardi And in forgiveness . . . if we are forgiven . . .
Do shame and remorse and guiltiness vanish in air?

Monaldo I am not the subject of an inquisition, Giacomo,
And do not intend to be.

Leopardi   I only wished to know
If you ever felt doubt, father.

Monaldo   Doubt about what?

Leopardi About yourself, Paolina, Carlo, Luigi, and me:
About this life of cruel incarceration,
Which you and mother have imposed upon us.

Monaldo I have done no more than any other father in the Marches
Assumes the right to do.

Leopardi   Yes, in this sullen prison of a province,
Our smaller prisons exist inside each other
Like Chinese boxes.

Monaldo   You are not imprisoned here.
Could a prisoner wander in at all hours as you do?

Leopardi Ah, yes, I had forgotten: I have recently been made free
Of the streets of Recanati, that pure exalted world.
And, oh, the beauties of its streets and people!
Certainly you and I should appreciate them,
Experienced travellers as we are: you, who have made
Journeys of twenty-five miles in every direction,
And I with my solitary jaunt to Macerata:
We are citizens of the world, father!

Monaldo I am neither moved nor impressed by your tasteless satire.
As for your jaunt to Macerata, with all my heart
I wish it had not happened. Since that day
You have been unrecognisable as the boy you were before.
Everyone has said so.

Leopardi   Unrecognisable?
Have I grown straight and tall?
Have I shed deformity? And are my eyes
As clear as those of other Recanati youths?

Monaldo Giacomo, I refuse to quarrel with you. Why should I?
　　　　Don't you realise, Giacomo, the life I had planned for us,
　　　　And hoped you would love as I would?

Leopardi　　　　　　　　　　　　　　Had such a thing a plan?
　　　　It seems the last unspeakable horror of all
　　　　That such an edifice of petty tyranny
　　　　Should have a plan for its construction.

Monaldo Whatever words I use you will always twist them.
　　　　It was to have been, I hope still may be, a refuge.

Leopardi A refuge from what? Are you frightened to say it, father?

Monaldo It need not be said in words.

Leopardi　　　　　　　　　　Oh, need it not?
　　　　How pleased she would be to be thought the ineffable.

Monaldo Giacomo, how can I speak to you? Have we no words in
　　　　　　　　　　　　　　　　　　　　common?

Leopardi Perhaps a few remain. I will try to use them.
　　　　You said you hoped to build a refuge for us.
　　　　But seeing that such a life was not for me,
　　　　Could you not count the battle honourably lost,
　　　　And let me go? I too need refuge,
　　　　And I do not find it here. Your own incarceration
　　　　Is not my business, father. If you make mine yours,
　　　　It should be to set me free. I will not be used,
　　　　And am therefore useless to you. That should be clear
　　　　To one who fought with honourable weapons.
　　　　But you, father: you do not!
　　　　　　　　　　　　　　You have given us
　　　　Hope for a day and a night; and in the morning
　　　　Have taken hope away. And the doors have shut again.

Monaldo You cannot say we have ever used force against you.

Leopardi No, you did not use force. Grief and beseeching:
　　　　Those were your weapons. What is it, in God's name,
　　　　That makes parental tears have such a force
　　　　As hungry children's have not? Those were the weapons
　　　　You never spared the use of. Will, hope, desire, nothing
　　　　Can hold against them.

Monaldo　　　　　　　　　What do you think to do?

Leopardi Give in: as I have always given in.
　　　　But do not think that even a captured citadel,
　　　　Starved out, father, as you have starved out me,

Do not think that I have not the sense to hide
Some precious part of my treasure under the dungeon stones
Where the conqueror can never find them;
Or that though I am a city you have occupied
I have no hope of deliverance. No, do not believe it!
And if I go on all my life to the very end,
As it seems may happen, under your squalid dominion:
Though the dances of hell weave round me, remember
You cannot drive from my mind that still calm vision
Of the life that should be mine, and shall not be shared by you.

Monaldo You are a hard and cruel son, Giacomo.
Do you not love your father any longer?

Leopardi You have no right to ask me such a question.
What do I know of love . . . ? Not a hundredth part
Of what I know of aimless desire and passion.
Oh, father, you cannot guess what you have done to me!
What do you know
Of the weeks of black misery that have engulfed me,
So that when I was blind I almost blessed the blindness,
That hid the other blackness of my life here?
What do you know of those hours that have been besieged
By acrid melancholy, where innominate monsters
Have lain and waited for me: where hooded figures
Have muttered censorious damnation at me?
What of the time when even these have retreated,
Leaving a blacker night of despair behind them,
Vacant and utterly featureless, lightless, only
Where I could only be certain that this was life,
My life, my life, for ever, and death out of sight.
What do you know of *that?* . . . But why do I ask what you
                                                    know?

You did know!

Monaldo   Giacomo!

Leopardi   And you thought you might be a refuge!
Knowing that the only refuge from that coiling night
Was the straight, simple daylight away from here:
Far, far away, if it meant even the ends of the earth.
Only away from here, and you, and mother!
I am not weeping, father, and I will not weep.
You shall not make me. I will bear what I have to bear.

(*pause*)
Will you let me go now? Go to my room, I mean . . .
I want to lie, alone, in the dark, in my bed.

Monaldo Yes, go to bed, Giacomo. You will not believe me now.
But I am sorry you are so unhappy. Good night . . . and God bless
you.

Leopardi (*firmly*) Good night, father.

Monaldo   Good night . . . Giacomo!

Leopardi (*from a slight distance: in hard tones*) Yes?

Monaldo Giacomo . . .

Leopardi (*nearer*) Yes?

Monaldo (*simply*)   It is rather dark in the upstairs corridor, Giacomo . . .
Would you like me to see you safely to your room?
(*pause*)

Leopardi (*suddenly in tears*) Yes, please, father.

(*pause*)

Adelaide Monaldo!

Monaldo (*approaching*) I am sorry if I woke you, Adelaide;
I thought you would be asleep.

Adelaide   Where have you been?

Monaldo I talked to Giacomo.

Adelaide   Giacomo went to bed an hour ago.

Monaldo I wanted to be alone for a while in the study.

Adelaide Well: what had he to say, and what had you?

Monaldo A good deal, Adelaide.

Adelaide   Well; I am waiting.
(*pause*)

Monaldo I shall send him to Rome.

Adelaide   I did not stay awake
To hear ridiculous jokes. Did you tell him
How gravely offended I am with his behaviour?

Monaldo He seemed, in some strange way or other,
To have divined that already.

Adelaide   And have you told him
Just what he may and may not do?

Monaldo I am sending him to Rome.
He shall go next month: or sooner, if he wishes.

Adelaide Am I to suppose you have taken leave of your senses?

Monaldo Adelaide! I have learnt many things tonight,
And some of them have been very new and shocking.
I would prefer, for once, if you will forgive me,
To assimilate them alone. I ask you not to try
To drown me or my decision in a show of temper,
Real or unreal. Tonight
Is not a time for you and me to repeat those duologues
That have become a ritual between us.
We still have the years in front of us for that . . .
Giacomo shall go to Rome. That is all I shall say.
If I lose him for ever, I may in the end gain something
Almost without his knowing. It is the only way.

Adelaide Monaldo!

Monaldo It may be years before I shall truly know
Whether it is not too late, too late already . . .
He shall go far away, my beloved child.

Leopardi

Part two: The Monument

An early version of *The Monument*, produced by Rayner Heppenstall, was broadcast on 7 March 1950. The version given here was first broadcast on 17 October 1950. The production was by Douglas Cleverdon. The cast was as follows:

GIACOMO LEOPARDI	*Marius Goring*
GIACOMO (as a boy)	*David Page*
MONALDO	*Carleton Hobbs*
ADELAIDE	*Gladys Young*
CARLO	*Derek Hart*
CARLO (as a boy)	*Jeremy Spenser*
PAOLINA	*Barbara Lott*
PIERFRANCESCO ('Pietruccio')	*John Charlesworth*
LUIGI	*Timothy Harley*
COUNTESS MALVEZZI	*Rachel Gurney*
ROSA PADOVANI	*Jill Balcon*
PIETRO GIORDANI	*James McKechnie*
BRIGHENTI	*Leonard Sachs*
PEPOLI	*Max Adrian*
ANTONIO RANIERI	*Leslie French*
FANNY TARGIONI-TOZZETTI	*Diana Maddox*
TARGIONI-TOZZETTI	*Robert Beaumont*
MADDALENA PELZET	*Margaretta Scott*
BIFFI	*Norman Shelley*
PAVESI	*Brian Haines*
FABRIZI	*Felix Felton*
BOTTI	*Max Adrian*
FANNY'S CHILDREN	*Ysanne Churchman* and *Molly Lawson*
MARIA	*Vida Hope*
LINA RANIERI	*Rachel Gurney*
MANNELLA	*Norman Shelley*

The date: 1826 to 1837.

The song for Fanny's children was composed by Antony Hopkins, and other music was composed and directed by John Hotchkiss.

(In the Accademia Felsinea at Bologna, 1826, Leopardi (28) is nearing the end of a public reading of a didactic poem. He does not take it too seriously. Echo)

Leopardi   *. . . and to this meditation I shall bear*
     My idle days. Even in the sadness of truth,
     There is delight. I speak of truth, and though
     My words may in your ears discover neither
     Welcome nor understanding . . . I shall not grieve.
     In me the ancient, fair desire for fame
     Lies spent already: goddess of vanity,
     Blinder than fortune and fate, blinder than love.
(much respectful, genteel clapping. Hold behind two old gentlemen)

Old Gentleman 1 *(deep voice)* What . . . was the poem . . . *about?*
Old Gentleman 2 *(deeper still)*   Truth. Truth, and that sort of thing.
Old Gentleman 1 *(profoundly)* Yes, I see. *(cautiously)*
     It was very good, didn't you think?
Old Gentleman 2 Oh, very.
Old Gentleman 1   What's the fellow's name?
Old Gentleman 2   Ah . . . *Count* Something or other.
Old Gentleman 1   Brilliant!
(clapping out behind next speeches, occasional laughter, murmurs, etc.)

Rosa *(a mocking, glamorous drawl)*
     Countess Malvezzi! . . . Well, well, what a pleasure!
Malvezzi Ah, Signora Padovani, it is very unusual
     To have you honouring the Academy with a visit.
     It isn't often we manage to inveigle *you*
     Into sitting and listening to poems.
Rosa   Indeed it isn't.
     But I promised Leopardi I would come.
Malvezzi Is he an acquaintance of yours?
Rosa   Yes, quite a friend.
Malvezzi How strange that he should never have mentioned you.
Rosa Ah, you know him too?
Malvezzi   He is one of my closest friends.
     He is always to be found at casa Malvezzi.

Rosa Not quite always, I think? He comes home sometimes.

Malvezzi Home?

Rosa   He has a little apartment in the same house as ours.

Malvezzi Well, that *is* unexpected. And he never remembered to mention
you.

Rosa I hope he remembered not to. One of the first things
I made him promise was never to talk about *me*.

Malvezzi We have, of course, many serious things to talk about.
There is, I think, no serious subject in life
That Leopardi and I have left wholly untouched.
How did you enjoy the poem he read tonight?
We've spent many hours together over that one.

Rosa I'm afraid I hardly listened. I was more engrossed
In watching the audience. One always is,
I think, on these occasions?

Malvezzi   Myself, never.
I was wholly absorbed in the poet's thought and expression.

Rosa I prefer his private thoughts and expressions myself.
I could write a book about some of the things he says;
I mean if I *could* write.

Malvezzi (*with reserve*)   Exactly, yes.

Rosa But it wouldn't, I'm afraid, be a book for publication;
Or at any rate not in Bologna.

Malvezzi   I am very glad
He goes in sometimes for lighter diversions.
Ah, there he is, making his way towards us.

Rosa Dear love, how he enjoys his popularity:
It is good for him to have so much fuss made of him;
He is blushing with pleasure . . .

Malvezzi (*superbly welcoming*)   Leopardi!

Leopardi Countess Malvezzi . . .

Rosa (*seductively gurgling*) Giacomino!

Leopardi Signora Padovani . . .

Rosa You have the whole of Bologna at your feet this evening,
Giacomo.

Leopardi Only because the platform is a little higher than their heads.
(*he and Rosa laugh a little*)

Rosa You mustn't let this solemn public see you laugh, Giacomo.

Leopardi Oh, they are not all solemn, by any means . . .
I hope you were pleased with the final version, Contessa?

(*pause*)

Malvezzi I cannot tell you how *deeply* moved I was.

Leopardi (*embarrassed*) The poem isn't, of course, *wholly* . . .

Malvezzi (*finely*)   The rhetorical force
  Which carries the verse through the most complex reasoning,
  And deposits it, like an athlete depositing a torch,
  Into the mind of the reader is of a kind to equal which,
   (*pause*)
  I suggest we must go right back to Alfieri.

Rosa (*cooing*) Yes, let us. Is he here?

Leopardi   Thank you, dear Countess Malvezzi.
  I hadn't ever thought of it in quite those terms perhaps,
  And I fear some passages are a little frivolous,
  But I hoped you were liking it all the time I was reading.

Malvezzi Liking it . . .? Dear poet!

Leopardi And . . . Ros . . . Signora Padovani . . . I hope *you* liked it.
  (*pause*)

Rosa (*intimately and jocosely*) Of course I liked it.
  (*pause*)
      (*even more so*) Why shouldn't I like it?

(*cross-fade rapidly to the conversation of Giordani, Pepoli and Brighenti*)

Pepoli Well, it has been a brilliant evening for your protégé, Giordani.

Giordani I can scarcely call him that any longer, Pepoli.
  If anything, I should be *his* protégé.

Brighenti Do you need protection, Giordani?

Giordani Always, Brighenti.

Brighenti   But you discovered him, didn't you?

Pepoli You knew him years ago, you said, in Recanati.

Giordani He was very different then.

Pepoli   How long ago was it?

Giordani Eight or nine years.

Brighenti   Has he always been deformed?

Giordani Not always. It is a great torment to him.
  He has curious illusions: that the life of happiness
  Is dependent on beauty, love and so on. He fears
  That he will be always shut out from such a life.

Pepoli I doubt if that is an illusion, Giordani.

67

Brighenti Or that he was wrong in such a prophecy.

Giordani Perhaps, Brighenti. Yes, you may be right.
What can you or I know of such a life as he must lead?
I have seen him during his periods of blindness.
I have seen him hunched unseeing in his chair,
And it seemed as if, relieved of being watched,
His other senses were creeping away from him:
His hearing and his touch, so that he barely heard
The words I said to him, or felt my hand in his.
If you want to see what Life can make of a life,
You should see him at such times.

Pepoli Yet when one is with him one forgets his ailments.

Giordani He never does.

Pepoli   One only notices the beautiful way he smiles.
It must be very strange to him to emerge like this
Into a world where his fame has preceded him.

Giordani He went to Rome two or three years ago.
But he always refuses to speak of it; he hated it.

Brighenti Who wouldn't?

Pepoli   He seems very happy to be in Bologna.
I hope we shan't turn his head.

Giordani   You won't do that.
He has, quite nakedly, that thirst for fame
Which you and I have carefully to disguise.

Pepoli (*in mock indignation*) I don't want fame.

Giordani (*ironically*)   No, neither do I . . .
But Giacomo's longing for fame is never . . . odious.

Brighenti Oh neither is yours, Giordani.

Pepoli   It's very beautiful.

Giordani I dare say it is, to generous people like you;
But it isn't half so beautiful as Giacomo's.
In Recanati, when I warned him of literary women,
He said very blankly, 'But I long for the praise of women.'

Pepoli He can't complain of the absence of such praise.
Countess Malvezzi's eyes pop out of her head
Whenever he goes to her appalling literary salons.

Brighenti And they say it isn't only literature they talk about.

Pepoli I think it is, dear boy, I think it is.

Giordani Well, whatever it is in the case of la Malvezzi
It won't be literature in the case of Rosa Padovani.

Brighenti I think he knows where he is with la Padovani.
He has an astounding capacity for mild flirtation.
Pepoli *Mild* flirtation must be a new experience
For *her.*
Giordani　　　　　He has a great capacity for happiness.
It is good to see him indulge himself in it.
Pepoli Then why is he going back to Recanati?
Giordani Is he? I hadn't heard he was!
Pepoli　　　　　　　　　　　　I think he is.
Giordani But who told you? This is very upsetting.
He said he had never been so happy as in Bologna.
He *can't* go away from here!
I shall go and ask him what it all means.
Brighenti Yes, do, Giordani.
　　　　(background chatter)
Pepoli　　　　　　　Tell him he can't go.
Brighenti *(calling after him)*　　　　　Tell him we shall all
Follow him if he goes away.
　　　　(cross to)

Malvezzi　　　　　　　　But, Leopardi,
It only emphasises the old difference
Between poetry and mere verse: there *is* a difference,
And we see it exemplified in . . .
Rosa *(loudly)*　　　　　　Why here is Signor Giordani!
Good evening, Signor Giordani!
Giordani *(shortly)*　　　　　Good evening to you, Signora.
Giacomo! Why are they saying you are going back to Recanati?
　　　(music and chatter out. Silence. Long pause)

I'm sorry if I embarrassed you in front of all those people.
But I wanted to know why you were going back to Recanati.
Leopardi You didn't embarrass me.
Giordani　　　　　　　You looked very confused.
Leopardi I didn't expect your question; that was all.
Giordani I supposed there must be some reason you wanted to hide.
Leopardi I have nothing to hide.
Giordani　　　　　　Are you forced to go back?
Leopardi I suppose you might call it forced.
Giordani　　　　　　　Is it money again?

69

Leopardi No: I am certainly very poor; but I contrive.

Giordani Are you still teaching that Greek merchant Latin?

Leopardi Yes. It's a wonderful conjunction, isn't it? I . . .

Giordani (*not to be put off*) Giacomo: why are you going back?

Can't you even tell *me*?

(*pause*)

Leopardi Hasn't it occurred to you that I might not know the reason?

Giordani You mean there is no reason?

Leopardi   I mean I have not discovered it.

Giordani I suppose you are worried about your sister, and your brothers?

Leopardi (*almost to himself*)

Paolina: unwanted by men, haunting the cold white walls.
Carlo: still trembling on the edge of his escape.
Luigi: watched, imprisoned, persecuted . . . Pietruccio:
Of course I am worried about them . . . But it is not they,
It is not affection alone that lures me back . . .

Giordani   *Lures* you?

(*brief pause*)

Leopardi Lures me.

Giordani (*comprehending, moved*) Don't, Giacomo, don't go and live in that

horrible darkness.

Leopardi And if I do not live in that horrible darkness,

Its darkness haunts my sleep. And sleeping and waking
Have both to be lived with. The dream fades in the day,
But if, night after night, the dream is always the same,
If the same horror lies each night beside you
And waits in patience for sleep to bring you to it
And at that moment becomes the whole of you,
Then it matters little how quickly each separate dream
Dissolves in the day, for you know that the day
Is only one of your two lives, whose alternation
No point in time or place on earth can destroy.
I shall go back.

Giordani   I see you must go back,

But, Giacomo . . .

Leopardi   Yes?

Giordani   It will not be for ever?

Leopardi I hope not, Giordani.

Giordani   Do not *creep* back, Giacomo.

Leopardi How else should I go, Giordani?

70

Giordani (*after a pause*)   Go in triumph.
    Not as a prodigal son. Go with a sword in your hand.
    Go . . . as a deliverer.
       (*pause*)
Leopardi (*quietly*)   And deliver Paolina,
    Deliver Carlo, Luigi, Pietruccio . . .
Giordani (*almost a whisper*)   Go in triumph.
Leopardi (*quietly*)
    With hurting heart and groin, with darkening senses,
    To go in triumph . . . (*passionately*) Good God, Giordani: *yes!*
       (*pause*)

Adelaide If that is what they told you, I hope you took no notice.
    Bologna is very well known for insincerity.
    It is not very kind of them to try to spoil you.
    You will become as vain as they are. How is your health?
    You seem to me to have an unhealthy flush.
    (*Leopardi speaks now with great self-possession*)
Leopardi No, I think it is really the flush of health, mother.
   Carlo You look wonderful, Giacomo; doesn't he, Paolina?
  Paolina (*softly*) Better than I've ever known him. Splendid!
Pierfrancesco   Giacomo the Magnificent!
Leopardi Thank you, Pietruccio, you look magnificent, too.
Monaldo You really are better in health than when you left us, Giacomo?
Leopardi My blindness is not as bad as I have sometimes known it.
    A good deal of the time I can even see, which is rather refreshing.
    But what is most interesting is that I have given up coughing blood.
    I rarely have indigestion; and I rarely lose my voice.
Adelaide   I see.
Leopardi (*easily*) I do, of course . . . sometimes have father's complaint.
Adelaide It is well you can be philosophical about these matters.
    They are sent for some good purpose.
Leopardi   Yes, indeed.
Adelaide You remember what I always told you as children.
Leopardi I can remember *most* of what you told us as children.
    Are you referring to any particular injunction?
Adelaide When you were ill, I never failed to tell you
    To carry your ailments not to me, but to God.
Leopardi Indeed I do so, mother, and with great fidelity;
    All except father's complaint, of course:

71

And ... *those*, I should be as reluctant to carry to the Almighty
As I should to you, mother.

Monaldo   Oh come, Giacomo,
What should I do without your mother?
She is splendid on these occasions, splendid.

Pierfrancesco What *is* father's complaint, mother? And why is it plural?
           (long giggle from Luigi)

Adelaide Luigi: I am not aware that your father's malady
Is a subject for amusement. You have ills of your own.
I do not think you would care for us to laugh at them.
You had better retire to your room.

Luigi   Yes, mother.

Leopardi *(concerned)* Have you been ill again, Luigi?

Luigi *(receding)*   Oh it was nothing.
Nothing at all, Giacomo ...

Leopardi   I think, Luigi,
I shall come and talk to you after you have gone to bed.
I am almost a connoisseur of illnesses.
We will compare experiences. May I visit him, mother?

Adelaide It is a matter of indifference to me.

Leopardi I gather I may, Luigi. Till later, then.
         ('*Good night, Luigi*', etc., from all)

Pierfrancesco Why did you come back to Recanati, Giacomo?

Leopardi Well, Pietruccio, one can't stay away from home for ever.

Pierfrancesco Why not?

Leopardi   Well, I like to see you all again.

Pierfrancesco   Why?

Leopardi Well, my dear, don't you ever want to see me?

Pierfrancesco Certainly I do. But that is scarcely a reason
    For *you* wanting to see *us*. We are not much to look at.

Leopardi You are a very great deal to look at, Pietruccio.

Pierfrancesco What, with there being six of us, you mean?

Leopardi *(laughing)*
Well, not wholly that, Pietruccio.

Pierfrancesco   Then wholly what?
    (pause)

Adelaide Why don't you answer him?

Leopardi   I mean, Pietruccio,
That I came home for a variety of reasons,
And it would be difficult to describe *any* of them.

72

Pierfrancesco Accurately, you mean.

Leopardi   Accurately.

Pierfrancesco   Yes ... I seem to know the feeling.

Carlo You are not usually inarticulate, Pietruccio.

Pierfrancesco No. But I used to be. Giacomo.

Leopardi   Yes?

Pierfrancesco Don't you find us all rather provincial ... ?

After Bologna, I mean.

(laughter, but not from Adelaide. Murmurs of 'Pietruccio!' These die
down)

Adelaide Why don't you answer him?

Leopardi   I was considering.

No, Pietruccio: I think that you would all add distinction

To the society of Bologna. Indeed you would.

Pierfrancesco Do you think Paolina would find a husband there?

Monaldo⎫
Carlo ⎭ Pietruccio!

Leopardi (loudly) Yes, Pietruccio, I was thinking at that very moment

What a wonderful success Paolina would have there.

Bologna would be at her feet.

Carlo   Of course it would.

Adelaide In that case it is possibly as well

That we entertain no idea of sending her there.

Monaldo (firmly) I hope that all my children may one day see Bologna.

I once went there myself.

Pierfrancesco   Carlo would be successful.

Wouldn't he, Giacomo?

Leopardi   I am sure he would.

Pierfrancesco He is very successful with the ladies of Recanati.

Did you know that, Giacomo? They smile at him in the street.

Adelaide Come, Pierfrancesco ... it is time you went to bed.

I know we rarely know where we are in this family,

But one thing is certain: you are not going to Bologna,

Unless of course your father insists to the contrary.

You are going to your bed in Recanati. Come.

Pierfrancesco (receding) Recanati must seem very dull after Bologna, mustn't it,
                                                 mother?

Adelaide That is neither here nor there.

Pierfrancesco   But they must each be somewhere, mother.

(door)

73

Monaldo Are you tired, Giacomo?
Leopardi   A little, father, yes.
Monaldo Then you won't really want to talk any more tonight.
Leopardi I am always ready to talk, and always glad to.
         I have missed you all far more than I can say.
         And sometimes almost more than I could bear.
         There was no day when I did not wish you were with me.
Monaldo Were you unhappy there, Giacomo?
Leopardi   No, father, no.
         Only I was rather confused, and am still confused,
         Less so than after Rome, but still confused.
         When things are clearer, I will say what I mean.
         I feel at the moment as if I had learnt only
         That cities are difficult. I must have learnt more than that.
         Now I am back perhaps I shall find out what.
         Only: please let me slip back into our life here
         As easily as I can; then I shall know what I am.
Monaldo What do you mean by 'cities are difficult'?
Leopardi I mean how hard they are for people like us to conquer.
         And until we have conquered them we cannot be happy.
Monaldo Or until we have conquered the desire for them.
Leopardi I feel that Bologna was still only a prelude.
   Carlo A prelude to what, Giacomo?
Leopardi   A prelude to ...
Monaldo Carlo, you will only tire your brother.
         I think you had better come along with me.
         Good night, Giacomo, I have missed you greatly.
         You won't go away again, will you? Not too soon, I mean.
Leopardi No, father.
Monaldo   Stay with us, Giacomo: stay for a long time.
Leopardi I shall, father.
Monaldo   Good night, Paolina. Come, Carlo.
         (good nights)
   Carlo I will come in a few minutes, father.
         (door)
Leopardi Why was Luigi ordered away like that,
         The minute he opened his mouth?
   Carlo   You know why.
         I wrote and told you about his escapades.
Leopardi You said they had forgiven him.

74

Carlo   They have, poor boy.
But forgiveness here is always rather worse than punishment,
As you should know, Giacomo: you have been forgiven often
                                        enough.

Paolina We are not allowed to be very often alone with him.
I expect they think our little brother may corrupt us.

Carlo (*sighing*) It's a very peculiar sensation here tonight.
As it always is whenever you return, Giacomo.
An air of expectation pervades the house,
As if mother were giving birth to another child.
Or no: it is, dare I say it, rather as if one were dying.

Leopardi Oh, don't worry, Carlo. I am not dying.

Carlo Well, I shall go to bed. Good night to you both.
    (*good nights exchanged. Door*)

Paolina (*in tones we have not heard her use before*)
    Well, you didn't find me a husband in Bologna, Giacomo.

Leopardi (*trying to banter*) Do you know why that was?

Paolina   I can imagine why.

Leopardi It is because I insist on the highest standards.
I will not let you marry less than a prince.

Paolina Oh, Giacomo, you would not joke on such a subject
If you had been here, if you had seen the efforts
That have been made to inveigle men to take me.

Leopardi Paolina!

Paolina   If you had seen mother's triumphant silences,
When father's attempts failed.

Leopardi   Paolina!

Paolina It is amazing how thin the family honour can wear,
When the question arises of marrying off a daughter:
Especially when there is so little money to give with her,
And neither her looks nor her accomplishments
Make her a very good bargain. I know you have suffered,
And I think I have suffered every moment with you.
But you cannot know what I have seen since you left;
The appraising glances of elderly widowers,
The tentative conversations under the eye of my parents;
Their disappointment that I show myself so badly.
It is not I they watch as I enter the room:

75

It is the face of the prospective purchaser.
It is worse when they cannot make up their minds at once.

Leopardi Paolina, you must not talk, you must not think like that!
There is no one in the world worth so much trouble.
You must not be hurt, Paolina!

Paolina (sobbing)   Why has my life gone wrong?

Leopardi It has not, darling, this is only a phase of it,
Only an intermission.

Paolina   Giacomo.

Leopardi   Yes?

Paolina Do you know those waking recapitulations
Of bygone disastrous scenes: how you proceed again,
How you prolong a dream, and try to twist it
From the hour of downfall, and contrive to avert
What in life was not averted? You change the accident,
The careless gesture, the unguarded word
That led to months of sorrow.

Leopardi   I know such hours, yes.

Paolina I have sometimes undreamt my whole life through,
And lived it as it might have been. I have lived yours too,
And Carlo's and Luigi's. But they do not alter.

Leopardi We must make them what we can. It is all I can say.
I know it does not help. Our lives are real:
We must try never to make them fantasies.

Paolina I am tiring you with my fantasies, Giacomo.
I must go to bed.

Leopardi   You can never tire me, Paolina.
Kiss me good night.

Paolina   Aren't you going up to bed?

Leopardi Yes, very shortly. I shall go and see Luigi first.

Paolina Till tomorrow, Giacomo.

Leopardi   Till tomorrow.

          (brief pause)

Monaldo Giacomo really is well, don't you think, my dear?

Adelaide   Is he?
Don't stand there dropping candlewax on the bed.

Monaldo I think he has found some sort of happiness in Bologna.

Adelaide It is useless to ask me for forgiveness;
Forgiveness can only come from the hand of God.

Monaldo Forgiveness, my dear? Have I said something wrong?

Adelaide I meant your son, of course. Get into bed.

Monaldo   Oh.
     He didn't seem to be asking forgiveness, my dear.
     I think he looked remarkably unrepentant.

Adelaide That is neither here nor there. Put out the light.
          (loud puff. Pause. Door, cautiously)

Leopardi Luigi?

  Luigi   Yes.

Leopardi   Aren't you in bed?

  Luigi   I am here at the window.

Leopardi What are you doing there? You will catch cold.

   Luigi I have my cloak. I was watching the street . . .
     Do you suppose if one jumped, it would kill one?

Leopardi Luigi, don't be foolish . . . Do you often
     Think thoughts like that?

   Luigi *(lightly)*   Quite often, yes.
     Whenever I am tired of my life: which is most of the time.

Leopardi Why on earth should you be tired of your life?

   Luigi I thought you would sympathise with such a feeling.
     Or at any rate that you would not reproach or blame me.

Leopardi I am not doing either of those things, Luigi;
     I am only begging you to talk in a happier way.

   Luigi That is scarcely the message of your writings, is it?
     I know that life here is not worth living.
     I have been almost cheered by the one single thought
     That you thought so, too; Giacomo, love,
     When I repeat your views, it is a little hard
     To find that you don't seem to acquiesce in them.
     Are you a fake, Giacomo?

Leopardi   I may be, yes.
     I would rather a thousand times that you thought me so,
     Than that I should hear you talk like this.
     You have everything to live for: you are young and handsome;
     And I did not write for *you*. You must not try
     To enter the blind circle in which I once moved.

   Luigi *Once* moved?

Leopardi   Yes. Luigi! Try to believe me.
     I know I cursed, when I knew no manner of life

77

Other than the life I lived in the trap of Recanati.
But there are other lives, Luigi. Here, at home,
I never knew that life could open like a flower,
As it did for me in Bologna; only wait a little:
There is, surely, something in life you hope for?

Luigi *(unmoved)* The wings of a dove. Can you provide those?

Leopardi Have you never had anything in life to make you happy?

Luigi Yes, Giacomo. But I shall not have it again.

Leopardi What sort of happiness?

Luigi   They surely wrote and told you?

        (pause)
When they discovered, three years ago,
That I used to climb out of the house at night
And pass the time in the company of whores,
I was almost as ashamed as the family. Delight
Had always been precarious; now it was certainly over,
And there would be no more risks, no more over-excitements.
And then, after the punishments and the weeping,
After the inquisitions and the silences,
I slowly realised what had been taken from me.
No, not the acts of pleasure, whatever you think;
But the immeasurable acts of charity.
You will have known how penniless I was . . .
        (pause)

Leopardi Yes?

Luigi   I was laughed out of my shame.

Leopardi   Shame?

Luigi That I could only have my girls when they could manage.
When they were not required by better-off customers.
By the time they had laughed me out of my shame at that,
Those nights were over. *Then*, I could begin to think,
Alone, in my bed, in a locked room, at night,
Of human courtesy, and where one finds it.

Leopardi There are other places to find it, Luigi:
I . . . won't deny you may have found where you say,
But . . . Luigi . . .

Luigi   Yes?

Leopardi   Only *wait* a little, hopefully.
Yes, I, Giacomo Leopardi, ask you to hope.
And I will take you to it in other places.

Luigi No, Giacomo . . . I have ceased to care.
We must all find a means of answering these things.
You have your life of fame, creation, the world;
Carlo is practical: he will escape;
Paolina may even now be rescued from here.
But my way has been found *for* me.

Leopardi   What way?

Luigi It is simply that I have not very much longer to live.

Leopardi Luigi! What wicked nonsense! You will live
Longer than anyone, you and Pietruccio.
When did you begin to think in that foolish way?

Luigi I even know that, Giacomo. Some time ago,
I noticed that mother had ceased to mention
My past iniquities; it was then I suspected.
And when that door was left unlocked, I was certain.

Leopardi (*quietly*) It cannot be true, and it shall not be true, Luigi.
Luigi: I will prove to you the delight even of this base world.

Luigi (*a little moved by the earnestness of Leopardi's tone*)
But even if you did, what could it matter to me?

Leopardi The first thing is that you shall know of it.
And then you will see perhaps some way we can win it for you.

Luigi Oh, Giacomo, how inconsequent you are . . .
(*pause*)

Leopardi It is not inconsequence. I will lead you, Luigi,
I will lead you out and away.

Luigi   It's like Virgil and Dante, isn't it?
Shall we ever see the stars?

(*pause*)

Leopardi Oh God, by this bed I have so often prayed by,
To you, oh God, who so rarely answer our prayers,
I pray to you again, oh God – or pray to whatever power
Outside us, that gives us strength – I pray you:
Help me to help them; deliver their deliverance
Into my hands. Help me to go away,
This time, oh God, not for myself alone. I know
That wherever I choose to go, if I have a choice,
Some inevitable city awaits my eyes,
Some unalterable spoken word awaits my ears,

79

One story, of many possible, now preparing,
Waits for my entrance. Let me enter, oh God, bravely,
And in my fight to survive, oh God, I pray you,
Let me never forget them, let me never forget
My young beloveds, still imprisoned here.
Let me never forget their sorrows, greater than mine,
Let me never forget them in the world preparing for me.

(*fade in Fanny Targioni, playing the piano*)

Fanny   Well, Ranieri?

Ranieri   Well, Fanny?

Fanny   Do you think my playing has improved?

Ranieri   It was always beautiful, Fanny: it is now impeccable.

Fanny   You are proud of your little Florentine friend?

Ranieri   I am very proud indeed of her, my dear.

Fanny   Then why will you not accompany me to the Opera Ball?

Ranieri   Fanny, my dear; I have already told you the reason.

Fanny   You do not expect me to believe that, do you?

Ranieri   Do you always suspect the motives of your friends?
Do you subject poor Targioni to similar inquisitions?

Fanny   And do not speak disrespectfully of my husband, Ranieri.
I assure you that that is forbidden.

Ranieri   I wasn't, my dear.
I was only wondering if I ought to commiserate with him.

Fanny   You impertinent creature. But you are quite, quite handsome,
                                     Ranieri,
And for want of a better companion I am glad to see you.
And you refuse to accompany me to the Opera Ball.
Who is this 'other engagement' you have to go to?

Ranieri   I am going to Pisa to meet Count Giacomo Leopardi.

Fanny   Haven't you enough aristocratic friends already?
There will be plenty of counts at the Opera Ball.

Ranieri   Fanny: you make it very hard to be patient with you.
I am not seeing Leopardi because he is a count,
But because he is a poet and a man of intellect;
He is very probably our greatest poet since Dante.

Fanny   Will you get me his autograph?

Ranieri   Fanny: you outrage me!
I think you must be the shallowest woman in Florence.

Fanny   Shallower even than your appalling actresses?

Ranieri My actresses, as you call them, are by no means shallow.
They may not have your advantages of breeding
Or the resources of your education, dear Fanny,
But continuous association with exalted art
Enlarges their culture and deepens their consciousness.

Fanny (*laughing*) Who taught you to recite that?

Ranieri   Fanny!

Fanny (*still laughing*) Did *they* teach you?
Is it a speech from one of their exalted plays?

Ranieri It is nothing of the kind; it is a simple observation,
Which I have made myself.

Fanny   It is very, *very* simple.
Dear Ranieri, I shall play to you again.

Ranieri Fanny . . .! And you wonder why I run away from you.
    (*Fanny laughs. Piano*)
The mere breath of coherent conversation
Will be like heaven after all this rattle and clatter.
    (*discord on piano*)

Fanny What a very disagreeable remark!

Ranieri If you will forgive me, I shall ring for my hat and cloak.

Fanny No, I will *not* forgive you. Come and sit here.
No: here, on the piano-seat. Now:
You have my permission to tell me about Leopardi.

Ranieri Leopardi's poems . . .

Fanny   I don't want to hear about his poems.
What is he like as a man?

Ranieri   He is said to be kind and gentle,
And very reticent.

Fanny   You are the stupidest person.
I mean: is he handsome and fascinating?

Ranieri No, dear Fanny, he is not like me at all.
    (*treble arpeggio, minor, up and down piano during next lines*)
He is said to be much pursued by women,
Though mainly, I understand, of the blue-stocking type.

Fanny And intellectual actresses, I suppose?
    (*she laughs*)
Will you bring him to see me?

Ranieri   That will depend.

Fanny   On what?

Ranieri On the nature of your behaviour from now till then.

81

Fanny Oh? (*sings, accompanying herself*) 'Io sono docile . . .'

Ranieri   No, Fanny dear, you are not.

Fanny 'Son rispettosa . . .'

Ranieri   And you are far from that.

Fanny Well, we shall see, when you bring your handsome poet.

Ranieri I am afraid, Fanny, that he is not at all handsome.

Fanny Not handsome!

Ranieri   No, Fanny; and he is sometimes almost blind.

Fanny Poor darling . . .

(*piano: 'Son rispettosa'*)

Ranieri   And he is said to be almost a hunchback.

Fanny (*recoiling*) What? Oh, I shouldn't like that at all.

(*soft glissando on piano*)

No, tell him to stay at home and write his poems.

I never know where to look if I see a hunchback.

Don't bring him here.

Ranieri   I shall go, Fanny.

Fanny No, don't go, Tonino: I shall be all alone.

Ranieri It will be good for you, Fanny: a little private thought

May bring you to your senses.

Fanny   I will meditate

Upon the resources of my education, shall I?

Ranieri You are a frivolous and shameless woman, Fanny. Goodbye.

Fanny You won't forget Leopardi's autograph, will you?

I already have Lord Byron's and Manzoni's:

It will be in honourable company.

Ranieri   You must ask him yourself.

Goodbye.

Fanny   You may give me one kiss on the cheek.

Ranieri (*doing so*) Goodbye.

Fanny (*with lingering sensuality*) Goodbye, Tonino. Leopardi, indeed!

(*door. After the briefest pause she attacks the piano angrily. Fade*)

Leopardi You are indeed the kindest of men, Ranieri.

I only wish you had come to Pisa earlier. It is a good place.

A place of unemphatic weather, unemphatic gaiety:

Even the leaning tower seems to say:

'Do not let us be too upright, too over-impressive;

Life is not worth such tension: let us incline a little,

Like a flower in a mild wind.' That is how it seems.

Ranieri (*laughs*) I have never been in Pisa before. I cannot say.

Leopardi It has been easy to be here. I am sorry to leave it.

Ranieri Then why do you go?

Leopardi   One always knows the moment:
          I have learnt all it has to say.

Ranieri   But you have been happy here?

Leopardi Yes, certainly. But happy with that sort of happiness
          That disappears when one discovers its cause.
          I found out why I have been happy here in Pisa.

Ranieri   Why have you been?

Leopardi One could laugh, if one did not weep, at its simple irony.
          It is like the place where I have been most *un*happy.
          It is only amazing that the reason took so long to seek.
          There is a road here I call the road of memories;
          It is like a road I have often traversed elsewhere,
          In a different mood . . . Pisa is Recanati.

Ranieri   But that is your home.

Leopardi That is my home.

Ranieri (*mystified*)   But, surely, Leopardi,
          Surely you were never unhappy at home?
               (*pause*)

Leopardi I . . . seem to remember an occasional awkward moment.

Ranieri But every family has those: they are quite unimportant.
          My family is in Naples. Being a liberal, of course,
          I am not allowed back there; but oh, Leopardi,
          I live for the day when I shall see them again.
          I always think of them as . . . (*he pauses*)

Leopardi   Yes?

Ranieri As a monument, Leopardi.

Leopardi (*impassively*)   A monument.

Ranieri (*sentimentally enthusiastic*)
          As a sculptured group under the sun of Naples . . .
          And an empty place among them: mine, Leopardi.

Leopardi (*as before*) Yours.

Ranieri   A monument in marble, permanent and fine.
          Mother, and father, and Paolina.

Leopardi (*almost in terror*)   Who?

Ranieri I have an adorable sister called Paolina.

Leopardi (*still a little shaken*)   So have I.

Ranieri You have? Well, that is a tie, Leopardi, isn't it?

83

Isn't it? But you have three younger brothers also.
Haven't you?
>   (*pause*)

Leopardi   I *had* three younger brothers, Ranieri.

Ranieri I...

Leopardi   A year ago, my second brother, Luigi,
Died... He died, contented, there, in Recanati.
He died of consumption: he was consumed.
He had nothing to live for. I might have shown him something;
I only showed him desperate examples.
I am unpardonably to blame, Ranieri.

Ranieri   You are not, Leopardi.

Leopardi He lived and died in that terrible dark place.
>   (*pause*)

Ranieri What shall you do, since you will not stay in Pisa?

Leopardi I shall go to Florence, and then to Recanati,
As I have always gone, again and again.

Ranieri No, Leopardi! If it is as you say,
You must never go back there... Forgive me, Leopardi:
But could you not stay with me for a time in Florence?
There are other worlds there than the worlds you know.
You might find something to care for in one of those worlds.

Leopardi (*gently*) I shall go to Recanati; perhaps I shall see you in Florence;
Or in another place, at another time.
But do not try to draw me into *your* world.
Do you promise me that, Ranieri?

Ranieri   Of course.

Leopardi It is not of course. You promise?

Ranieri   I promise.
>   (*long pause: jangle of doorbell. Door*)

Janitor (*hoarse and old*) Good evening, sir. Can I help you?

Leopardi Signor Ranieri lives in this house, I believe?

Janitor Yes, sir. On the second floor.

Leopardi   I will go up.

Janitor Yes, sir. Would you like me to show you the way?

Leopardi No, thank you. I think I can find it myself.

Janitor The large door on the right at the top of the staircase.

Leopardi (*receding*) Thank you. I shall find it...
>   (*pause: knock at the door, rather heavy. Pause*)

(*another knock, heavier. Brief pause*)
(*disappointed*) Not there. So it is hail and farewell . . .

(*door opens suddenly*)
Ranieri (*surprised and pleased*) Leopardi! I didn't know you were in
Florence!

Leopardi Ranieri! Once more.
Didn't you get my note?
Ranieri No. Did you send one?
Let me take your cloak . . .
Leopardi I didn't come sooner . . .
I have not been the best of company.
Ranieri Well, I have never known better.
Maddalena (*off*) Who is it, Tonio?
Leopardi Are you sure you haven't better at the moment?
I can easily come tomorrow.
Ranieri No: I want you to meet Maddalena.
Leopardi Maddalena?
Ranieri Maddalena Pelzet.
Leopardi She is an actress, isn't she?
Ranieri She is, Leopardi. (*sotto voce*) *Yes*, my dear . . .
(*he breaks off as Maddalena, a swooping contralto, approaches*)
Maddalena Who *is* it, Antonio? Who is it?
Ranieri Maddalena, dear, may I present
Count Giacomo Leopardi! Signora Pelzet.
Leopardi Signora.
Maddalena Leopardi!
We have talked of *no one else!* Antonio!
You can tidy the room and then go and sit in the corner.
I have no more time for you this evening. I shall sit here,
And listen to Leopardi.
Ranieri He will listen to you, you mean.
I can never get a word in edgewise, Leopardi.
Maddalena You will not be called on to try. Pick up that cushion.
I have never known such a man for sitting on the floor.
There. Are you comfortable, Leopardi?
No, of course you are not. Antonio, bring the decanter,
And put it over here.
Ranieri There you are, my dear.
Is there anything else I can do?

Maddalena   Not at the moment.
            Leopardi: I shall give you a glass of Ranieri's horrible wine.
            And now tell me, my friend:
            Have you been writing any more of those beautiful poems?
    Leopardi (*overcome*) I . . . am always trying . . .
Maddalena (*interrupting triumphantly*)   Of course you are.
            There is always something to learn: it is what I tell Ranieri.
    Ranieri I am perfectly willing to be taught.
Maddalena   (You common creature.)
            Leopardi: I have always prayed to meet you,
            Ever since the night when I read aloud, at a party,
            Those wonderful lines of yours on Údine:
            (*declaiming*) 'Dead, yes: but never vanquished,
            We shall fall free; and armed; and all together.'
                (*Ranieri laughs loudly*)
            I am not aware that I have said anything funny, Ranieri?
    Ranieri No, dear; only the poem happens to be by someone else.
Maddalena By whom?
    Ranieri   Vincenzo Monti, dear.
Maddalena   Leopardi, is this true?
    Leopardi I'm afraid it is, signora.
Maddalena   How extraordinary.
            But you wrote a poem very *like* that, didn't you?
    Leopardi Extremely like, signora.
Maddalena (*triumphantly*)   What did I tell you?
            And now, I suppose, Antonio Ranieri,
            You will immediately tell the others when they arrive,
            That I made myself foolish in front of this great, great Man?
            I am sure that Leopardi will spare my feelings?
    Leopardi Of course I will, signora.
Maddalena (*intimately*) I liked you for saying that. Thank you.
    Leopardi (*disturbed*) Did you say there were other people coming?
    Ranieri Yes, Leopardi, it's to be a great occasion
    Leopardi I am sure I had better not stay . . .
Maddalena   Of course you must stay.
    Ranieri You must stay, Leopardi. It won't be a large gathering.
            But a few friends of mine are coming in after the theatre,
            And a few of the actors with them; they'll be here quite soon.
            It's an intellectual gathering.
Maddalena (*impressively*)   Biffi is coming.

86

Leopardi Biffi?

Ranieri   Maddalena's leading man.

Maddalena I'm having a night off tonight. Cartieri
           Is doing my part. (*sharply*) You haven't asked *her*, Ranieri?

Ranieri No, dear, of course not.

Leopardi (*vaguely*)   Is she not nice, perhaps . . . ?

Maddalena My dear, she's perfectly charming. And even as an actress,
           It's possible she may one day show considerable promise.
           But, you do understand, she's not very good at a party.

Ranieri And we particularly couldn't have her here tonight.

Leopardi Why, what is going to happen?

Ranieri   Biffi and Maddalena
           Are giving a little recital of their favourite scenes.

Maddalena (*plaintively*) Ranieri insisted on it, the tiresome *Man*.

Leopardi I am glad he did. What are you going to act?

Maddalena (*eagerly*) We're beginning with the suffocation scene from
                     Shakespeare's *Otello*.

           You know it, of course?

Leopardi   Yes, very well.

Maddalena And then the death scene from Alfieri's *Cleopatra*:
           And the poison scene, of course, from *Lucrezia Borgia;*
           And after that, if there's time, the scene of the murders –
           (*exuberant knocking at door. Cries of 'Ranieri', etc.*)
           Why, they are here already!

Ranieri   I'll go to the door.

Maddalena No, no, Tonio, you stay here; I'll let them in.

Leopardi (*agitated*) Ranieri, I dare not stay. Is there another way out?

Ranieri My dear Leopardi, why should you not stay?
           (*greetings in background*)

Leopardi I am desperately ill at ease, Ranieri, I cannot meet people.
           You promised me you would not . . .

Ranieri   Please stay, Leopardi,
           If only for a little . . . I will protect you:
           It will be no more than being at a concert.
           (*conversation held behind*)

Maddalena Botti! How nice to see you away from the theatre for once.
           Dear Botti! (*sharply*) How was she?

Botti   Dreadful, my dear, dreadful.

Maddalena Darling! How could she be? But you're so *prejudiced*.
           Botti, this is Count Giacomo Leopardi:

87

And this is Botti. I want you to like each other
So very much.

Leopardi   I am sure we shall. How do you do, sir?

Botti   How do? Is there anything to drink, Maddalena?

Maddalena   It's right in front of your eyes, you stupid man.
           And where is Biffi? I must go and find my Biffi.

Ranieri   Maria! Teresa! I am so glad you could come.
           What a long time to stay away!

Maria   It seems like months.

Teresa   Like months . . . and, oh, what a lovely new carpet!

Ranieri   You honour it with your tread, my dear Teresa.

Teresa   Ranieri!

Ranieri   My dear, may I present Count Giacomo Leopardi?
           Signorina Teresa Santi; Signorina Maria Santi.

Leopardi   Signorine.

Maria   But Count Leopardi, what a pleasure to meet you!
           We have read your poems so often.

Leopardi (*pleased*)   Have you?

Maria   Oh yes: that dear little poem about the Hillside.

Teresa   And that dear little poem about the Sparrow.

Maria   What a genuine pleasure to have you here in Florence!

Leopardi   It is kind of you to say so.

Maddalena (*loudly*) Biffi! Where are you? Fabrizi, dear, where's Biffi?

Fabrizi   He's out in the hall, darling.

Pavesi   Just making himself look nice.

Maddalena   He always looks nice. Biffi! (*receding*) I want you, Biffi!

Ranieri   I hope you're not too exhausted for a drink, Pavesi?
           Nor you, Fabrizi?

Pavesi   I'm never exhausted, dear boy.

Fabrizi   But it doesn't look much as if we could get at the table.

Ranieri   Leopardi, I want you to meet Pavesi. Pavesi: Leopardi.
           And this is Fabrizi . . . Fabrizi: Leopardi.

(*greetings: 'How do you do?' 'Enchanted', etc.*)

Leopardi   How do you do? I have been to your theatre,
           And seen you often, though of course you won't have seen me.

Pavesi   Ah, but we know your writings, Leopardi.

Fabrizi   Yes, of course.

Leopardi   And I have been thinking that no one ever read them.

Maddalena (*approaching*) Here's Biffi! I've found my Biffi at last.

Do you know what he was doing? He was *patting his cheeks* in the hall.

Biffi (*bass clarinet*) Maddalena, you really are a ridiculous woman.

Ranieri Welcome, Biffi. How kind of you to come.

Biffi Nuttatall, dear boy.

Ranieri   This is Count Giacomo Leopardi:
Signor Armando Biffi.

Leopardi   How do you do, sir?
I am very enchanted to meet you.

Biffi (*indifferently*)   D'do.

Ranieri Leopardi has seen you many times, of course, Biffi.
And you will have read his poems.

Biffi   I don't think so, no.

Maddalena Leopardi is one of my best friends, Biffi;
I want you to like each other *so very much.*

Biffi Good.

Maddalena   I've told him we're doing the last scene from *Otello*.

Leopardi I am looking forward to it very much.

Biffi (*bored*)   Good.

Leopardi Very much. It must be incomparably difficult to act.

Biffi Yes, there are some bits of it not very easy;
The words don't give one very much help of course.

Leopardi I imagine it's very beautiful in the original.

Biffi Oh, the original's much worse. I think we've improved on that.

Pavesi Yes, Botti's translation is simply superb.

Biffi   Of course, yes.

Botti It's the plot, of course, that matters.

Biffi   Yes, of course.

Fabrizi And the plot, of course, is anglicised beyond recognition.

Biffi
Pavesi⎰ Oh yes, of course, of course, yes.

Botti And that whole century, of course, had no sense of style.

The others Oh no, of course not, of course not, no, of course not.

Maddalena Come over here, Leopardi, away from these trumpeting
                                        elephants.
I want you to meet the dearest woman in the world:
This is my darling Fanny Targioni.
I want you to like each other *so very much* . . .

Leopardi   Signora . . .

Fanny (*after a brief pause*) Count Leopardi, how charming to find you here.
Ranieri has told me about you, and given me your books.

89

Leopardi I am happy to think of your looking at them.

Fanny And of course I do look at them. . . . You must autograph them
for me.

Maddalena (*cheerfully*) I want you to *love* each other. I must flee . . .

Fanny Won't you come and sit here?

Leopardi Thank you, may I?

Fanny Isn't it exciting to be going to have a private performance?

Leopardi Ah, signora, then you are not one of the company?

Fanny (*laughing*) Good heavens, no. I'm only a humble spectator.

Ranieri Don't believe her, Leopardi, she's going to play the piano.

Fanny Oh, you won't really hear me.

I am just going to play the music during the acting.
You won't notice me at all. Ah, here is my husband.
This is Count Giacomo Leopardi, darling.

Targioni (*vaguely*) Ah, very pleased.

Can I come and sit down? No, don't move, Leopardi. There.
Tell me, Leopardi; you . . . *write*, or something, don't you?

Leopardi Yes.

Targioni (*kindly*) I thought as much. I haven't time for writing myself.
To do it, I mean; though of course I should very much like to . . .
You going away, Fanny?

Fanny I am going to try the piano.

Forgive me, Count Leopardi.

Leopardi Signora.

Fanny No, don't get up.

Leopardi How charming your wife is, Signor Targioni.

Targioni (*absently*) Who, Fanny? Oh yes, she's very charming, very.
I've often thought of trying *my* hand at poetry,
Something rather lengthy, you know, on the lines of Tasso.
(*piano behind*)
Something that would keep one occupied for some years.

Leopardi (*agreeably*) It would do, yes.

Targioni (*helplessly*) But, of course, there's never the time . . .
I don't know what Fanny's supposed to be doing at that piano.

Leopardi I think she's going to accompany the acting.

Targioni Oh yes? She ought to be at home looking after the children.

Leopardi She looks so very young to be a mother.

Targioni (*laughing dimly*) Oh yes, she's well preserved.
Don't tell her I said so, though.
That wouldn't do at all . . . Can you see . . . ?

Leopardi Thank you.
           (*background conversation out. Piano up. Hold behind Leopardi*)

           (*to himself*) She is a wife and a mother . . .
           This city is lived in by her; the streets know where she goes,
           And are indifferent to her. This room
           Ignores what it contains. Only the keys
           Yield music to her small white hands. This curious man beside me,
           Whenever he likes can take those hands in his.
           His hands are close to mine . . . Her face
           Could twist my heart and turn my days to fever . . .
           Othello: Cassio: Iago: Desdemona . . .
           'It is the cause, it is the cause, my soul . . .'
               (*music*)

Biffi *Oh my profoundest soul, the reason is as follows:*
      I need not mention it, you bright fugitive stars;
      But the reason is as follows. Not that I intend
      To let her blood (tremendous Heaven!) stain
      The snow-white marble of her morbid skin. No, no!
      But die she must, alas, or she will drive
      Yet more unfortunate desperates to their doom . . .
      Extinguish this light . . . Then . . . extinguish that!
      The one can be be relighted, not the other,
      If I should change my mind. No, fair Desdaymona,
      Thee once blown out, unscrupulous plan of Nature,
      Not even Prometheus's omnipotent pants
      Could fan thy vital flame. The rose, once picked,
      Must die upon the ground. While still upon the tree,
      Let me inhale its perfume, as of balsam.
         (loud kiss)
      Look thus when dead, and I will murder thee,
      And then continue to love thee. One final kiss. Just one.
         (loud kiss)
      Sweet, fatal creature; the tears I weep are painful.
         (sob)
      Ah me, Desdaymona awakes at last.

Maddalena (as Desdemona) *Is that Otello there?*
     Biffi   *Desdaymona: it is he.*
Maddalena *Art thou prepared for rest?*
     Biffi (on fade) *Desdaymona: hast thou prayed?*

91

Leopardi (*to himself over from 'Sweet, fatal creature'*)
    'So sweet was ne'er so fatal. I must weep,
    But they are cruel tears.' Shall I one day
    Weep also for this evening's work? Oh not just yet, not now,
    Now while her hands rest on the waiting keyboard,
    Sweet and fatal.
       (*bring up Biffi and Maddalena*)
Maddalena (loudly) *Speakst thou of murder? Speakst thou of murder then?*
   Biffi Desdaymona: I do.
Maddalena   *Help me, oh Holy Mother!*
   Biffi I echo thee: amen.
Maddalena I trust thy slaughterous thoughts turn not towards me?
   Biffi (like a drum-roll) *Berrrumph!*
Maddalena (vox angelica) *A mortal fear steals o'er me.*
    (more deeply) *Well know I*
    The dreadful portent as thy large white eye
    Swerves in its sooty socket. I am not guilty,
    And wherefore should I fear? Yet none the less,
    (vox angelica) *A mortal fear steals o'er me.*
   Biffi (loudly) *Think of thy sins!*
Maddalena (passionately) *My only sin is Love!*
   Biffi (crescendo) *And for that sin thou to thy death shalt go!*
     (rapid fade on '*to thy death shalt go*' . . . hold)
  Leopardi (*to himself, over from 'that sin'*)
    'Think on thy sins . . .
    They are loves I bear to you.'
    I could build up whole cathedrals of thought about her
    On the only thing I know of her: that she is good.
    She did not fear my glance;
    Nor did she, as the other women did,
    Stare in my eyes to avoid the horror elsewhere . . .

    (*fade into piano playing children's song. Two little girls, Fanny's*
    daughters, are singing the last verse of a song)
  Girls   *Little bird, my little dove,*
                Little dove, as white as snow:
                See, I have you in my hands,
                And I shall not let you go.
  (dim.)   *And I shall not let you go.*
  (pp.)   *And I shall not let you go.*

(piano out)

Girls Oh, another, mamma! Please, darling!

Fanny *(laughing)* Don't you see, darlings, a visitor has just come in.
Count Leopardi, how good of you to call.
There darlings, that must be all for today.

Girl I No, mamma, please let us stay.

Girl II   Please go on playing.

Leopardi   I should love them to stay.

Girl II There, mamma, the gentleman would love us to stay.

Fanny He would soon repent if you did. Go along.
I will come and see you before you go to bed.

Girl I *(receding)* Mamma, it is always the same . . . oh, *please!*

*(they retire, grumbling a little: and we hear one of them say in
wonderment as they vanish from hearing)*

Girl II Did you see, Carla, he had a hump on his back?

Fanny *(quickly)* Come and sit by the window, Count Leopardi.
How very kind of you to remember me.
Where is Ranieri? Is he down below?
I expect the children will waylay him; they usually do.

Leopardi I am afraid I came alone. Did you expect Ranieri?

Fanny No. But he often comes; I thought he had brought you.

Leopardi No . . .

(embarrassed pause)

Fanny   I hope you enjoyed the acting the other night!

Leopardi I preferred the music.

Fanny *(laughing)* Oh, what a shocking thing to say!
I hope you didn't say that to the others?

Leopardi   No.

Fanny You thought I acquitted myself efficiently?

Leopardi   That I hardly noticed.

Fanny You never noticed how I was playing? Count Leopardi,
You will never make a courtier!

Leopardi I only noticed that among those people,
Almost only you seemed real.

Fanny *(delighted)*   What nonsense, Leopardi!

Leopardi Yes: there they sat in their unreal, well-learnt postures.
They had forgotten how to live, so much each gesture
Came from some other life they had enacted.

Fanny Can you say that of . . . Pavesi?

93

Leopardi	Pavesi sat

Sideways to the dark wall, presenting his best profile
With practised nonchalancy.

Fanny   And Pietro Fabrizi?

Leopardi Fabrizi could not cease pressing his long white fingers
Against his lustrous hair.

Fanny (pleased)   What malice, Leopardi!
Biffi, at any rate, never bothers about his appearance.
    (both laugh)

Leopardi Sound is enough for Biffi. He lets down into a well
A voice deeper than any human feeling ever called for.

Fanny I see you have them all anatomised.
What you must think of us *untalented* people
I cannot bear to think. How pale we must seem.

Leopardi No, Signora Targioni; you seemed like a genuine flower
Among so many wax ones.

Fanny (demurely)   I think we should leave this subject . . .
And where is Ranieri?

Leopardi   He is engaged this afternoon.
I suppose you know I have gone to live with him?

Fanny No. I thought you were leaving Florence very shortly?

Leopardi I suppose I am . . . strictly . . . yet it seems foolish
To go away from here . . . at the height of the season.

Fanny Of course it is. I am glad you are staying.

Leopardi Ranieri has not only offered me hospitality;
He helps me invaluably with the difficulties of my work.
As I expect he told you, I do not always see well.
I think he must be the kindest person on earth.

Fanny Perhaps he is another real flower
Among the wax ones . . . ?
    (they laugh slightly)

Leopardi Yes, he is real indeed . . . poor boy.

Fanny 'Poor boy'? Why do you say 'Poor boy'?

Leopardi I was thinking . . . *(he pauses)*

Fanny (softly) Thinking what? What were you thinking?

Leopardi His infatuation for that stupid Maddalena:
Where will that lead him?

Fanny (much amazed)   *Infatuation?*
For Maddalena Pelzet? What are you thinking of?
Ranieri knows Maddalena to be . . .

94

<table>
<tr><td>Leopardi</td><td>Whatever she is.</td></tr>
</table>

Leopardi   Whatever she is.
Which can scarcely matter to a man in love with her . . .

Fanny   In love? Ranieri in love with Maddalena Pelzet?
Ah, Count Leopardi, you must indeed be a poet
If you can be so romantic as all that . . .
(*laughing*)   Ranieri and Maddalena . . . !

Maddalena (*loudly*) Antonio Ranieri! Will you please leave me alone!
Ranieri   Maddalena!
Maddalena (*as though freeing herself*) No! Go and sit over there!
I have never known a man so inconsiderate.
Ranieri   You can scarcely call *me* inconsiderate.
Maddalena   I shall call you what I like. No, go away.
Ranieri   Maddalena, do be kind to me.
Maddalena   I was kind to you yesterday.
There isn't a kinder woman in Florence than I am.
Ranieri   There isn't a more tormenting one.
Maddalena   Ranieri, I will not tolerate bad temper.
I do not ask you to torment yourself;
I cannot help what you feel.
Ranieri   It would serve you right
If I went and consoled myself with someone else.
Maddalena   By all means do so; I should be very glad
If someone would take you off my hands a little.
Ranieri   Maddalena, you don't mean that!
Maddalena   Of course I mean it.
I would prefer to devote myself to my art.
Now, then, *sulk.*
Ranieri   I am not sulking.
You are such a child yourself you can't tell the difference
Between childish sulking and genuine wounded feeling.
Maddalena (*magnificently*) I, Maddalena Pelzet, *childish!*
Do you know whom you are addressing, my friend?
(*dramatic pause. Then softly*)
Listen; and perhaps I may be able to tell you.
When I was sixteen, I was still a poor girl,
Orphaned, unfriended, with only my good looks,
And my little brothers and sisters, crying for food.
A poor girl, with only her star to guide her,
Forced to defend herself against the advances

	Of at least two-thirds of the men in her native village.
	Can you think what that means to a poor girl of fifteen?
Ranieri	Oh, Maddalena!
Maddalena	That was the life I led.
	That was the childhood of the one you have just called childish.
	That. Was the childhood. Of the one. You have just.
	Called childish.
Ranieri	Maddalena!
Maddalena	(*softly*) That was Maddalena, a poor girl of fourteen.
	(*fierily*) When I was seventeen, I had already acted Medea!
	I had played Cleopatra by the time I was twenty!
	I had acted Antigone and Lucrezia Borgia
	Before I was twenty-two. Did I say 'acted'?
	Acted? I had *been* these women, I had *lived* them!
	I, childish Maddalena Pelzet . . .
Ranieri (*abjectly*)	I am sorry, my darling.
Maddalena	Yes, I have been a child. It was a child, perhaps,
	Who came, night after night, to your apartment,
	To be what you called kind. I was a child,
	And, like a child, deceived.
Ranieri	No!
Maddalena (*pathetically*)	Deceived.
	I had thought, when I gave myself so freely to you,
	You would be always kind and gentle with me,
	A refuge from a pursuing world, a shelter for innocence,
	And someone who would understand my Art.
	But are you, *are* you?
Ranieri	I promise I will try.
	Please, please forgive me this once, Maddalena?
Maddalena	Forgive. How often have I heard that word!
	My God, how often! I entrusted myself to you,
	And found out what you are. You, Ranieri, you
	Are sensual, jealous, and insatiable.
	You are as bad as my husband.
Ranieri	Maddalena, my darling,
	I deserve all you say; only please forgive me.
Maddalena	And now I must go to the theatre; I must paint my face,
	And put on the squalid rags of poor Electra.
	That is what I have to do when I go from here.
	(*with satirical casualness*) Just that.

Ranieri (*anxiously*) I can call for you afterwards?
　　　(*pause*)
Maddalena (*significantly*) No, Ranieri, not tonight.
Ranieri　　　　　　　　　　　　Maddalena!
Maddalena Do you think I could face you after this afternoon?
Ranieri But, Maddalena, you are coming back tonight?
　　　You can't . . . Maddalena!
Maddalena　　　　　　　We shall see, my dear.
　　　My Art, perhaps, will give me a little counsel:
　　　It sometimes seems the only thing I have . . .
Ranieri My darling!
Maddalena　　　　　No: don't come near me now . . .
　　　Good-bye . . . Antonio Ranieri.
　　　(*door*)

Ranieri What have I done? Oh God in Heaven, what have I done?

　　(*briefest pause. Door*)

Leopardi (*gaily*) Hello, Ranieri!
Ranieri (*dully*)　　　　　Oh . . . you're back, Leopardi.
Leopardi Yes. I nearly bumped into Maddalena on the staircase.
　　　How radiant she always looks! She was singing.
Ranieri Singing!
Leopardi　　　Yes: and she gave me a kiss.
　　　She said she wouldn't be back till just after midnight.
Ranieri (*joyfully*) Midnight! Oh Leopardi, thank God!
　　　Leopardi: isn't Maddalena a wonderful woman?
　　　Isn't she fine and noble? Isn't she . . . *rare?*
Leopardi She is everything you say; of course she is.
　　　But what I like best about your wonderful woman, Ranieri,
　　　Is that she makes you so happy. That is what matters.
Ranieri I am not worthy of her the tiniest bit.
Leopardi What nonsense, man.
Ranieri (*cheerfully*)　　　　No, I am not, I am not.
　　　Let us have some chocolate, shall we? It's just over here.
　　　(*from a very slight distance*)
　　　You are looking very happy too; where have you been?

Leopardi I . . . I paid a call on Signora Targioni.
Ranieri (nearer: absently) A call on whom?
Leopardi   Signora Targioni . . .
Ranieri (uninterested)   Oh, Fanny. . . .

      (band-music: clean start, then down, and hold through scene)
Leopardi (approaching) Fanny ! . . . Oh, I am sorry; I shouldn't have called
                                             you that.
Fanny (laughing) Not in a public garden, certainly not . . .
   But perhaps if you are a good boy, you may in private.
   There. Isn't that kind of me?
Leopardi   It is very kind . . . Signora Targioni.
Fanny And did you get me the autographs you promised?
Leopardi Yes, all but two. I am afraid that some of them
   I have had to cut off from the bottoms of letters.
   I hope you don't mind?
Fanny   Of course I don't.
Leopardi They are rather delayed; I had to send home for them.
   I will bring them round.
Fanny   Oh, I can send for them.
   And when are you *going* home?
Leopardi   I . . . hardly know.
   I seem to have indefinitely postponed *that*.
Fanny (roguishly) I hope you are not forgetting your duties, Leopardi?
   Just because your family is so far away.
Leopardi They are never far away.
Fanny   But they are in Recanati.
Leopardi They are never far away, even when you are here.
Fanny I? *(laughing)* What have *I* to do with it?
Leopardi I mean: anybody.
Fanny (in mock offendedness) Oh . . .
Leopardi (slowly and firmly)   Ranieri says,
   One's family is like a monument . . . and certainly
   They have that permanence; and when they die,
   They are only stilled. They do not go away.
   Ranieri is winged and free; he like a bird can hover
   Over the immutable carven group. But I am grounded.
   I carry their stone with me; I am touched to stone by them.
   And there they are *still* . . . And here they still *are*.

Fanny (efficiently stemming the conversation)
    Yes: you poets are always stony-hearted.
    I have always said so.
    (before he can protest: incisively)
            And where *is* Ranieri? Why isn't he with you?
     (brief pause)
Leopardi (reluctantly) He is at home.
Fanny   Why are you not with him?
Leopardi I usually come out in the afternoon.
Fanny   Why?
Leopardi (embarrassed) Oh, I . . . I somehow think he prefers it.
Fanny Prefers to be left alone? That isn't like Ranieri . . .
     (brief pause)
    Does he *say* he wants to be left alone?
Leopardi He . . . isn't always alone, Fanny . . . Signora Targioni.
Fanny (steelily) Oh . . . *(graciously)* . . . Well, goodbye, Count Leopardi.
Leopardi Goodbye Signora Targioni . . .
    (music still in: slightly up: but still behind)

Leopardi (slowly) And now she goes
    Between the insensible stone and the heedless fountain,
    By the trees that do not see her, as she passes
    Where I dare not go with her, where I only follow,
    To let the shadows that have fallen upon her path
    Fall upon mine a moment after . . .

    (music up and out)

Ranieri (much distressed) I waited in three hours this afternoon.
    She never came. Why do we love people, Giacomo?
    Why do we love them at all?
Leopardi   When I discover that,
    I will tell you.
Ranieri   She could twist me round her finger.
    Oh, Giacomo, if you only knew what I go through!
    It is worse than any previous love-affair.
    Far, far worse.
Leopardi   You must be patient with her.
Ranieri Giacomo: wouldn't you like to leave all this?
Leopardi Leave what?

99

Ranieri   Florence, Tuscany, the whole damned lot?
Giacomo: think: in a month the police will allow me back
In Naples. Home, home, home! (*affectionately*) Come with me,
                              Giacomo!

Leopardi (*disconcerted, softly*)
I had never thought that we might go to Naples.
Ranieri (*genially*) Well, think about it now. My sister longs to meet you.
Leopardi (*uncertainly*) No, Tonio. No. I don't want to go to Naples.
Ranieri Why? (*as Leopardi does not answer*)
        You don't want to stay in Florence, surely?
Leopardi Yes, Tonio. I want to stay in Florence.
Ranieri (*helplessly*) Good God. You are the least predictable of men.
I could never . . .
Leopardi (*dully*) I will stay in Florence. I will face it out.
        (*brief pause*)
Ranieri Face what out? . . . Giacomo, why do you look like that?
Face what out?
        (*door*)
(*angrily*) Maddalena! Where have you been?
Maddalena (*slowly, after a dangerous pause*)
Leopardi: you are a poet and a gentleman.
Do you ever speak to a woman as this man does?
        (*pause. Fade in*)

Fanny (*gurgling seductively*)
It is the only thing for it, Giacomo, the only thing.
I have thought it all over; I am sure it is the only thing.
We must have a little conspiracy. Do you like conspiracies?
Leopardi It all depends who my fellow-conspirators are.
I think I could always conspire with *you*, Fanny.
Fanny We must try, then. Just Giacomo and Fanny, eh?
Leopardi Giacomo and Fanny.
Fanny   We must of course pretend
That it is only a little game that we are playing.
We must try to *rescue* him from Maddalena.
It will, after all, be only for his own good.
Leopardi I have already tried my hardest with him.
I am very affectionate towards him, and I do not care
To see him ruining himself like this.
But if I suggest that, he tries to be tough and buoyant,

And pretend he doesn't suffer.
He takes very little notice of what I say.

Fanny (*slightly irritated*)
There must be some approach, some little suggestion . . .

Leopardi I have already reminded him many times
That Maddalena is married and is a mother.

Fanny (*coldly*) You told him that?

Leopardi   He knew.

Fanny   I mean you mentioned it?

Leopardi Yes.

Fanny   Did you think it mattered?

Leopardi   A little, perhaps.

Fanny (*reasonably*) Giacomo, dear, have you ever been in love?

Leopardi   Yes.

Fanny How many times?

Leopardi   Twice. Three times, I think.

Fanny Then tell me truthfully: and *truthfully*, mind:
How many of them were unmarried girls?

        (*pause*)

Leopardi (*huskily*)   None of them were.

Fanny Thank you. I think you will see then, Giacomo,
That that is not the point at all. No, my dear,
It is not the point at *all* . . . Now, *Maddalena* . . .

(*cross promptly to Maddalena*)

Maddalena Say it, then! Say it, say it, say it, if you want to!
You will only be sorry for it.

Ranieri   I shall *not* be sorry!

Maddalena That at least will be something new. Go on: say it.
You have said it often enough; say it again.

Ranieri I will *not* say it!

Maddalena   Would you like me to say it for you?

Ranieri No!

Maddalena   Then say it yourself.

Ranieri   I will not say anything.

Maddalena How does it go? 'It would serve you right . . .'
Are those the words? 'It would serve you right . . .'

Ranieri It *would* serve you right!

Maddalena (*quickly*)   What would, darling?

Ranieri (*savagely*) If I went and consoled myself with someone else.

101

Maddalena There then. Perhaps you'll feel better now you've said it.

Ranieri You are a devil, Maddalena, a ruthless devil.

Maddalena (*laughing comfortably*) That was what Botti said about my
                                            Clytemnestra.

Well, go and console yourself. I shall not mind.

Go and console yourself with Fanny Targioni.

I am sure you would find her only too willing to help.

Go and push poor little Giacomo out of the way.

She must be tired of winding him round her finger.

Let her wind you instead.

Ranieri   She is very kind to Giacomo.

Maddalena Very well then, let her be kind to you.

I am sure she is a very kind person.

Ranieri She is not spoilt, as you are.

Maddalena (*after an icy pause*) Did I hear you say spoilt?

Was *spoilt* the word you used?

(*pause*)

Fanny That is not the point, Giacomo, you know it is not.

Maddalena is nothing but a spoilt and vicious woman.

Leopardi She is spoilt, certainly, but she is not vicious.

And who would not be spoilt with such a talent?

Fanny   The point, Leopardi . . .

Leopardi Fanny!

Fanny Giacomo, then: the point – but what is the use of talking?

Leopardi I know the point, Fanny, as well as you do.

Fanny What do you mean?

Leopardi   I know it as well as you.

I think I find it even harder to bear.

Fanny I don't understand what you mean, Giacomo.

Leopardi Suppose Ranieri were to leave Maddalena,

Or – as is more likely – she were to leave him?

Fanny Well?

Leopardi   What do you imagine would happen to him?

Fanny I imagine he would very soon come to his senses.

Leopardi Coming to one's senses may not mean being happy,

Which I think is what you mean. One may come to one's senses,

And see that the reality of life is only heartbreak;

And that where the heart has held itself together,

It has done so only by the strength of an illusion.

Fanny I think you are describing yourself, not Ranieri.
Ranieri would quickly find some consolation.
Leopardi He would perhaps. (*in a low voice*)
There, I have injured you.
Fanny   Injured me! Giacomo:
Do you think that I am the kind of woman
Who devotes herself to consoling rejected lovers?
Leopardi Must you always try to twist my words, Fanny?
Fanny Your words seem to me very twisted already.
Leopardi Then I will try to say some very straight ones.
Fanny I do not think you had better, Giacomo.
You are trying to force confessions out of me,
And the confessions you expect would not be true ones.
You want me to say I am in love with Tonio.
Well, I am not, do you see: I am no more in love with him,
Than you are with me.
Leopardi   Oh, Fanny, Fanny, Fanny!
Do you know what you are saying?
Fanny   I usually do.
Do you think I am mentally defective as well as immoral?
(*with a sudden change of tone*)
Giacomo: You are being very naughty this afternoon.
Do you know what I'm going to do?
Leopardi   No, Fanny.
Fanny I am going to give you a kiss. Come here, sir.
No: do not try to make love: I am very angry.
And now go back to your seat, and I will tell you a story.
I see I must treat you just like one of the children. Listen.
Leopardi With all my ears.
Fanny So. Once upon a time, and not very long ago,
There lived in Florence a rather good-looking young woman.
Her name began with an F. She was much sought after,
And among her favourite admirers was a handsome young
                                                            man,
Whose name began with an R. And among her friends
Was a little hunchback magician whose name began with an L.
(*promptly to Ranieri*)

Ranieri (*passionately*) You can't deny it, Maddalena, you can't deny it!

103

Maddalena I was not attempting to deny anything,
　　　　　So far as I am aware.
　　Ranieri　　　　　　　　　His name begins with a V.
　　　　　I saw it on a letter.
Maddalena　　　　　　　　　You will find many strange things,
　　　　　If you always read my private correspondence.
　　Ranieri I was not trying to pry into your affairs.
　　　　　You left the letter on your dressing-table.
　　　　　Who is he?
Maddalena　　　　　　Who is who?
　　Ranieri　　　　　　　　　V.
Maddalena (*yawning*) There are many people
　　　　　Whose names begin with a V.
　　Ranieri　　　　　　　　　Maddalena!
Maddalena If you really want to know what a little thought would have told
　　　　　　　　　　　　　　　　　　you;
　　　　　My husband's name begins with a V, does it not?
　　Ranieri Maddalena! Oh, Maddalena, thank God!
Maddalena I do not know why you say thank God.
　　　　　(*pause*)
　　Ranieri What do you mean?
　　　　　(*pause*)
Maddalena (*slowly*)　　　　　Had it ever occurred to you
　　　　　That I might go back to him?
　　　　　(*pause*)
　　　　　(*brief silence. Music*)

　　Ranieri Damn them, Giacomo, damn the whole lot of them,
　　　　　They are none of them more than cunning strumpets and bitches.
　　　　　They drain one of the power either to stay or to go.
Leopardi Tonio, I cannot bear that you should break yourself like this.
　　　　　I know that Maddalena is adorable . . .
　　Ranieri　　　　　　　　　There you are wrong.
　　　　　They are none of them adorable.
Leopardi　　　　　　　　At all events,
　　　　　You must not let yourself be killed by her.
　　Ranieri Let her go back to him; what should I care?
　　　　　There are always other women in the world.
　　　　　It is friendship that counts, friendship between men,
　　　　　Like you and me. Love is very easy to find.

I would give it all up, I almost think,
To take you to Naples, and nurse you back to health.
Leopardi You shall certainly not sacrifice yourself for me.
And do not seek cheap loves, I beg of you, Tonio.
Ranieri I never do: I insist on long courtships.
Leopardi You are incorrigible, Tonio.
Ranieri   Who would forgo
The pleasures of the chase and the overtaking?
Oh, Giacomo, how perpetually adorable they are:
The walk in the public garden, the balconied evening,
The borrowed book, the accidental meeting:
You know these things, Giacomo, you must know them.
Leopardi I think I know my own variations of them.
Ranieri And the first personal joke: 'Ah, you *would* say that, Ranieri.'
'Oh Signor Ranieri, that is just like you.'
Or, 'I thought about you at the theatre the other night,
When one of the actors said so-and-so.'
And, Giacomo, isn't it a wonderful moment,
When the first reference to one's earlier loves is made?
Leopardi   Is it?
Ranieri That is a great step forward.
Leopardi   Forward to what?
Ranieri   To the final investment.
The final great preliminary dinner,
The suffocating blow-out, in whose extravagance,
The practised taste must always recognise
The ultimate cadence of the mating-call.
And the night, Giacomo, the night!
The exquisite smooth glide to the needlepoint of seduction!
And in the depths of satisfaction or disappointment,
The charming element of politeness always persisting,
For you know it will never in either case be required again.
And then the languor and the separate thoughts,
The soft words murmured from the cleared throat:
'I'm afraid we've behaved very badly to poor Federigo.'
'Shall you tell him?' 'I shall have to tell him.'
'Do you love me, darling?' And the final great Amen:
'*I am not quite sure.*'
(*triumphantly*)   And you know you have *won*!
And, ah, the joy of that final celebration,

105

The second fall-to in the early morning . . .

Leopardi (*shouting*)   Tonio, stop!
You cannot mean this horrible rigmarole.
It has nothing to do with love.

Ranieri   You mustn't blame me
If I try to protect myself by strategy.
I know that things between me and Maddalena are at an end.
I am taking the best way to prepare myself.

Leopardi What you say is squalid and disgusting.
Love is not the repetition of a formula.

Ranieri I didn't mean to be disgusting, I assure you.
But I suppose I am being misunderstood, as usual.

Leopardi I think I understand you.

Ranieri   I was only trying
To describe the poetry in these things, Giacomo,
And how in the midst of the prose one longs for the poetry again.
You do see that, Giacomo? (*earnestly*) You do see it?
(*pause*)

Leopardi Fanny . . .

Fanny (*welcoming*) Ah, Giacomo, I have so hoped you would come
                                                            today.

Leopardi You don't always hope that, I am afraid, Fanny.

Fanny Ah, but I have been moody and quarrelsome lately.
You must forgive me. I am glad to see you today.
I have made a decision at last which I think will please you.

Leopardi Have you?

Fanny   Yes, yes, I have decided. My poor little brain
Must be no longer occupied as it has been.
There have been whole days, as you must have known, Giacomo,
When I have thought of nothing else but Ranieri.
That is not as it should be.

Leopardi   It is natural:
He is handsome and lovable.

Fanny   That is beside the point,
It is neither wise nor dignified for me, a woman with children –
And my children are very dear to me: I think you know that?

Leopardi They are also dear to me, as is this room,
And everything inside it.

Fanny   Dear friend.
No, it is not wise for the mother of a family
To allow such intrusions on her thoughts as I have done.
I certainly felt nothing of the kind about my husband,
Even when we were both much younger than Ranieri.

Leopardi Those thoughts are not accessible to youth.

Fanny Whatever sort of thoughts they are, they are over.
There is only one thought truly beautiful, only one thing
More beautiful than love, than poetry, than summer,
More beautiful than anything else in the world.

Leopardi (*wistfully*) Friendship?

Fanny (*gravely and priggishly*) No, Giacomo; *home.*
The place we always return to in the end,
When we are tired of being naughty children:
And as you will guess, what I feel most of all is . . . freedom.
Yes, I feel a genuine happiness, untroubled by the thoughts
That have troubled me so long. Be glad for me Giacomo.

Leopardi I am very glad for you. (*unsteadily*) Dare I say as well,
That I am also glad for myself?

Fanny (*gaily*)   Long-suffering Giacomo:
There will be no more tedious expeditions for you to make,
No more proddings and temptings, never again.
Of course you are glad. Ranieri can be left
To stew with that fat Maddalena.

Leopardi   That will not last much longer.

Fanny What? How do you know?

Leopardi   I . . . I *do* know, Fanny.

            (*pause*)

Fanny I see . . . What do you think he will do?

Leopardi (*with difficulty*)   He . . . is adaptable.
I am very glad that he is. I think that . . . some new attachment
May grow with such force that the thought of Maddalena
Will soon be extirpated from his mind.

Fanny You mean . . . there is someone else?

Leopardi   No, Fanny.

Fanny Who told you this?

Leopardi   It is something I have noticed.

Fanny And yet you never told me?

Leopardi   There seemed . . .
No reason why I should, Fanny.

107

Fanny (*after a pause, lightly*)   No, none at all . . .
I remember the first time that you came here, Giacomo.
I expect you will have forgotten.

Leopardi   Forgotten?
How should I ever forget? I only wonder
That you remember. You sat with your furs thrown back
And the children around you. You were wearing a blue gown.

Fanny It was green rather than blue.

Leopardi   It was long ago, Fanny.

Fanny Three whole years. Well, that world which you as a poet
Saw to be vain and empty, I in my slow little way
Also see to be foolish. And when I see a world
I do not care for, what do I do?

Leopardi   Leave it, I hope, my dear.

Fanny I turn my back, collect my cloak and go.
It is what I am doing now, and without regret.
Ranieri has become too stupid to be borne with.
He is inside that world, and he can stay there.

Leopardi But Ranieri . . .

Fanny   Please, Giacomo, I have said that he can stay
                                                        there.
Please spare me from hearing his name again.
Or rather . . . (*intimately*) let us both, like an exorcism,
Say his name once together – just for fun –
And then let silence have him.

Leopardi (*aghast, softly*) Such a childish game, Fanny!

Fanny A childish game, that is all. Are you ready? One, two, three . . .

Leopardi⎱ (*whispers*) Ranieri.
Fanny⎰ (*whispers*)   Ranieri . . .

There, he is gone! How fresh the room seems without him.
But, oh dear, how silly it all seems. How glad I am
To get back to my children and my dear husband:
To be Home once more, once more . . . like a tired child.
You must know that feeling, Giacomo, must have known it,
Every time you have gone back to Recanati.
You must have known the calm, the peace, the reality
Of real society, with real *people*.

Leopardi (*an echo*)   Real people.

Fanny And so . . . I know you will understand what I have to say.

You are a poet: I sometimes think you understand everything.
Giacomo.

Leopardi (*simply*)   Yes, Fanny?

Fanny   It is time to say goodbye.

Leopardi Yes, you must be tired: yet you never look less than radiant.
Shall I come at the same time tomorrow?

Fanny I meant – don't be perverse, dear friend, you know what I
                                                                    meant –
I meant, of course, goodbye for ever.
        (*pause*)

Leopardi (*suddenly and sharply*) No, Fanny, no!

Fanny I must not see you again. You must see, Giacomo . . .

Leopardi No, no!

Fanny . . . That that is out of the question.

Leopardi   Why?

Fanny You don't make things very easy for your friend, Giacomo.
I am not, in any case, used to be spoken to like that.

Leopardi Why must I be turned abruptly aside like this?

Fanny I have to consider my happiness, Giacomo.

Leopardi And mine?

Fanny   Your happiness is not my concern, Giacomo.
We each have to find our own.

Leopardi (*passionately and rapidly*) But not alone, Fanny.
These afternoons are all I have ever had,
And all I have asked for, all I ask for now.
Don't you believe me? You could prove it, Fanny . . .
Oh, Fanny, men I know have turned their heads on their pillow
At the point of death, they have turned and said to their wives,
'Thank you, my love, for my thirty years of happiness,'
And have gone into death smiling. Oh, my darling . . .

Fanny   Giacomo!

Leopardi You could take in your hands all the years I have lived till now,
You could turn every one of them inside out,
Examine every day: you would find my happy days,
Torn from a sea, and set on a narrow beach,
And all their tiny number spent with you . . .
Must happiness be so absolute
That you cannot admit a moment of inconvenience
Into your perfect day for one who loves you?

Fanny Giacomo!

Leopardi   Did you think I could leave that word unsaid for ever?
  Fanny I did not hear it.
Leopardi   Fanny!
  Fanny   I did not hear it, Giacomo.
         Nor should I ever hear it in your presence.
Children (*in distance*) Mamma! Mamma! Where are you?
Leopardi Please, please, let me come tomorrow, Fanny.
         I promise you I will not . . .
          (*children calling as before, but nearer*)
  Fanny *Those* are the voices I intend to listen to!
         Not yours, Giacomo. Not Ranieri's. *Those!*
Children (*bursting into the room*) Where have you been, Mamma?
              Mamma, where have you been?
  Fanny (*loud, hideous welcome*) My darlings! My darlings!
            Carla! Annina! My darlings!

Leopardi (*with great simplicity*)
         I know, and have always known, I should loathe a woman
         Who could caress this hideous, shapeless lump.
         Yes, there would be
         In such a love a desperate perversion,
         Which would, God knows how quickly, quench my own
                             passion.
         But how can I say that now, now she is gone for ever,
         Now, when such words might comfort and sustain me,
         How can I say them now, when every way
         Failure and desert lie . . . ?

         Here I am lost among iron, clanging streets,
         Which proffer to me only a choice between
         This mighty prison or that.
         And this is Florence; and I will not stay in Florence.
         And there: in the other desert: Recanati.
         How easy it always was to return to that stone safety,
         To take up my position on the plinth,
         There in the vacant space that waited for me
         And beckoned me to my habitual resentment:
         How easy it was . . . the only place in the world.
         'A monument in marble, permanent and fine.'
         And that is home: and I will not go back home.

Though this be the end of the world I will not go back,
And I will not stay.
                        Oh heaven, emptied of God,
Oh hidden ugly Power that orders our common ill,
Give me strength to move, once only. Give me the strength
To go with my friend to Naples. Give me the strength of the
                                                        damned

To shift my place in hell.

   (*Naples music up*)

   (*Maria is a servant-girl of twelve with an unpleasant voice. In his
   scene with her, Leopardi, now four years older, is impassive, colour-
   less and arid in tone, refusing to be irritated*)

Maria (*imperiously*) Count Giacomo! Count Giacomo!
Leopardi   Is that Maria?
   Maria Yes. Open the door. I want to come in.
Leopardi Can you come back again a little later?
   Maria No, I must come in now. Unlock the door.
Leopardi Come in, Maria . . .
        (*door unlocked*)
                        Did you want something?
   Maria It's rude to lock your door in somebody else's house.
        I know why you did it.
Leopardi   I did it for no special reason, Maria.
   Maria Yes, you did. Why?
Leopardi I am not accustomed, Maria, to answer for my actions
        To children of eleven.
   Maria   I am twelve, not eleven.
        And I know why you did it.
Leopardi Well then, we both know why. What did you want,
        Maria? Did you want to dust the room?
   Maria   What are you writing?
Leopardi Nothing very important.
   Maria   Is it a poem?
Leopardi   It is trying to be.
   Maria (*laughs*) You're not very clever if you can't make it do what you
                                                        want.

        You're a poet, aren't you?
Leopardi   Yes.

III

Maria   And you can't write a poem?
Leopardi I said I was trying to write a poem.
Maria   I think poets are silly.
        And poems are silly too. (*slyly, after a pause*) You don't like us, do
                                                                          you?
Leopardi Of course I like you.
  Maria (*slowly*)   No, you don't; you don't like us at all.
        Do you . . . m'm? Do you . . . m'm?
Leopardi   Of course I do.
        I should scarcely say so, if I didn't, should I?
  Maria (*jeering*) 'I should scarcely say so, if I didn't, should I?'
        And you don't like *them*, either.
Leopardi   Them?
  Maria   Do you?
        Signor Ranieri and his sister. You don't like them.
Leopardi What nonsense, Maria. I am devoted to them.
  Maria   You have to say that.
        They'd send you back to Recanati if you didn't
        And there you'd stay and you'd stay and you'd stay,
        Till you was dead. So you have to say you like us,
        So you can stay in Naples, and
        (*she is overcome by a snigger*)
                                      die of the plague, instead.
        (*she continues to snigger*)
Leopardi Maria, be quiet.
  Maria (*sharply*) And you don't like Naples either.
        You don't like Naples, and you don't like Recanati.
        You don't like us, and you don't like anybody,
        'Cepting yourself.
Leopardi   I like everyone except myself.
  Maria Why do you like me then?
Leopardi   Your manners are so charming.
  Maria Do you want to kiss me?
Leopardi   No, thank you.
  Maria   Why?
Leopardi We are not much given to kissing in my family.
  Maria Everybody kisses everybody in Naples.
Leopardi I hope they enjoy it.
  Maria   You're not a man, really, are you?
Leopardi No?

Maria (*an exaggerated imitation*) No-o-o? . . . (*slowly*)
Why, boys of nine know more than you do, down in Santa
Lucia.
(*with pride*) I've seen them.
Leopardi Maria, if you came to tidy the room,
Will you kindly do it, and go?
Maria Don't you bully me.
Nobody can't bully nobody while the plague's on.
The priest said so. Everybody can say what they like.
My dad said so, justafore he died.
'You be happy while you can,' he said. 'You have a good time.'
Lina (*approaching*) Maria! Maria! Where are you?
Maria I'm here, signorina.
I'm dusting Count Giacomo's room; and a fine mess it's in.
Lina (*entering; her voice is warm and charming; she speaks to Maria almost
with deference*)
Maria, we have to have luncheon rather early today.
Will you go and lay the table as soon as you can?
Maria I suppose so . . . Signorina . . .
Lina Yes?
Maria He's bin saying he doesn't like you and your brother . . .
Leopardi Maria!
Lina Run along, Maria, there's a good girl.
You mustn't try to tease Count Giacomo. He's been very ill.
Maria He'll be iller yet. They took off two hundred last night.
I thought that'd make him flinch.
Lina (*sharply*) Go along.
(*door*)
I am so sorry, sorry, sorry, Giacomo, my dear.
Has she been a nuisance again?
Leopardi Not very, no.
Lina The plague brings out all the evil one had always known,
And sharpens and refines it.
Leopardi But never in you, my dear.
You are always an angel, and you always will be.
Lina Ah, you don't know me.
Leopardi (*affectionately*) I think I do, Lina.
Lina We shall all be angels when we get to Torre del Greco;
The carriage will be round at half past two.
Are you looking forward to it, Giacomo?

113

Leopardi   Immeasurably.
   Lina It will be like getting out of a prison, won't it?
Leopardi Naples has not been a prison, Paolina.
   Lina (*protesting with a laugh*)
        Lina, Giacomo, not Paolina. Tonio's sister, not yours.
        I thought we settled that years ago.
Leopardi Lina, yes, I am sorry: Lina, Lina, Lina.
        I was only remembering the day I first came here,
        And how I had thought whether to go to Recanati,
        Or whether to come here . . . I am glad it was here.
   Lina You must have thought of Recanati often this morning:
        That was the fourth time you have called me Paolina.
Leopardi Ah, Lina, you would not mind if you knew her.
   Lina I do not mind now. Perhaps when you are better,
        Next year, perhaps, you will be able to go and see her.
Leopardi I shall never see her again.
   Lina   Nonsense, Giacomo.
        I only insist that she doesn't make you forget me.
Leopardi (*musing*) You are not a bit alike really, you and Tonio.
   Lina People say we are very alike.
Leopardi   No, you are not.
      (*door*)
   Lina Here is Tonio . . . Tonio. Giacomo is saying again
        That we are not alike.
  Ranieri   He says that to tease you, dear,
        And to flatter me.
   Lina   If you were a good brother,
        You would challenge him to a duel.
  Ranieri   Very true;
        Giacomo, the minute you leave this room,
        You must regard me as your first duelling opponent.
        We will fight it out on the terrace at Torre del Greco.
Leopardi (*gaily*) Yes, yes, you can have choice of weapons!
        And I will have one hand tied behind my back.
  Ranieri A promise, a promise?
Leopardi (*loudly*)   A promise, Carlo!
  Ranieri (*a mock threat*) *What* did you call me?
   Lina (*triumphantly*)   There!
        He calls you Carlo, and me Paolina.
        I do not think his thoughts are with us at all.

Leopardi (*lapsing into absentness*) You would not mind if you knew.
  Ranieri That remains to be seen: and when we do . . .
    Lina Is everything ready, Tonio?
Ranieri   Everything, yes.
Leopardi (*eagerly*)   Is it?
  Ranieri In seven hours' time we shall be in Torre.
Leopardi Thank God.
  Ranieri   You have no idea of the trouble I've had.
      The whole of the port area is to be sealed off,
      Except for priests and doctors. It will be a tedious journey
      For you, Giacomo, round by the hill-roads.
Leopardi How many deaths were there yesterday?
  Ranieri   I didn't ask. I couldn't.
Leopardi (*suddenly*) Have they disinfected the carriage?
  Ranieri   Of course they have.
      In any case it has been nowhere near infection.
Leopardi Who disinfected it?
  Ranieri   Michele.
Leopardi   Are you sure he washed himself
      Before he did it?
  Ranieri   I am sure he did, Giacomo, dear,
      Don't let's have all this over again.
    Lina I am glad Giacomo's frightened of the cholera.
Leopardi (*harshly*)   Why?
    Lina It shows you are no longer in love with death,
      As you were when you came here. Oh, Giacomo,
      I am sorry you are distressed. Of course I am,
      But at least it is reassuring.
Leopardi   I will die my own death.
      I will not share it with the rest of men.
    Lina You are not going to die at all. Now put your papers together,
      And come down and eat a great luncheon; there is something
                               special.
      You will need all the strength you can get for the journey.
Leopardi I dread the thought of it.
    Lina   But you do want to go, Giacomo?
      All yesterday you talked of nothing but going there.
Leopardi I long for it, yes: you know how much I want it:
      The broom-flower and the pines and our tiny villetta.
      I have only to close my eyes to see it there:

115

The bay, the serene great arms of Posillipo and Sorrento,
That girl who sings all day at her loom down below;
Capri and Ischia, like dozing cats in the sunshine.
Of course I long for it, Lina dear.

Lina   You shall have it tonight.
Ranieri And now for luncheon.
Leopardi (*docilely*)   I will collect my papers.
Lina (*receding*)   Don't hurry too much . . .
            (*door*)

Leopardi (*quietly*) Will it ever be certainly there, my house of peace?
            The servants docile and good, a beloved view from the window.
            A cypress-walk, the sun on the balustrade,
            The distant sea, and a daily boat-sail plying . . .
            Or is the image of *their* fate mine: the wanderers:
            Tasso dustily toiling from court to court; Ariosto
            Touting his trade among the cardinals;
            Petrarch always between Italy and Avignon;
            Cavalcanti, wistfully dying in the marshes;
            And Dante, eating the salty foreign bread . . .
            In the shame of political obloquy, in the terror
            Of the torturer's rack, in the flight and the assumed name,
            In the grip of physical or moral disaster,
            In the breathing-spaces of such worlds, they forced
            Their words from out of their hearts: all wondering,
            'How does it happen I have come so far,
            And by a route so strange?'
               (*brief pause. Bring up mild laughter*)

            Well, it's the first time you've ever given me ice-cream at
                                                    luncheon,
            Why don't you let me have it every day?
            I should always be well if you did. I could eat
            Ice-cream for breakfast, for luncheon and for dinner.
            I know why you did it. I know.
Ranieri   Why?
Leopardi   I know.
Lina   Why, Giacomo?
Leopardi So that I shouldn't be naughty on the journey.
Ranieri I shall not be the one to deny it.

Leopardi (*mouth full*)   In that case,
　　　I had better have some more.
　　Lina   No, Giacomo, you cannot.
　　　If you are good, we may get some on the way.
Leopardi (*earnestly*) There's a very good place for it just outside Vico.
　　　We should be there by five. Though how can I wait till five?
　　Lina It will still be daylight by the time we get to Torre.
　　　It will be exactly as it was the last time.
　Ranieri Exactly as it was; and waiting for us.
　　Lina And waiting especially for little Giacomo.
Leopardi (*lost in thought*) Waiting, yes . . . as it has waited every time.
　　Lina Every time? What do you mean? We have only been there once.
Leopardi I have been back there every time save one.
　　Lina Back where?
Leopardi   To Recanati. I went back there
　　　After Rome. After Bologna, Florence, Milan, Pisa, always.
　　　I went back there save once.
　　Lina   You foolish Giacomo,
　　　I don't think we are talking about the same things.
　　　Are you ready?
Leopardi   Yes.
　　Lina   Then let us leave the table,
　　　And wait in the other room till the carriage comes.
　　　Then we shall escape Maria's gracious overtures.
　　　Is there any point in our taking those grapes, Tonio?
　Ranieri No, there are some in the basket, with the wine.
　　　Shall I help you up, Giacomo?
　　　　(*pause*)
　　　Giacomo!
　　　　(*pause*)
　　　　　　Giacomo, do answer me!
Leopardi (*softly*)   Tonio . . .
　Ranieri   Yes?
Leopardi   Tonio . . .
　Ranieri (*anxiously*) Yes, Giacomo, what is it?
Leopardi Tonio, don't be alarmed, please, will you?
　　　But please send for Doctor Mannella immediately.
　　　Will you send for him at once, please?
　　　　(*silence*)
　　Lina (*sharply, terrified*) Giacomo!

117

Leopardi   Dear Lina, there is no cause for worry.
   I only want . . . reassurance . . .
 Ranieri   I will go myself.
Leopardi (*trying to joke*) Mannella will tell you
   That asthmatics always have very very long lives.
   It is quite true.
 Ranieri   Stay with him, Lina.
  Lina   Yes.
Leopardi It is quite true. I never had asthma till lately.
   Do you think it has been sent as a life-preserver?
  Lina Giacomo.
Leopardi   It is not the *vox cholerica* in my throat.
   I am so well used to my own familiars,
   I should have recognised an interloper.
   Lina . . .
  Lina   Yes, Giacomo?
Leopardi   Isn't it rather dark in here?
  Lina No, Giacomo, I don't think so, my dear.
Leopardi Oh . . . I can't see you very well,
   But I am sure you are looking shocked, Lina.
   (*she is sobbing: he tries to comfort her*)
     You are so kind and sweet, Lina.
   Be cheerful too. Why, usually it's the reverse.
   You are usually trying to comfort selfish me.
   Think, Lina, this evening we shall be in Recanati.
  Lina In Torre del Greco, my dear.
Leopardi   In Torre del Greco, I meant.
  Lina Are you in pain, Giacomo?
Leopardi   No, Lina . . . Where's your brother?
  Lina He has gone for Doctor Mannella.
Leopardi He shouldn't have done that . . . It was a mistake.
   I can't see them very well, Lina.
  Lina   See whom, Giacomo?
Leopardi   I saw them there . . . again and again:
   And yet . . . I carry so much of their stone about with me,
   I cannot move very easily in the world of others.
   And they are lingering in a stony sunset.
   They cannot come to me. They keep their distance.
   How far they seem from me, how far, how far!
   Carved and frozen in an unmoving action.

Lina Giacomo, speak to me!

Leopardi   I saw them there . . . again and again.
Paolina: still haunting about the cold white walls.
Carlo: still trembling on the edge of his escape,
Pierfrancesco, a gallant boy fighting . . .
And under the stone, under the ground, under the life,
Luigi forever dead; and the two lost infants,
Unintelligible, undecipherable fragments of life, lost:
Long dead, and the living dead still over them,
Still. Mother: more silent and still each day and year,
And at her side, in and under her glance . . .
Oh, my father . . .
    (*door*)

Ranieri   Lina, here is Mannella.
I met him on the way . . . How is he now?

Lina   I am frightened, Tonio.
Doctor Mannella . . .

Mannella   Count Leopardi . . .

Leopardi   Oh, my father . . .

Mannella You sent for me, Count Leopardi?

Lina   His lips are moving:

Leopardi Tonio, Lina, why don't you speak to me?
Tonio . . . no, you will not answer me . . .
I have no place among you.

Ranieri   Giacomo, speak to me.

Leopardi They will not answer . . . There is my place:
By Paolina's side, my eyes on Carlo,
My hand in the warm young hand of Pierfrancesco,
And father's arm round my shoulders, hiding my sorrow,
Shielding my shame; that is my place,
And I must not go there . . . Oh, my father . . .

Mannella (*whispering*) Signor Ranieri, send for the priest at once.

Lina (*wailing*)   Doctor Mannella, no!
It isn't true, it can't be true: only a few minutes ago,
He was talking of going to Torre del Greco,
We were going this afternoon . . . Doctor!
It is not the plague?

Mannella No, it is not the plague, but I am afraid, my dear,
You must do as I say.
    (*the following sequence gains very rapidly in speed*)

Leopardi (*loudly*) Ranieri!

Ranieri Giacomo!

Leopardi Ranieri: open the shutters!

Ranieri They are open already, Giacomo.

Leopardi Open the shutters.

Ranieri (*receding*) They are open already, Giacomo.

Carlo (*echo*) They are open already, Giacomo.

Ranieri (*distant*) They are open already, Giacomo.

Carlo (*echo*) They are open already, Giacomo.

Leopardi (*loudly*) Lina: open the shutters.

Lina Yes, Giacomo.

Paolina (*echo*) Yes, Giacomo.

Lina Yes, Giacomo.

Paolina (*echo*) Yes, Giacomo.

Leopardi Paolina!

Lina (*near*) Yes, Giacomo.

Leopardi Carlo!

Ranieri (*near*) Yes, Giacomo.

Leopardi I cannot see them. Open the shutters.

Carlo (*echo*) They are open already, Giacomo.

Paolina (*echo*) Giacomo, darling, my darling, they are open.

Leopardi Carlo! . . . Carlo! . . . Carlo!

Carlo (*boy*) (*laughs*)

Leopardi Carlo . . .

Carlo (*boy*) What have birthdays to do with it?

Leopardi Everything.

Adelaide Why don't you answer him?

Leopardi Everything.

Adelaide Why don't you answer him?

Leopardi Everything, mother, everything.

Carlo (*boy*) (*laughs*)

(*following speeches at utmost speed but extremely clearly*)

Leopardi Carlo, be quiet!

Paolina What is the matter, Giacomo?

Monaldo You are tired, Giacomo.

Carlo (*man*) It is as if one were dying.

Leopardi I am not dying, Carlo. It was my birthday.

Why was Luigi sent out of the room like that?

Monaldo You are tired, Giacomo.

Luigi It is simply that I have not very much longer to live.

Paolina I have sometimes undreamt my whole life through.

Leopardi And lived it as it might have been.

Paolina   I have lived yours too.

Leopardi I ask you to hope!

Luigi   Are you a fake, Giacomo?

Monaldo You are tired, Giacomo.

Leopardi   I ask you to hope!

Paolina   And Carlo's and Luigi's.

Carlo (boy) (*laughs*)

Carlo (man) I shall challenge you to a duel, Giacomo.

Leopardi There are other lives, Carlo.

Luigi   Are you a fake?

Leopardi I will prove it!

Pierfrancesco   Accurately, you mean?

Adelaide Why don't you answer him?

Pierfrancesco Giacomo the Magnificent!

Leopardi Don't speak to me like that! Paolina: open the shutters!

Lina They are open, Giacomo.

Ranieri They are open.

All except
Monaldo and } (*confusedly*) They are open, they are open, they are open!
Adelaide

     (*sudden silence – very brief. The rest of the scene is taken at normal speed*)

Paolina Oh, Giacomo, you would not joke on such a subject,
If you had been here, if you had seen the efforts
That have been made to inveigle men to take me,
If you had seen mother's triumphant silences,
When father's attempts failed.

Leopardi   Paolina!
You will not open them. Mother, open the shutters for me!
It is my birthday, mother; please, today, mother . . .

Adelaide If that is what they told you, I hope you took no notice.
It is not very kind of them to try to spoil you.
You will become as vain as they are. How is your health?
You seem to me to have an unhealthy flush.

Leopardi They cannot move, they try, they cannot move.
Father, you are hard as stone.

Monaldo   You are tired, Giacomo.
And you won't want to talk tonight, let us wait till morning.

121

I have missed you, Giacomo, I have missed you greatly,
Stay with us, Giacomo, stay for a long time.

Leopardi Carlo, Carlo, where are you?

Carlo An air of expectation pervades the house.
As if mother were giving birth to another child.
Or no: it is, dare I say it, rather as if one were dying.

Leopardi Pier . . . francesco, Pietruccio: be brave, my brother.

Pierfrancesco Why did you come back to Recanati, Giacomo?
Don't you find us all rather provincial?

Leopardi Luigi . . . Luigi . . . why don't you answer me?

Luigi (after a pause, tonelessly)
It is simply that I have not very much longer to live.

Leopardi The other one, Giacomo, Giacomino.
Open for him, for me, for him! Oh, Giacomo.
What could I tell you? What could I not tell you now?
And will you have known already? Can I not talk to you now?
The eager senses of youth were strong inside us;
Bright eye on the belfry, ours were brighter yet,
Oh, were they not, Giacomo, Giacomo, were they not?
We could feel the day unbearably flower inside us,
In joy, in joy, in joy against the heart.

Giacomo (close at hand: jubilantly)
Bright . . . glancing . . . morning!

Leopardi (a great cry of relief) Ah . . . !

Giacomo Oh morning, morning, across the twittering rooftops.
Oh slumbering, umbered city.

Leopardi Oh Recanati . . . !
I saw you in the morning light for a moment,
A festival of the spirit. And then the shutters closed.

Giacomo And now there are once more thirty thousand shutters,
All closed in Recanati. Peace, gentle city!
My birthdays have all slipped from me.

Leopardi And all the cities are silent under the sun,
Florence and Pisa, Rome and Bologna, peaceful.

Giacomo And Recanati and Naples are here in the sun!

Leopardi I can turn my whole life round and live it again;
Surely I can, I can . . . for it is morning . . .

Giacomo Soft glance across the town . . .

Leopardi Surely I can . . . ?

Giacomo Long look across the watch-tower . . .

Leopardi   Surely I can . . . ?
Giacomo Bright eye on the belfry . . .
Leopardi   Surely I can . . . ?
     For it is morning at last.
                Oh morning!
  Both   (*in voices of triumph*)
     Oh morning, morning . . . and it is morning again!

The Streets of Pompeii

To Rosalind Shanks and Carlo Cura

The Streets of Pompeii was first broadcast on 16 March 1952; and in a new production on 22 April 1955. The version given here was first broadcast on 20 February 1970, with the following cast:

THE SIBYL OF CUMAE	*Flora Robson*
ATTILIO	*Carlo Cura*
FRANCESCA	*Rosalind Shanks*
THE TRAVELLER	*Marius Goring*
MACFARLANE	*John Laurie*
MACBRIDE	*Frank Duncan*
THE LIZARD	*Carleton Hobbs*
JUDY	*Hilda Kriseman*
MARGERY	*Deborah Dallas*
BILL	*Derek Seaton*
WALTER	*David Spenser*
GUIDE	*Hector Ross*
MERCHANT	*Godfrey Kenton*
HIS WIFE	*Kathleen Helme*
HIS DAUGHTER	*Deborah Dallas*
AN OLD MAN	*Malcolm Hayes*
THE SILENT OLD GENTLEMAN	*Carleton Hobbs*
THE SILENT OLD LADY	*Kathleen Helme*

In all cases the production was by Douglas Cleverdon, with music by Anthony Smith-Masters. In the earlier versions of the script, Attilio and Francesca were played by Robert Rietty and Gwen Cherrell.

(music: clarinet: pastorale)

The Sibyl of   Once more, once more, once more:
  Cumae   These plains once more with barren ashes covered,
           Once more the lava, once more turned to stone;
           The traveller's feet once more clink over it,
           Once more, once more.
           And the snake nests and coils in the sun's heat,
           The rabbit seeks its familiar winding home
           Once more.

           And once, once, once:
           The garden and the palace and the noise
           Of the once prince, once powerful, broke this air:
           The temple and the arena and the house,
           Once, once.
           And the merchant went through the street in the early morning,
           The sailor lolled in the wineshop,
           Once.

           And to this place,
           Let him come bravely now, whose wont it is
           To praise man's power and chance; here let him see
           How the harsh Nurse covers her children's eyes.
           On these bright shores full-painted let him see
           Here of the human race
           The magnificent, progressive destinies.

           (Music: violent orchestral tutti.
           Long decrescendo of drums down behind Sibyl.
           Hold drums.
           Orchestral tutti, as at first entrance.
           It is almost at once reinforced by the voices of a great crowd in
           terrified flight. What they say is largely indistinct.)
  Voices *(confusedly)* It is destruction again. It is the mountain.
           It is earth and fire upon us. It is the mountain.
           My father, where are you? Where are my children?
           My mother has fallen, fallen. Father, my father.

127

To the sea, to the sea. Is there time? Is there time?
It is the mountain. We shall never be saved,
We shall never, never . . . It is the mountain.
The mountain, the mountain has burst!
Oh, mother, my mother, my mother, my mother, my mother.
The mountain again, the mountain, the mountain.
> (*at an abrupt point of climax, both orchestra and voices suddenly out. Silence.*)

Attilio Can I help you? You have a thorn in your hand?
Francesca   No, it is nothing, thank you.
I scratched my arm on a thistle there by the gate.
But it is nothing.
Attilio   But it is bleeding.
Francesca   Only a little.
Attilio Let me give you my handkerchief.
Francesca   No, thank you, it is . . .
Attilio It is very clean. I have not used it yet.
You see? It is still folded, where my mother ironed it.
Francesca No, but I must not take . . .
Attilio   *Ehi, non importa.*
A handkerchief, that is all.
Francesca   But . . .
Attilio   *Non importa.*
Look: I will put it round your arm, like that.
Otherwise the blood will run all down your wrist.
One can bleed to death.
Francesca   Not from a scratch.
Attilio Yes, it is very dangerous. Have you a pin?
Francesca No. I am sorry.
Attilio   Then I will tie a knot.
Francesca Thank you. But it will spoil your handkerchief.
Attilio No, it is not a serious handkerchief.
Francesca   I hope not.
Attilio There.
Francesca   Thank you.
Attilio   *Niente.*
Francesca   But it will . . .
Attilio   You like Pompei?

Francesca Yes, very much. But I have not seen it yet.
  Attilio I have been here five days in succession.
    It is very interesting and historical.
Francesca It is a marvel they have excavated so much.
  Attilio They will excavate more.
Francesca   Yes, it is wonderful.
    It is very dead and ancient.
  Attilio   Beautiful, however.
Francesca Yes, it is very beautiful. In this weather
    It is very beautiful, extended here in the sunlight.
      (*fade on last line*)

  Attilio And she is beautiful also. Her dark hair shines,
    And flashes in dusky gold about her shoulders.
    And when she smiles, what she discloses of laughter
    Is less than she conceals. Does she deride me?
    When I touched her arm, here in the hot, dead street,
    It was living and firm and white and smooth and simple,
    And cool and damp like mushrooms in my hands.

Francesca It is very beautiful, extended here in the sunlight.
    And you have been here five times already.
  Attilio My father and uncle are architects in Naples.
    And I must study the structures.
Francesca   Ah yes, you study them.
  Attilio But also for pleasure. I am very contented here.
    I am very contented at Pompei and Ercolano.
      (*fade on last line*)

Francesca Is he always contented? His eyes are shining.
    Oh, handsome boy, when he took my arm in his hand,
    And bent his head, I saw above his eyebrows
    A dew as faint as down. And he took my arm.
    Perhaps we shall never touch each other again.
    Only, perhaps, if we shake hands at parting.

  Attilio I am very contented at Pompei and Ercolano.
    You do not know the excavations yet?
Francesca   Not yet.
  Attilio Perhaps we could make a short walk together then?

Francesca Thank you, but I ought to wait for my friend.
　　　　　She is rather late.
　Attilio　　　　　　　Perhaps she will not come.
Francesca Oh, yes, she promised.
　Attilio　　　　　　　Perhaps she has already gone.
Francesca She would not go without me.
　Attilio　　　　　　　*Perhaps*
　　　　　She has already started to look for you in the ruins.
Francesca Y-yes.
　Attilio　　　And if we make a short walk together,
　　　　　We shall certainly find her. She will probably be in the Forum.
Francesca Yes, very well . . . I . . .
　Attilio　　　　　　　　I will show you the best places.
　　　　　We will go up the Harbour Street and into the Forum,
　　　　　And if we see her I will drop behind.
Francesca (*relieved*)　　　　　　　Yes. Thank you.
　Attilio *Andiamo allora. Io mi chiamo Attilio; come si chiama Lei?*
　　　　　(*fade*)

Traveller They go. As they pass through the dark tunnel, they exchange
　　　　　names, and politely felicitate each other on the possession of them.
　　　　　He is called Attilio, she Francesca . . . They emerge into the
　　　　　sunlight of the Street of the Harbour, and here they exchange
　　　　　ages: he is seventeen, she fifteen. They touch briefly but appreci-
　　　　　atively on the gulf of years between them, and pass on to a
　　　　　comparison of place of origin, number of family, occupation of
　　　　　father, and so on. They are both from Naples; she has come out
　　　　　by the train that morning, he is at present staying with relations
　　　　　not far away, on the hill of Boscoreale . . . The brilliant light of
　　　　　the day pours down on them, and the shadows of the broken
　　　　　columns of the Basilica pass over them as they ascend the lumpy
　　　　　sidewalk towards the Forum. At the end of a wall, Vesuvius
　　　　　becomes visible, and automatically they turn their eyes north to
　　　　　regard him across the ruins of the temple of Apollo.

　Attilio　　　　　　　　And this is the temple of Apollo.
Francesca Ah yes, Apollo.
　Attilio　　　　　　It is not a great thing, of course.
　　　　　It is a simple enneastyle peripteros.
Francesca A simple . . . ?

Attilio (*reassuringly*) Oh, yes. The podium has a certain interest;
     Only now, of course, it . . . But look, Francesca, look!
Francesca At what?
  Attilio (*amused*) The foreigners.
Francesca   But there are always foreigners.
  Attilio But look at that lady there!
Francesca   What is she doing?
         (*he bursts into laughter*)
  Attilio She has climbed up on to the plinth of Apollo's statue.
Francesca She is sitting on his foot, with her arm curled round his leg.
  Attilio And her head against his thigh!
Francesca   Is she . . . exalted, perhaps?
  Attilio No, they are making a photograph of her.
     Judy (*off*) I'm ready, if you are!
      Bill (*off*) O.K., Judy.
Francesca (*entranced*) *Ah, che strani* . . .
     They are Austrian, perhaps?
  Attilio   No, I think they are English:
     The gentlemen's shorts are so long.
Francesca   Oh.
  Attilio Let us go on to the Forum. It is just round the corner.
     (*fade on last line. Clarinet. Hold behind*)

  Sibyl Here to the light of heaven returns
     From underground the skeleton
     Of dead Pompeii, disinterred
     By avarice or piety
     From underneath oblivion.
     Here in the Forum's emptiness,
     Erect the pilgrim stands between
     The fallen colonnades and sees
     With a long look the smokeless hill,
     The cloven summit threatening still
     The shattered fragments of this place.

Traveller Vesuvius: quenched and smooth-breasted in the summer air.
     It has changed many times overnight, and can change again.
     Those smooth slopes, dotted with intrepid white houses, have
     still in them the power to burst open, to split from crest to base,
     to discharge their insane and unimaginable fire and filth upon

the swarming, ardent life of the bay, and in a single night to extinguish a million people, who yet live and multiply there unconcerned.

Sibyl   Oh, sons of men,
　　If I remember here your state on earth,
　　How should I think of you, what should you seem?
　　The soil you tread bears witness.

Traveller Earthquake: here in the Forum, here alone perhaps, are the successive fates of the town clear to the searching and expert young glance of Attilio. In the days of the Emperor Nero, this was a great public place, flanked by colonnades, admonished by temples, presided over by the statues of the powerful. In the year 63 of the Christian era, a vast earthquake tossed down the colonnades like daffodil-stalks to the ground and, crashing stone against stone, half-devastated the crowded, thriving town.

Sibyl   Here let him see
　　How the harsh Nurse covers her children's eyes.
　　When he least fears her, she
　　With one light gesture shakes away half his life . . .
　　And with one other, and how little stronger,
　　Gives him annihilation.

Traveller Eruption: sixteen years after the earthquake, the rebuilding of the city yet but half-completed, the mountain broke open, and obliterated the work, the city and the men . . . In the months after their fear had subsided (and fear vanishes quickly in this bright air) the survivors returned. Over the grey impacted desert of their labours still rose a little of what they had done: blackened capital and architrave, bruised entablature and pediment, disfigured abacus, metope, echinus. They stripped away all they might use elsewhere, and bore it off. Perhaps they were looters . . .

　　Others dug downwards where they believed their houses to have been, broke when they could through the grey hardness to the packed, soft nests of pumice-stones, the *lapilli*, beneath; here they disinterred what they could, hacking their way through the bright pictured walls from room to room. Then they gave up, and the night of centuries fell over the place, till even where it had been was forgotten. All this the Forum and the adjacent streets laconically record; the half-finished granaries, the shattered achievements, the ravished treasures. But does the place yield up its vanished people? Not here, not yet. Here is only that other death, scarcely less solemn, scarcely less pitiful: the death of places.

Attilio Yes, there are a lot of people here this morning.
Francesca Do you know any of them?
Attilio   Only by sight.
            I often see the two over there, by the temple.
Francesca The old gentleman and lady in the straw hats?
Attilio Yes. They are also English; they are very nice.
            They never speak to anyone, or to each other.
            But they think a great deal. They are very intelligent.
            I think they are an archaeologist and his consort.
            They are very white and clean. Do you like them?
Francesca   Yes, very much.
Attilio And is your friend here, Francesca?
Francesca   I . . . cannot see her. No.
Attilio What is her name?
Francesca   Mariagrazia.
Attilio Well, we shall find her.
Francesca   Perhaps I should go back?
Attilio No. She will be over there in the north, in the rich quarter.
            She is probably with the crowds at the house of the brothers
                                             Vettius.
Francesca Ah, I have heard of them. I have seen pictures.
Attilio Yes, everyone goes there. There are many big houses
            In that part of Pompei. The businessmen lived there.
            It was convenient, and near the Forum:
            The House of the Dancing Faun, the House of the Gilded Cupids,
            The House of the Silver Wedding: they are all over there.
Francesca You do not seem to think very highly of them?
Attilio But yes, of course I do. But . . . I like, *better*,
            The places that are rather difficult to understand.

133

Like this Forum for example. Like that great white marble
rectangle

Just standing there by itself . . . over there through the columns.
Come and see . . .

   (*brief pause*)

Francesca   What beautiful marble flowers and leaves all round it!
It is like a great white picture-frame without a picture.

Attilio   They call it the Edifice of Eumachia.
They say she was a priestess. She and her son –

Francesca   Her *son?*

Attilio   (*maturely*) Oh, yes. They are said to have given it to the populace.
Donated it, they say. But of course they don't *know.*

Francesca   Who don't know?

Attilio   The guide-books. The experts.
They don't really know, I think. That is why I like it.
I like things from the past to have a little mystery still.

Francesca   There is a Villa of the Mysteries.

Attilio   Ah, but that is a different kind.
Mysteries there mean secret rites, the rites of Bacchus,
Of Dionysus . . .

MacBride   (*suddenly*) Ye'll pardon me, young gentleman . . .

Attilio   Signore?

MacBride   Pardon me for interrupting,
But we heard ye mention the Villa of the Mysteries.

MacFarlane   Can ye tell us the way there? We left our guide-book
Back at the hotel.

Attilio   Yes, with pleasure.

MacBride   Thank you.

Attilio   You must go over there to the left, and under the archway.

MacFarlane   Under the archway; ay.

Attilio   And keep straight on to the Street of Fortune.

MacFarlane   The Street of Fortune. Ye'll remember that, MacBride?

MacBride   The Street of Fortune.

Attilio   Then turn to the left: *così.*

MacFarlane   Così.

Attilio   Così. Until you come to the end of the excavations,
And turn to the right, *così*, and go straight on,
And always straight, and straight, until you come
To the Ercolano Gate. There is no gate there any more;
And keep straight on along the Street of the *Tombs.*

And at the end you find the Villa of the Mysteries.
It is far.

MacBride   Well, it seems pretty easy to find.

Attilio It is easy, but far.

MacFarlane   Well, thank you, thank you.

Attilio *Prego, signore, prego.*

MacFarlane   M'm?

Attilio   Don't mention it.

MacBride Thank you. Good morning.

       (*they all say good morning. Briefest pause*)

Attilio (*calling*) Oh, *signori!*

MacBride (*distant*) Er . . . yes?

Attilio   Would you like to borrow my guide-book?

MacBride Pardon?

Attilio   Would you like to borrow my guide-book?

MacBride It's very kind of ye. But . . . how would we get it to ye back?

Attilio Get it . . .?

MacBride   Get it to ye back. Afterward.

Attilio (*who has not understood*)   I . . .

MacFarlane How would we *re-give* it to ye?

Attilio   *Ah, capisco!*

     (*smiling*) Oh, we shall meet again. I am here every day.

MacBride We might easily miss each other.

MacFarlane   It's a big place, P'm-pee-eye.

Attilio Oh, you can leave it at the gate. The gatemen all know me.
Or I can call for it at the hotel. I live very near.

MacBride Ah . . . (*firmly polite*) No, thank ye. I think we can manage
                                  without.

MacFarlane We're only just having a wee look around the place.

MacBride But thank you all the same. It was very thoughtful.

Attilio Not at all.

MacFarlane   And thank ye for the direction.

Attilio *Prego, prego.*

MacBride   Good morning.

     (*further good mornings exchanged, MacBride and MacFarlane
     retreating*)

Francesca How strange that they would not borrow the guide-book.
I wonder why.

Attilio	*Chissà* . . . ?

Attilio   *Chissà* . . . ?

Francesca Were they Americans?

Attilio   No, no. They were pure English.

Francesca   Ah, yes?

Attilio Yes, one can tell by the accent. Well . . .
And now we must look again for Mariagrazia.
She will be at the House of the Brothers Vettius. *Andiamo?*
(*slight fade on last line*)

MacFarlane Extraordinary thing, MacBride, the way the young laddie wanted to make ye take his guide-book like that. What do ye suppose to have been the motive behind such a gesture?

MacBride There may have been several motives, of course. The Latin races have always been noted for the ambiguity of their utterance and action. It may have been the preliminary to some form of black-mail or other.

MacFarlane I had thought of that. I suppose he was trying to scrape some kind of an acquaintance with us, which we may have found very difficult to shake off later?

MacBride Especially if he had presented himself at the hotel to collect the guide-book. You noticed he was gey and ready with that as an alternative suggestion?

MacFarlane Yes, it's mysterious. Though he seemed a reasonably agreeable and cleanly young lad. Still, ye can't be too careful. Just look back over your shoulder in an inconspicuous manner, will ye, and see if they're following us.

MacBride Eh . . . *nooo*. No. They seem to be making their way to the congeries of buildings over to the north.

MacFarlane Good. It was the presence of the young girl I did not quite trust.

MacBride Ye mean she may have been some sort of a *decoy* like?

MacFarlane Well, *he* may have been a decoy for *her* . . . I suppose that *was* a guide-book he held out to ye . . . ?
(*fade out on last line*)

Traveller Attilio and Francesca have left the Forum, and are approaching the Street of Nola. Some shared instinct tempts them to loiter a little as they go, giving this or that object on the way an intense and detailed examination which they know it does not always merit . . . The sun is higher, and the shadows in the street are shorter.

(*music: clarinet alone briefly. Long last note behind Traveller's first words.*)

Antiquity. Is it thus that the Land of the Dead will look at our first glimpse of it? At the moment of release into that long vacation, is it thus we shall see that country? . . . Set out in empty streets, the fractured grey boxes of strangers' houses lining them, into eternity? Each containing something we cannot see, even though all seems shamelessly and horribly broken open to the still, new air, the new, still air of the morning, the vagueness and the lightness of morning, of a holiday morning in a strange land.

Francesca (*almost a monotone*) It is very dead and ancient.
  Attilio (*likewise*)   Beautiful, however.
Francesca Yes, it is very beautiful. In this weather
          It is very beautiful, extended here in the sunlight . . .

Traveller Which floods the hither-and-thithering streets; long, long or short; narrow, narrow or wide; straight, straight or curved . . . There are stepping-stones across them; for water, always water, coursed all day and all night through these streets. Water gurgling and clucking in the streets, and the lull of water all through the night.

    Sibyl And everywhere dryness succeeds,
       And dryness through the long, long street,
       And heat and dryness on the stone.
       The only flow, the flood of sun.
       And everywhere the grass and weeds
       Fight for and win their killing life.

Traveller Emptiness: water and fire gone; vacancy of earth and air. Empty.

    Sibyl Stand for a moment in this street:
       You are alone.
       The broken houses, hovels now,
       Or towering still, are all about.
       Peer through the gated door . . .
       Vestibule, fauces, atrium . . .
       The broken fount, the pillared hall,
       Actaeon on the scarlet wall,

137

The locked Priapus in the box,
The frantic, barking, silent dog
Mosaicked on the long, dead floor.
Empty indeed this silent home.

Traveller Silence: water and fire gone; vacancy of earth and air ... And from out of the house of Sallust, a lizard runs, pauses, hesitates, a lizard palpitates on the stone, runs, silently, silently, rustles between two grasses, skims up the wall, a lizard, pausing on the stone, waits, palpitates in the sun.

The Lizard In-out-in-out-in-out. Breathe gently. In-out-in-out. Careful. Watch. Where? Stone, under belly. Good. Hot, all over back. Good. Yes ... Noise? No. Grip. Sand? Sand under claw? Yes. Nice ... Can wriggle? Yes. Good. Dirt, all under belly. Cold, all over back. Dark. Breathe gently. Good. In-out-in-out-in-out-in-out ...
   (fade)

Traveller Emptiness. Alone. And then at the end of the street, round the corner, voices again, the world.

Judy *(off)* Bill we're going down here!
Bill *(off)* O.K., Judy, we'll catch you up later.

The Lizard *(off)* ... In-out-in-out-in-out-in-out. Noise? ... Yes. Better ... *skip.*

Traveller Voices round the corner again, figures emerging idly, casually, few, into the street again; and again the light bright skeins of life are knitted together again.

Judy *(abrupt and bossy)* Margery! Margery!
Margery *(dim and fluffy)* Yes, dear? Sorry. I was peeping through this gate. It's locked. Should I ask the guide to unlock it?
Judy Are there any statues inside?
Margery Don't *think* so. Can't quite see.
Judy Well, don't bother if there aren't any statues. How many more can we do?
Margery More what, dear?
Judy Snaps.
Margery Oh, yes. I'll just peep at the cam. It says number seven.

138

Judy One left then. And eight on the other roll. Nine. Should be
   basta.
Margery We won't use them all here, will we?
   Judy Depends. I told Mum we'd get a snap of one or other of us, with
   every damned statue in Pompeii. (*stoutly*) And we will. Where's
   Walter?
Margery He and Bill seem to be looking at something with the guide.
   Judy Stealing a march. Come on. Let's go back. Hi! Walter! Bill!
   What do you think you're doing?
Walter (*distant*) It's O.K., Judy!
Margery Walter's waving to us not to go.
   Judy Not to go? My foot. What do they think they're up to? Come on.
   To horse for Herculaneum!
Margery Oh, Ju-*dee* . . .
            (*slight fade*)

Walter It's O.K., Judy, it's O.K.! We're just coming!
   Bill Damn, are they coming back? We'd better go on.
         (*to Guide*) Sorry, *scusi.*
Guide Signore?
   Bill I think we'd better get along. The girls . . . *signorina* . . . *vengo*,
         you know . . .
Guide Ah, *sissignò!* The ladies. It is better go on, yes. Another time.
   Bill Yes, quite. Don't say anything about it to the . . .
Guide Nononoh.
   Judy (*approaching*) What are you two up to? What is it?
Walter Nothing, Judy, nothing.
   Judy Come off it. What is it?
Walter We were just chatting.
   Judy On the subject of what?
   Bill Oh, nothing.
   Judy On the subject of what?
   Bill The man was just showing us . . . well . . .
   Judy Showing you what?
Walter Nothing, old girl, nothing. Now, are we going to take . . .
   Judy Showing you what?
            (*brief pause*)
Guide (*helpfully*) It was a liddle stone obscenity. Perhaps the ladies also
         laike to . . . ?

139

Walter⎫ No, don't bother, not really in their line.
   Bill⎭ No, we must get on, or we'll never get round the place . . .
   Judy It was that thing on the wall there.
Margery Ju-*dee* . . .
   Bill Damn it, Judy, don't *point* like that!
   Judy Well, think we don't know what that is? (*to the guide*) Continuary.
 Guide *Sissignorina, sicuro* . . . (*impressively*) This . . . is phallus.
   Bill Do look, Margery, such a whopping great lizard on the wall there behind you.
   Judy You shut up.
 Guide It is a small stone phallus, affissed to side of the door. *Naow:* you unnerstand that we fine two kind of phallus at Pompei . . .
   Judy Really?
 Guide One is phallus with wings. De other is phallus with*out* wings.
   Judy I get it.
 Guide *Naow:* when we fine phallus with wings, it h'means much harvest, a very great fruits, a good corn and wine this year. We say in Italian language *la fecondità.*
   Judy And in English, fecundity. Same word.
 Guide *Eh già?* That I have not knowed. *Naow:* when we have phallus *without* wings, it h'means a house of gay life.
Walter Care to stroll on a bit, Bill?
   Bill M'm? Yes, let's.
 Guide This, ladies . . . is phallus without wings. It h'means, gay time with girl. Oh yes. 'Ere, in this 'ouse we have foun' immoral pictures. They are now put into the Museum of Naples. For safe. Here the gentlemen of the ancient days have always come for nice time, for divertiment with girl.
   Judy Loopernary, in fact.
 Guide (*pleased*) Yes, yes, yes. *Lupanare.*
   Judy M'm. Pretty good.
 Guide An' if you wish, signorina, you can buy small bronce rrripproduction, with or without wing, at gate.
   Judy Oh, good.
Margery Judy, you *wouldn't* . . .
   Judy Yes, why not? Embarrass old Walter.
 Guide Then I show you the boy who sell them. They are quaite, quaite pret-ty, *anche molto artistico* . . . Many English laike to take them home for their friends . . .

     (*fade on last words. Brief pause*)

The Lizard In-out-in-out-in-out. Breathe gently. Careful. In. Out. In. Out.
Stone, under belly. Good. Hot, all over back. Nice. Near leaf.
Noise? No. Can wriggle? Yes. Safe. Good. Stop now. In-out-
in-out-in-out. Gently. Stone. Yes.
(*music: clarinet, briefly solo. Down behind Traveller*)

Traveller Noonday. The streets stretching away in the distance, to the
mountain, to the hills, to the sea, to the plain, to the pine-trees.
Steady descent of heat upon tufa, limestone, brick, travertine,
opus reticulatum, dust and earth. Here the excavators have dug
well, here they have sometimes pieced together with excellent
certainty. Here they have failed, been defeated. Here is a place,
one of many, lost beyond conjecture, unredeemable.

Sibyl What was that broken place, that there
Meanly indicates a room?
A small uncertain wilderness,
An unrecapturable thought,
Where seeding grass and arid bloom
Between the undeciphered stones
Cluster about the humps of earth
And shake in this unshaken air.

Traveller Oblivion: neglected space in the street, shabbiness of uninter-
pretable past. And bright beside it the wine-bar, the thermo-
polium, recovered, clear, definite; jolly the smooth counter,
jolly the big containers, jolly the brown earthenware amphorae,
clean and stacked side-by-side in jollity, jolly the polished marble.
Here the out-of-work sailor lounged, scratched his thigh, spat
in the gutter, bored. And the owner twitted him for incapacity,
and meeting his resentful gaze, raised his eyebrows inquiringly,
suggestingly, suggesting coolness, jolly coolness of room upstairs. Gay time with girl. Or agony with girl. Or boredom with
girl. If he revisited this small cube of earth and air, it would be
the same still, now as then.

Sibyl Here is the spot; and all around,
Nightmare silence in the ear,
Scentless and familiar heat.
But the touch and sight remain
Now as then.

141

The ghost returning here has found
Along the devastated lane
One familiar place untouched,
One shining corner that again
Can stir once more an ancient pain.

Traveller Hallucination: the single known and burning point in a waste of
extinction. Fancies start up in the unreal heat, are warmed for a
moment in the glowing sun, and evaporate on the listless air.
Attilio . . .

Francesca Attilio . . .
Attilio Francesca?
    (*pause*)
Attilio What were you going to say?
Francesca Oh nothing . . . Something silly.
Attilio *Ah, no* . . . What was it? *Dica.*
Francesca I suddenly had the feeling . . .
Attilio *Dica, dica.*
Francesca Only for a second,
As I looked at the fallen house we have just passed,
That if they dug hard enough . . . *into the air above it,*
It would reveal the tops of the houses.
Attilio *Anch'io!*
    (*both laugh*)
Yes, I have felt that too.
We must invent an aerial pick and shovel,
And see what we shall find!
Francesca I wish we could see
What it all looks like from above, from up in the air,
I wish we could see *ourselves*, going in and out of the houses.
Attilio (*authoritatively*) We would look like bees going in and out of a
honeycomb.
Francesca Ah, yes; I would love to see it. Would you?
Attilio (*thoughtfully*) No.
Francesca Why?
Attilio Because then we should know where Mariagrazia is.
Francesca *Ehi, basta* . . .

Traveller Honeycomb. From above, from up in the air: ourselves going in and out of the houses. And into the cells of the honeycomb, wander the visitors, the bees. Climb into the upper air. The streets of the city stretch below us, and that is how they look: purposeful, busy, intent. Invisible from here the boredom, the vagueness, the pleasure, the flippancy, the amazement, the disappointment, the wondering how much longer it will be necessary to stay, the increase of hunger, the vague indigestion, the sudden suspicion of what Joan's real reason for going to Venice by herself after saying she would be all the summer in Portofino was. Etc. But nothing of this is apparent from above. Absorbed, lively, purposeful, the bees perform their allotted tasks, in and out of the cells of the honeycomb.

Sometimes they pause and rest. At the intersection of the Street of Stabia and the Street of Nola, stand the old gentleman and lady whose whiteness, cleanness, intelligence and silence have earlier in the day won the approval of Attilio and Francesca; they appear engrossed in a long contemplation of the small dry public fountain there. Away to the west of them Judy, Margery, Walter and Bill have entered the House of the Dancing Faun, in whose airy centre, looking strangely small and misplaced, the divine little dancer raises his green arms and snaps in drunken bliss his eternal fingers ... Judy has observed the curling tail above the little wild creature's exquisite rump. She has decreed that a photograph be taken of this, with Walter crouched in the impluvium beside it, smiling uncertainly ...

Walter Like this, Judy?
Judy No, crouch down, Walter, crouch right down.
Walter Oh, hell ...

Traveller To the north-west, MacBride and MacFarlane have arrived within four hundred yards of the Villa of the Mysteries. They have remembered Attilio's directions and have followed them with care and exactitude. Attilio himself is now loitering in the street outside the House of the Vettii; Francesca has left him and entered the house, among the swarming bees, to discover if here indeed is the elusive Mariagrazia. She returns. No Mariagrazia; Attilio grins broadly, and she tries not to. They enter the house together, and he keeps close beside her as they make their way through the knots of people.

143

Francesca And there are paintings on all the walls, Attilio . . . !
I did not think the houses would be so large.
Attilio They look very undistinguished from the outside;
And there are many larger than this. However, this one
Is always the most crowded, because of the postcard stall.
You must see the pictures of the *amorini*:
You will like them . . .
Francesca Yes, I have heard of them . . .

Traveller The House of the Vettii: here once the two brothers passed their days and nights, walked, lay, drank, ate, and gave their orders. Aulus Vettius Restitutus, Aulus Vettius Conviva, freedmen, manumitted by the same master. In some way they made their pile, bought the noble patrician house, took it over lock and stock as it stood. It was theirs. To the pictures and ornaments, which had been the best that money could buy and the artist create, they added the worst. It was theirs. Attilio knows as much; but is troubled by other thoughts about them. He follows Francesca, who wanders entranced before the frescoes of the tiny *amorini*, the long delicious trail of winged domesticated Cupids: Cupids gathering and expressing the grapes, Cupids bartering oil and wine, tasting and sampling, Cupids hammering and weighing gold, Cupids driving the stag-drawn chariots . . . Attilio stands beside her, as she bends to contemplate them.

Francesca *Ma guardi, che bello . . . !*
Attilio *(to himself)* Francesca, her name is Francesca . . .
Francesca And this one, Attilio, look . . .
Attilio The one in the chariot, yes.
Francesca He is drawn by leaping dolphins over the sea.
How bravely he pounds them!
Attilio *Eh già, non c'è male.*
Francesca *(with a sigh)* Ah, sweet *amorini* . . .
Attilio *(to himself)* Francesca, her name is *Francesca* . . .
Her smiles come and go,
Watching the antics of the little beguiling creatures,
Dimpling her smooth warm cheek. *Francesca* . . .
She must not pursue the round of the house like the rest,
The House of the Vetti, house of the dirty brothers.

I will not think . . . She must not see what we saw . . .
It was a joke when I went there with Giancarlo,
With Edoardo and the boys: it was all right for us.
Though I wish I had never . . . Look, how her smiles
Flit over the curves of her mouth, as over the mouth of a baby,
Starting and starting again . . . She must not know what is there,
I must not think of that room while she is here.
Why did they build such a place, the filthy pair?
Evil old men, spewing their clever new sins
Over drunken girls. And their paintings, their little lewd
           paintings . . .
 No, for the love of God, not for *Francesca* . . .
  (*the last word loudly*)

Francesca   Did you call me, Attilio?
 Attilio (*recovering himself*) Yes . . . What do you think of the garden?
Francesca The garden. I like the boy with the duck.
  But it looks very *crowded* with statues
  For such a small garden? As though they were all on sale.
 Attilio (*an outburst of disgust*) Ah, what can you expect!
Francesca (*disconcerted*)   Expect?
 Attilio When you think who they were . . .
Francesca   Who?
 Attilio   The Vetti!
Francesca But I thought they were a great ancient family,
  Like the . . . well, like . . .
 Attilio   Like the Gracchi?
Francesca   Yes.
 Attilio   *Not they!*
Francesca But they had this beautiful house.
 Attilio   They ruined it.
  They were vile.
Francesca   But they liked beautiful pictures.
  Look at the other wall there . . .
 Attilio (*impatiently*)   I see it.
  But I do not understand painting in any case.
  At least, I mean, I mean, I mean . . . (*breaks off*)
Francesca (*mystified*)   Yes?
 Attilio (*rapidly*)   I mean, *ehi, in somma,*
  I know who Giotto was and who Leonardo,
  I know the difference between Bellini and Mantegna,

And even between Tintoretto and Veronese,
Who are often very alike; and Greco and Caravaggio . . .
    (*pause*)
Francesca And Pintoricchio?
    (*pause*)
Attilio (*deflated*) Pintoricchio: no.
    (*pause*)
Francesca (*placidly*) I can tell Pintoricchio.
Attilio   *Ehi, brava* . . .
    (*distressed*) Let us go, Francesca, let us go somewhere else.
    Si soffoca qui dentro . . .
Francesca (*concerned*) Of course, Attilio, but . . .
Attilio   I am suffocating here.
    (*fade on last line: drum roll*)

Traveller They go. And a vague sense of menace accompanies them. They leave unlooked at, among the luminous blue-green splendours of the paintings on the walls, one before whom it might have soothed Attilio to linger. It is the painting of Ixion's mother, draped, hooded, and sorrowful, small and ignored. Beside her towers the brown figure of Mercury, nude and plebeian. Behind them Hephaestus binds her son to the everlasting wheel. No one regards her. Her hand is raised, and her eyes are lifted in recognition of eternal calamity . . . It is, twelve centuries early, the ageless, immemorial gesture and look of the Madonna, the posture of suffering maternity; the long tenderness, now incapable to save; the onset of inextinguishable grief. The *Pietà*. The *Addolorata*. An agony known to Titian; and to Bellini and Mantegna, between whom Attilio can distinguish. Known to them all in time, but known here long before, already: known also, the means for its expression.
    (*brief pause*)
MacBride and MacFarlane have reached their destination, the Villa of the Mysteries.

MacFarlane Ay, we do have to pay a further entrance-fee.
MacBride Ay – I thought as much.

Traveller It stands on a separate island of stone, an islanded country-house among the fields, the greatest of the houses here fetched up from the past. It stood on a point of land which in those days fell sharply away to the sea, and the splendour of the bay spread out in swept blue flatnesses before it: Capri, Ischia, Procida, Nisida, Posillipo, advancing and receding through the atmosphere. It is not easy to guess at the succession of lives that were lived here, the existences that beat and declined through its ninety rooms: its sound, as it filled with a crowd of guests singing and drinking, its silence perhaps, as countless slaves whispered their way about the expiring wants of some ageing man or woman dying in loneliness here. And was it so, indeed? And who was entertained? And did the visitors come, muffled, after dark, for a forbidden purpose? Or were there none?

It is not the grand atria, the peristyles, the baths, we have come to see. There are as good elsewhere; you will not remember one from another. It is the great ante-room to the nuptial chamber. The whole of the ancient world has nothing to show us like the strange and startling centre to this abode. Enter it quickly: see if you can catch a movement of drapery or limb among the figures that crowd its walls. You cannot. However softly you enter, all movement in the room ceases the second before. Nevertheless enter.

(*drum-roll*)

Sibyl   Slowly round the painted wall,
Spreads the cold voluptuous dream,
Silence of arrested feast,
Quiet of arrested dance,
Anger of arrested lust.
The minutes of the hour are stilled,
The minute held, but not the hour,
While all the time a Time ticks on.
The persons of the drama raise
Their eyes to your intrusion here,
Tacitly scan enough to know,
In the erotic silent pause,
Definite, precise and clear,
The nature of your appetite,
While all the time a Time ticks on.
Traveller   Ticks on. Ticks on.

Sibyl The minute held, but not the hour.
Traveller Ticks on. Ticks on.
    Sibyl While all the time a Time
Traveller   ticks on.
         The room stands still.
         Panic and calm.
    Sibyl Not calm.
Traveller Panic. Presence of Pan.
    Sibyl And of another.
Traveller   No, not yet.
    Sibyl He is here.
Traveller   I say: not yet.
    Sibyl Look behind you.
Traveller   He is here.
    Sibyl Name him.
Traveller   Bacchus.
         (*one loud drumbeat*)
    Sibyl Answer: what is here for you?
Traveller The persons of the drama.
    Sibyl   You
         Know them?
Traveller   Yes. I know them all.
    Sibyl And their names?
Traveller   I cannot name
         Anyone among them. But
         I know their faces, one by one.
    Sibyl How many are there?
Traveller   Twenty-nine.
    Sibyl There are thirty.
Traveller   With myself.
    Sibyl Name them.
Traveller   No. I cannot name
         Anyone among them.
    Sibyl   You
         Know their faces.
Traveller   No. Not now.
    Sibyl Nothing of them you can tell.
         Nothing of them.
Traveller   Yes. I can.
    Sibyl But not the faces.

Traveller   Not the names.
        Not the faces.
  Sibyl   Not the names.
Traveller Not the faces, not the names.
  Sibyl What then?
Traveller   Only one thing remains.
  Sibyl And that thing
Traveller   I dare not say.
  Sibyl It is their eyes.
Traveller The silent face, the silent look
         Out of the wall from them to me
         And in the wall from them to them
         The silent ocular interchange
         The silent recognising eye
         And the silent thought behind the eye
         Out of the wall from them to me.
  Sibyl And the young satyr's sidelong glance
         Who lifts the syrinx to his lips.
Traveller The watchful, knowing, smiling gaze
         Of him who lifts a hideous mask,
  Sibyl And shows behind, the evil face;
         Silenus with the blank brute stare,
Traveller And the maiden's indrawn breath
         Of terror as she sees him there.

     (one drumbeat)

MacBride I would not say, MacFarlane, that the evidence about the true nature of the pictures is what I would call *conclusive* at any point. Even when ye have settled whether ye should start *here* on the wall and go round to *there*, or whether, as Professor Maiuri asserts, ye should start *there* and go round to *here*, no, I would not say that the evidence as to the true nature of the chamber is conclusive.

MacFarlane I take your point.

MacBride Good. As you know, strong claims have been made that the lady of the house was a high priestess of the Bacchic cult, which, however, we know to have been forbidden by the Roman law of the time. And if the cult were a secret practice, it seems very extraordinary that the ritual-chamber should have been in so *exposed* a position.

MacFarlane The professor says that it is the antechamber to the nuptial al*cove*, where the lord and lady each night retired to rest.

MacBride But does it not seem to you possible that the frescoes may have perhaps had no *religious* significance at all?

MacFarlane (*profoundly, after thought*). Ah. Ye mean that the lord and lady will have had to pass *through* this chamber as they retired to rest and may likely have been strongly impressed on the way by the erotic nature of some of the scenes depicted?

MacBride Well, something of that I was thinking, maybe.

MacFarlane Do I understand ye to suggest then that the motive for the highly spectacular decoration of the chamber was primarily aphrodisiac?

MacBride I would not like to be dogmatic on the point. But ye may recall other occasions where extremely famous artists were expressly engaged for such a purpose. There are numerous examples here in P'm-pee-eye. And ye may call to mind the Palace of the T outside Mantua, where the painter Giulio Romano (he is mentioned in Shakespeare) was employed to decorate the bedchamber with frescoes conducive to a greater degree of earnestness in the conjugal performance of the occupants.

MacFarlane It would certainly explain the suggestive nature of some of the scenes delineated here: for example the comparative abandonment of the scene between Bacchus and I-forget-the-young-woman's-name, and the partial revelation, a wee bit further on, of the stylised symbol of the male organ of generation; and the act of flagellation yonder, and so forth ... (*very thoughtfully*) But I would not understand in that case the presence of the wee nude boy. He is said to be reading aloud from a papyrus the rites of initiation.

MacBride There can be no certainty on the point. It may be, not a papyrus, but some small piece of children's literature given to him to distract his attention from the orgiastic character of the activities around him.

MacFarlane But, MacBride, though I agree that the room could not be kept secret if it was the gathering for some forbidden religious ritual, would not the same objection obtain if the room were purely aphrodisiac in its purpose?

MacBride Och, there's always the possibility of an intentional ambiguity

in such an apartment. To the more delicate and mystical-minded
of his visitors, the host would probably have pointed out the
religious significance of the scenes, while to the non-religious, or
to the police inspector, he may have asserted them to have been
no more than pornographic in intention.

MacFarlane I see. Yes, maybe. It's very remarkable there should be no
mention in the guide-books of such an interpretation. (*fade*)

(*fade in Attilio. He still speaks with some impatience, but has
partially recovered*)

Attilio Oh, Francesca, yes, I know there are beautiful pictures here at
Pompei;
But ... all those eternal paintings of birds and flowers,
And sad little moonlit landscapes on the walls ...
They must have been done by a set of idle women
Dilettanti, with nothing better to do all day
Than imitate painters, like German spinsters in Capri,
Who can only paint cliffs, and trellised arbours and seascapes:
(*his voice deepening with melancholy*)
Ehi ... the kind of pictures my *sister* always paints
For my cousins' birthdays,
(*tragically*)   in *water-colours*.

Francesca (*suddenly but placidly*)
And when they have nothing important to say any longer,
The great painters leave out the people and paint only the
scenery,
And where Carlo Crivelli gives us the Madonna and Baby
surrounded by vegetables,
They give us only the vegetables and leave out the Madonna
and Baby,
And less and less even of those, till they try to say
That a mountain in France means just as much as Saint
Jerome,
Or a newspaper and a bottle as the mystery of the Creation:
(*conclusively*) It is a decadence.

Attilio (*after a pause of amazement*)
How ... how do you *know* that, Francesca?

Francesca (*earnestly*) My father says so.
He is a little angry about it.

Attilio   And he has reason.

151

Francesca Yes. My mother says that he has always reason . . .
And she is sometimes a little angry about *that*.
   (*brief pause*)
Attilio Shall I meet your father, perhaps?
Francesca (*shy once more*)   Perhaps . . . I expect so.
Attilio When?
Francesca   I . . . don't know.
Attilio   Tomorrow?
Francesca   N-no, not tomorrow.
Attilio Then the day after tomorrow?
Francesca (*evasively*)   . . . Soon.
Attilio And you think that your father will like me, Francesca?
Francesca I think so . . . I expect so.
Attilio (*passionately*) I am *not* bad-tempered, Francesca.
I do not know why I spoke as I spoke just now
In that horrible . . . I never speak like that
To anyone at all.
Francesca   *Ehi*, Attilio, it was nothing.
Attilio And naturally I would put on my long trousers;
I only wear these when I stay at Boscoreale.
And a tie, and my jacket, and my proper shoes.
Francesca (*smiling*) He would not mind what you wore.
Attilio   Oh, yes, it is very important.
Francesca   Not to my father.
Attilio And I will put some brilliantine on my hair:
A great quantity in fact.
Francesca (*like a passage from Dante, sadly*) Ma, Attilio,
A me non piace mai la brillantina.
Attilio   Not *like* it!
Francesca No, never.
Attilio   Oh.
Francesca   No.
Attilio (*dully*)   Then water?
Francesca   Yes . . . Attilio, look!
Attilio What is it?
Francesca   The old gentleman and lady whom we saw.
They are coming along the street.
Attilio   How white they are!
And properly clean.
Francesca   Yes. And they are still quite, quite silent.

Attilio Ah, they never speak. They are very intelligent.
I like them.

Francesca   And I.

Attilio   They are coming from the House of the Silver
Wedding.

Francesca Do you suppose they spoke to each other inside?

Attilio Oh, no, I am sure . . .

Francesca   Sh . . . They will hear what we are saying.

Attilio (*loudly*) So shall we inspect the House of the Silver Wedding?
It is so called because it was discovered
In 1892 –

Francesca (*similarly*) Ah, yes, how interesting.

Attilio   – The year
Of the silver wedding of the King and Queen.

Francesca Ah, yes.

Attilio   And at that point the excavations stop.
You see? The road is closed in just there.
Did you notice, Francesca? Did they look at us as they passed?

Francesca Yes, both of them.

Attilio   Good. They are very intelligent.
An English archaeologist and his consort,
I am sure they are . . . I am glad they noticed . . .

The Lizard (*fade in*) In-out-in-out-in-out-in-out. Breathe gently. Careful. Noise? Noise? Gone. Good. Hot, all over back. Good. M'm under belly? (*suspiciously*) M'm? M'm? Stone? No. M'm under belly? What? Bad. Better . . . *skip.*

Traveller The heat increases . . . confusing the senses. It is time for the ingurgitation of great quantities of food, for the imbibition of appreciable draughts of wine, for digestive repose. The white old gentleman and lady, having passed, looked at, and been re-approved by Attilio and Francesca, make their way slowly, but always intelligently, through streets as silent as themselves, to emerge at last, cleanly, at the Harbour Gate. They are nearly out of sight. And as they pass out of hearing, they – it might almost seem? – yes, it is wellnigh certain – they begin to speak. They have gone to their hotel. Two and a half hours will pass before they return . . . Attilio and Francesca, unweary, only a little hungry, have clambered up onto unexcavated ground and are making their way south-east in the direction of the amphitheatre. Alive and upright, incessant in speech and gesture, they walk over the land of the dead. Seven yards below them, wherever they go, lie the imprisoned skeletons in their black nests, prone or supine, silent, immobile.

Seven yards below them, the dead wait in their dead houses, their dead money scattered round them. The rain of filth that killed their bodies preserved their forms. Inside the black encasement that petrified quickly round them, the decay of flesh and blood proceeded, leaving only the skeleton therein, the dead butterflies inside the black cocoons. Eighteen centuries later, when the discoverer's pick struck against bone, he would suspend his labours, liquid plaster would be poured into the hollow shape about the bones, and allowed to harden there. And the dark husk of death might then be broken open. There they lay, in their unchosen extinction: the dead face of an ordinary person, even of a suicide, is triumphant in comparison. Here is a man who died alone, face down. Here is the naked form of a young girl, her head pressed against the bosom of an older woman. Here is a dog, strangled at the chain, twisted on its back, its legs like those of a broken upturned stool, its long jaws open in agony . . .

Through the grass and the weeds and the wild flowers they go, the young ones, through the heat of the sun and the windless air. The distances quiver and dance in the heat . . .

(*music: clarinet and strings. Interlude. During a quiet passage:*)

The Lizard (*faded up and down*) In-out-in-out-in-out-in-out-in-out. Sleep. Sleep. Sleep. Sleep. Sleep . . .

Traveller Afternoon. Much has happened. MacBride and MacFarlane have long ago returned from the Villa of the Mysteries, and for some time past have been carefully inspecting Region Six . . . Judy and Walter, followed at a distance of eighteen yards by Margery and Bill, have wandered along the Street of the Consul and emerged into the spacious avenue beyond the Herculaneum Gate: the Street of the Tombs. They have dismissed their guide. Rather glad he's gone, to tell you the honest. Nice chap, but enough is as good as. Got a bit bored, too, with all those streets,

one after another. Very interesting, of course; but all the same, after all, aren't they? I mean, when you've seen one...
(*cross-fade to Margery*)

Margery I mean, when you've seen one, you've had it.
   Bill Couldn't agree more. Still, it's a bit fresher here, anyway, more open.
Margery Yes... Jolly hot, though, all the same.
   Bill Yes, mustn't get sunstroke...
Margery Well, the *real* danger is, when you stay away from the beach all day like this, *some* parts of you get browner than the others.
   Bill Oh, well...
Margery Well, it is worrying, isn't it? I mean, you don't want a sort of a *pattern*.
   Bill No, I suppose not.
Margery What a long way in front old Judy and Walter are getting!
   Bill Energy, the energy of it...
Margery (*brightly*) Lot of ruins about still.
   Bill You'd think Jerry had been here, almost. Was, of course, during the war. Bombs dropped here, too.
Margery Ours?
   Bill Oh, yes. of course. Accident, of course.
Margery Can't have made much difference anyway, when you come to think.
   Bill ... Oh, look, Margery, there's a bit of jolly dee. Three pillars set up there in a nice curve.
Margery Nice curved seat, too.
   Bill How about a nice sit-down?
Margery Oh, yes...
   Bill That's better. Good to take the weight off your legs.
Margery Don't talk to me about weight! All that macaroni! Gosh! Where are Judy and Walter?
   Bill Oh, just up there. They'll be back.
      (*cross-fade to Traveller*)

Traveller Just up there. They'll be back... And as they sit at ease on the seat of the exedra of the Priestess Mamia, Bill, looking with deceptive intensity before him, suddenly runs the fingers of his right hand, in sportive manner, up Margery's spine.

Margery (*sharply*) Oo! Oo! Oo!

Bill Hahaha! That caught you out. Poor old Marge.

Margery Oh dear, Bill, you really shouldn't. Oh dear.

Bill (*roguishly*) What did you think it was?

Margery I made *sure* it was a liz.

Bill Hahaha!

Margery I can't bear them. They skip about everywhere.

Bill Oh, they're all right. I like lizards. Like me to catch one for you?

Margery Yes, and see me faint.

Bill Sh! There's one just behind you.

Margery Where!

Bill There.

Margery Oh dear. Looking right at us, sideways.

Bill BOH!!

Margery Oh, it's running right up that pillar!

The Lizard Upupupupupupupupupupupupupupupupupup ... up ... up ... up ... up. Stop. In-out-in-out-in-out. Where? Stone, yes. Careful. Can wriggle? Yes. Wriggle. Careful.

(*music*)

Margery I wouldn't like Judy to know, of course, 'cause she *is* so keen on getting the snaps of all the statues. But I really don't *like* Pom-pay.

Bill Well, it's jolly interesting, you know. I like coming to places like this. So long as I don't have to know what they're all about.

Margery I know. But it's the ruins *I* don't like.

Bill Well, sweetie, it's *all* ruins.

Margery That's what I mean. I don't like the atmos.

Bill Oh, it's all right.

Margery No, it's not. I don't like churchyards either.

Judy (*off*) Margery! Margery! Come on!

Bill There's old Judy calling us.

Margery Why doesn't she come back?

Bill I think she wants us to go on. Whatever for?

Margery Oh, *I* see what it is. (*affectionately*) Dear old Judy.

Bill What's up?

Margery She's found another statch, on a tombstone. Come on. No rest for the wicked.

(*fade before end of line*)

Traveller It is the sad gaunt statue of a woman, holding about her the heavy draperies of the tomb, standing mysterious and alone among the ferns, one hand raised nearly to her face, and with an expression which seems to say that she is trying to remember this place she has returned to. She seems, from death, to be regarding life, and wondering if she has ever known it aright. *What were we?*

Sibyl What was that bitter point in time
That bore the name of life?
Mysterious, tremendous,
Lost in our thought that hidden country lies;
As in our day of life there lay
The secret land of death. And as in life
Our souls drew back from death, so now they draw
Back from the flame of life.
     (*no fade in*)

Judy (*in determined tones*) I want to be cremated.

Walter Oh, really?

Judy Yes, cremated; and have my ashes scattered.

Walter What, *now*, do you mean?

Judy (*coldly*) Don't be funny.

Walter (*contritely*) Sorry, old girl. It slipped out.

Judy I'm quite sincere about it. Always have been. I don't like all this Tomb business.

Walter Oh, I dunno . . .

Judy Well, *I* do. No marble dames over *my* last resting place, thank you all the same.

Walter Well, she looks just *like* you, Judy.

Judy Some hopes . . . Where *are* they?

Walter They're just coming. (*calls*) Bi-ill! Come on!

Margery} (*fairly distant*) Com-ing!
and Bill} We're here!

Judy Dawdling about. Is that roll of film in all right, can you see?

Walter Perfectly O.K.

Judy Mother'll like this one.

Margery (*approaching*) Oh, dear, all these *stones*. I keep slipping.

Bill Margery says she wants her din.

Judy Where've you been?

Bill Oh, plodding along slowly. Some of us aren't so young as the rest of us.

Judy Up to no good, I expect, as usual.

157

Margery (*reproachfully*) Ju-*dee!*

   Judy Well, come on, we haven't all day to waste. Margery, go and stand over by that marble female, and let me take a snap.

Margery (*firmly*) No, Judy, not by a *tomb.*

   Judy Why not?

Margery Well, it's *morb.*

   Judy It's what?

Margery Morb.

   Judy Nonsense!

Margery (*rebelliously*) Well, I'm not going in among all those fern-things without any stockings on, no thank you. Besides I'm not going to be taken with my arms round a lady, it's silly.

   Judy Margery, *look here* . . . !

   Bill (*pacifically*) *I'll* go. I'll go, Judy. There's nothing I'd like better.

   Judy O.K. then. Hurry up. Then we can have a bite to eat.

Walter Shall I take it, Judy, or will you?

   Judy I will. You O.K., Bill?

   Bill (*some yards off*) Yes, O.K!

   Judy You're sticking your behind out again.

   Bill Sorry!

Walter What's she like, Bill?

   Bill She's as cold as old Judy!

   Judy (*sotto voce*) Silly great ass.

Walter Pretend she's Marilyn Monroe, Bill!

Margery Or Gina Lollobrij.

   Judy Shut up you two. Now. Ready . . . Hold it. Ready . . .

Walter *Click.*

Margery Click.

Traveller Click. The camera clicks in the Street of the Tombs. And at the same second, a mile and a half to the south-east, Attilio and Francesca reach, click, the top of the amphitheatre wall; and at the same second, a mile to the south, the clean old gentleman and lady raise, click, to their silent lips a glass of white wine, served by an intelligent waiter; and in the same second, three quarters of a mile to the east-south-east, MacBride emerges, click, from a roofless, empty, deserted and unidentified house in the Street of the Baker, and rejoins his companion MacFarlane, who is waiting two yards nine inches to the west: click.

MacBride (*with a slight cough*) Well, well, I don't think anybody could raise any objection to *that*, even supposing they knew.

MacFarlane Och no, man. It's not as if it were one of the more valuable excavations.

MacBride And after all, there's no other provision made.

MacFarlane And ye cannot be expected to go all the way back to the hotel.

MacBride No, certainly not . . . Let us make our way over to the Street of Abundance, will we, and take a peep at the New Excavations, so called? (*as they proceed*) You're not feeling the heat too much?

MacFarlane No, no. It's down here, I think.

MacBride Ay, must be.

MacFarlane I was thinking while ye were gone, MacBride, that it's very remarkable that Europe in the Middle Ages should so strangely have lost sight of the *art* of sanitation: it had clearly been brought to a high pitch of perfection in the ancient world.

MacBride Ye cannot, I think, judge all places from P'm-pee-eye. The ready availability of running water must have tended to solve problems that the more inland towns may well have found insuperable.

MacFarlane I catch your drift.

MacBride It seems fairly plain they must have been somewhat uninhibited in their sanitary habits as between the sexes.

MacFarlane But that, I have noticed to be a phenomenon by no means uncommon in Italy even today. You may recall the very exposed nature of the urinal at the back of the Piazza Brà, at Verona.

MacBride Ay. So much so that on the one occasion I attempted to utilise it personally, I was unable to commence.

MacFarlane It would seem from P'm-pee-eye that the simplest form of the convenience was a broken amphora inserted and embedded into the cement of a corner-wall at a cross-roads, as a sort of elongated chamber-pot.

MacBride A position which must have rendered it, if anything, even more conspicuous than the contemporary object at Verona.

MacFarlane Certainly. It is, no doubt, the origin of the line in the poet Catullus: *nunc in quadriviis et angiportis.*

MacBride How would you translate that?

MacFarlane Well . . . say . . . 'Now in the quadrivia and the angiportae.'

MacBride Och, yes. I see.

MacFarlane The former being a cross-roads and the latter a blind-alley where the object was situated.

MacBride How does it go on?

MacFarlane I cannot remember. It is one of the poems dedicated to Lesbia, the young lady with whom the unfortunate poet was for a time infatuated.

MacBride But I wouldn't understand the connection a young *lady* might have with the object in question; ye would say from its shape and incidence . . .

(*fade, well before the end of the speech*)

Traveller They proceed to the New Excavations at the eastern end of the Street of Abundance. They are not appreciably hungry, though it is now a quarter past two. In any case, MacFarlane remembers another poem, which runs as follows:

MacFarlane
In great heat,
Never eat.

Traveller This poem is not by Catullus. MacFarlane's grandfather composed it in the hot summer of 1870, the year of the Franco-Prussian War; and MacBride agrees that it would be a folly in an unfamiliar country recklessly to overload the digestive organs and incur thereby the risk of enteric disturbance, difficult to cope with adequately when in almost daily movement from place to place.

This risk, however, has been taken by Judy, Walter, Bill and Margery, who have picnicked heartily from their luncheon-basket in a shady dell near the monument of the Istacidii. Stone glimmers all around them, beyond the trees; the sky blazes white overhead. Nice to get into the shade. Almost cool for the first time today. (*fade*)

Judy Almost cool for the first time today.

Walter Yes, lovely spot, lovely.

Margery Bit eerie, though.

Walter Oh, I don't know . . .

Bill Lizards.

Margery Oh Bill, *no:* don't be silly.

Judy Are we going on?

Walter What, already? After all that *vino?*

Bill Give a young man a chance in life, Judy.

Judy All right, then, mind if I slip my shoes off, boys and girls?

Walter Do.

    Bill Do.

    Judy Ah ... That's a relief.

  Walter Blister O.K., Judy?

    Judy As near as.

  Walter Good.

    Judy And I don't know about my other little playmates, but here's me for ten minutes' shut-eye.

    Bill That's an idea. Helps the digestion.

  Walter I'm asleep already. And please don't wake me if I snore.

      (*pause*)

Margery (*dreamily*) A little siesta ... under the trees ... We shall be just like the four lovers – (*hastily*) the two couples, in *Midsummer Night's Dream*, by Shakespeare, shan't we?

    Bill (*profoundly*) M'm ...

Margery (*half-asleep*) We did it at school ... for Commem ... in the open air, just outside the cricket pav ... I did Helena – the tall one ... I must have been awful ... though I got a good crit. in the mag ... I like acting ... wouldn't like to take it up though ... for one thing, a girl I know at RADA ...

    Judy (*quietly*) Margery.

      (*pause*)

Margery (*mildly*) Yes, dear? ...

      (*pause*)

    Judy Shut ... *up.*

      (*pause*)

Margery O.K.

      (*pause*)

      (*clarinet in, hold, and then down behind speech. Eventually out.*)

Traveller Far away, on the southern slope of the shadowless amphi-theatre, Attilio and Francesca sit. They are a long way away, but you cannot miss them. He talks to her, she listens, she talks also. From time to time they glance down into the great stone-girt oval space, perfect, simple and emphatic. There was the entrance for the gladiators, there the entrance for the beasts; somewhere the emperors must have sat, if ever they came down this way.

   Sibyl Here the bright day is even apt
       For sudden strangeness. It is said

The traveller sitting with his book,
Or dozing on the arena's lip,
Has lifted up a casual eye,
And seen substantial in the day,
Legions of passionate soldiery
Gazing intent with open mouth
Before them at the combatants.
The vision instantaneous
Instantly goes; but not before
He through the summer air has caught
The sound of their triumphant roar.
    (drum up full and abruptly out.
    Clarinet loudly replaces it without a break.
    Hold, and out without fading)

Francesca He sleeps, Attilio sleeps, sleeps lightly, sleeps by me.
I must not watch him, and I must, as there he lies.
I must not watch too long, lest when he wakes, his eyes
Open to mine. I must not. It must not be.
I must watch instead the lizard or the tree,
Or the stones he knows so well: which recognise
The warm bright glance, affectionate and wise,
He turns upon them; so that I may not see
The sunlight fall on his mouth, nor the surrender
To sleep of his dark hair, nor clear and sweet
The curve of his silent cheek, the golden splendour
Of his throat and his arms and his thighs and his sandalled feet.
I will watch the lizard, or the stone, or the sky above him,
Lest he should see, when he wakes, dear Attilio, how dearly I
                                   love him.

(diminuendo on last line. Very brief pause)

The Lizard (drowsily) Breathe gently. Careful. In-out-in-out. Hot, all over
back. Noise? No. Sleep? Yes. Just a bit. Watch. No better . . . *skip.*
Attilio (waking) Francesca, Francesca, something ran over my hand . . .
did you see . . . ? A lizard per- *(breaks off, and finishes the word in a
whisper)* haps . . .
    (brief pause)

Attilio She sleeps, Francesca sleeps, beside me, sleeps in grace.
I can see her how she is when I am away.
I can watch her as I have wanted to watch her all day.
And she will not know how well I know her face.
Secret her sleep. I am not there. All trace,
All thought of me is banished . . . I only stay
To be the first thing in her waking eyes; I only may
Protect till then that sleep in which I have no place.
Now I could hurt her, and will not; will not seek
To lay my hand softly on her soft breast;
I will not press my cheek against her cheek;
I will even her shining hair leave uncaressed;
I will not . . . I will only . . . oh, Francesca, can it do you harm,
If I place a kiss, like a whisper, into your open palm?

(*pause. She wakes*)

Francesca Attilio . . .
    (*long pause*)
  Attilio Francesca.

Traveller Do not move. This minute hold.
      In this concave of grass and stone,
      May your love and may this hour
      That slaughterous bloody past atone.
  Sibyl No, do not move. This minute hold.
      Do not remember, nor retrace
      That far-back day, when such-as-you
      Sank in destruction in this place.

      (*music: sudden orchestral tutti, as in the first pages. During the drum
      decrescendo after it, voices are heard intermittently and dispersedly,
      gradually merging into a confused panic, as they converge from
      different points*)

Voices It is the mountain!
    It is the mountain; it is the fire again!
    It is destruction; it is upon us again!
    Father, where are you?
    Where are my children?

163

The people are crowding the streets.
We shall never be saved!
It is the last destruction!
My mother, my mother has fallen.
We shall never be saved.
The mountain has burst!
Where, where are my children, help me to find my children.
The temple has collapsed, and the priests are fleeing!
My mother, my mother.
It is the mountain . . .!
　　(*eruption crash: then down behind Sibyl*)

Sibyl These plains once more with barren ashes covered,
Once more the lava, once more turned to stone.
Let him come now, and now, whose wont it is
To praise man's power and chance, here let him see
How the harsh Nurse covers her children's eyes.
　　(*music: eruption crash*)

Traveller And one alone in his darkened house wrote on the wall the words
'Sodom and Gomorrah.' There were many for whom in the
darkness, and the rain of stones and water, there could be no
escape; priests hid behind the altar, men and women huddled in
the cellars, the gladiators in the barracks; all who remained
indoors, collecting their treasures, were doomed to suffocation.
　　(*drums crescendo, orchestral flash, drums down. Hold through scene
　　irregularly in background*)

Merchant Hold the torch up! Hold the torch *up*, you fool! I can't see what
I'm pulling out of the chest. You – take these bags, carefully.
Slave Yes, master.
Merchant You can carry more than that; take these as well. And when we
go out into the street, keep close to me, don't move unless you
see me. Where . . .
Wife (*approaching*) Lucius, Lucius, we shall be trapped if you insist on
staying any longer; please, my darling . . .
Merchant Be quiet!
Daughter Papa, papa, don't make me stay here . . .
Merchant Be quiet, I tell you, both of you. And when we go out, Marcus,
and Horatius – are you listening?

Slave Yes master, yes master.

Merchant Keep three paces in front of me, keep there all the time. Hold the torch up, I told you!

Slave Essir.

Merchant Well, *hold* it, *hold* it, then! Here, for God's sake, give it to *him*, give it to the other one, you feeble imbecile.

(*sudden outcry from four or five female voices at door of room*)

Female Slaves Mistress, mistress, we daren't stay any longer!

The streets are crowded with people, mistress!

We shall never get away, mistress, if we don't go now.

It is so dark.

We are all frightened. It is everyone now for himself, they are saying!

Can we go, mistress, can we have your leave to go?

Merchant For the love of God, send those women out! Send them out! Let the stupid whores lose their own way in the dark. Am I to leave my money and jewels for a set of dirty slaves?

Two Female Slaves We're as good as dirty you! You great dirty monster!

Merchant Send them out! Send them out! When we get back, by ...

Wife Go, my dears, go.

Daughter Mother, let me go with them, I'm frightened here.

Wife Stay with me here, darling, it will be safer.

Female Slaves (*receding*) Good-bye, mistress, God bless you; how shall we get into the Forum? Etc., etc.

Merchant Take this statue, and stand by the door with it, and wait for me; don't let it go, it's the most precious one in the whole of ...

Wife Lucius! We dare not wait any longer. Lock the doors, and come.

Merchant I'm not leaving my silver here, don't think it! They'll be looting the place the minute our backs are turned. Hold the torch up, Lucretia!

Daughter Papa ...

Merchant Be a good girl and take this little bag, it is full of your mother's jewels. Marcus! Marcus, where are you?

Slave (*sudden outburst*) No! No! No! Who are you! Take your statues yourself! And your money and your jewels. You'll be as naked as we are in an hour's time; take them. The girl was right. We're as good as dirty you any dirty day. Take them. I won't touch them, I'm going, I'm going! (*in terror*) Don't touch me!

Wife⎫ Lucius!
Daughter⎰ Papa! No! Don't hurt him! Aaaah!
        (the slave is knocked over and is heard hysterically moaning)
Merchant The filthy bastard, I hope I've done for him.
    Wife Lucius, in the name of Heaven, will . . .
Merchant Go! Go! Go, if you want to; but, by God, if we ever get out of
        this, I can tell . . .
Daughter I can't see anything. Papa! I can't see anything!
        (eruption crash. Drums behind. Lose after a few words)

Traveller The hot wet ash suffocated them as they lay or cowered, their
        clothes pulled over their heads for protection. Or it caught them
        as they stumbled in their flight. It pressed them down, surrounded
        them, engulfed them, found out every curve of their bodies, and
        settled there and hardened, pressing inch by inch round their
        lives . . . The last fraction of breathed-in air passed out again in a
        bubble from their mouths into the filthy blackness, and the filth
        that had already closed their eyes and filled their ears and nostrils,
        occupied their last point of struggle: against their clenched teeth.
        That done, it mounted over them, piled itself heavily upon them,
        holding them, alone or embraced. It filled the streets, and the
        alleys, the theatres, the baths and the temples and the great open
        spaces: there they lay: in the cellar, in the doorway, under
        the temple arch, in the colonnade: some huddled together in
        hopelessness. And some were not with others, not even near
        them . . .

Old Man I must have fallen. I cannot move my arms. Are my eyes open?
        I don't think so. I don't think they are. I must be helped. If I were
        not so thirsty. I said I never would ask them for help. I never
        wanted to be a burden to them. Now I must. It is hard to breathe,
        but I think I must cry out to them. Yes. Ah. *(a sharp soft bark
        merely)* They will hear it and come. *(pause)* Again: ah. Perhaps
        they can't hear. Then louder: ah. *(it is no louder in fact)* Aah. On
        the ship at Tarentum, the wine dripped on the floor from the
        captain's table, and we lay and let it pour into our mouths . . .
        Ah . . . In the moonlit orchard near Capua, I took you, and your
        mouth was cool against mine because it was night-time . . . Ah . . .
        All along the shore the waves bent back, ah, in a long white frill,
        and the water sparkled all the way to Sorrentum and you

bounced me in the water, crying, 'You are five years old today!'
Ah. Ah. Ah.

>   (*silence*)

Francesca Attilio . . .

>   (*long pause*)

> *Attilio* Francesca.

>   (*pause*)

Traveller They have not moved. His head remains bent over her hand; and
she still feels the gentle, exact print of his lips on her palm. After
a little while he raises his head, and their eyes meet, each seeing
in the other's a light they have not seen in faces before. She lifts
the hand he has kissed, and places the back of it against his cheek,
as though to discover if it is as real as she has believed.

>   (*pause*)

Francesca Attilio . . .

> *Attilio* Francesca?

Francesca (*solemnly and gently*)
>   You said you would show me . . . The Friangular Torum.

> *Attilio* (*sweetly*) The what?

Francesca (*carefully*)   The Fri-angu–
>   (*they both giggle*)
>   The Triangular Forum.

> *Attilio* (*briskly*) No: the Friangular Torum!

Francesca   *Ehi*, Attilio . . .

> *Attilio*   I shall see you tomorrow?

Francesca It . . . is possible.

> *Attilio*   But probably?

Francesca   *Ehi* . . .

> *Attilio* Yes. Let us see each other tomorrow. Here?

Francesca That may be difficult.

> *Attilio*   Then I will come to Naples.
>   We can see the pictures from Pompei in the Museum.
>   And I can come and meet your father.

Francesca   But . . .

> *Attilio*   Yes.
>   It is better at once. I am older than you, Francesca.

Francesca Nearly two years. That is nice.

> *Attilio*   Certainly. It is best.

167

But it is a grave responsibility for me.
It is better to have these things in black and white.
You said you had five elder sisters.

Francesca Yes.

Attilio Very well:
Your parents will be very glad that you should be promised.
Yes?

Francesca Perhaps.

Attilio Certainly. And now may I kiss you?
You permit it?

Francesca A little one.

Attilio (*agreeably*) Yes . . . Ah, Francesca.
(*juvenile kiss*)

Thank you.

Francesca Prego.

Attilio (*happily*) And now we will go to the Friangular Torum.

Francesca Perhaps we shall see the clean old gentleman and lady.

Attilio Yes. And we will call on our way at the Temple of Isis,
Which I love very much.

Francesca Egyptian!

Attilio Egyptian! Yes!
(*sings exuberantly*) Immenso, immenso Phthà,
Del mondo spirto fecondator!
(*she joins in as they recede on a very long fade*)

Both Ah! Ah!
Noi t'invochiamo . . .

Traveller (*cheerfully*) Never, never, *never* have the buildings in the Oriental
Quarter of the New Excavations shone more brightly than they
do this evening, as Attilio and Francesca pass between them; the
scarlet frescoes in the street seem like works of art; the red
political slogans on the walls have the radiance of a new-found,
unexpected sincerity. And indeed, in the cool wind that wanders
around the city after even the hottest day, when the evening
seems to open, relent and bless, an air of happiness, of duty well
done, pervades the place. Through the deepening evening, the
pilgrims are making their way through the streets to the entrance
gates. MacBride and MacFarlane, for example: they have come
to the end of a long day, no minute wasted, no hour idly spent,
a day of profit and refreshment to the mind.

MacBride ... and in fact, MacFarlane, I think it might be well said that throughout the ancient world we find, as regards their physical life, a frank mixture of the practical and the sordid in almost equal proportions; in so far as ye can demarcate proportion in such matters.

MacFarlane The ancient world made no disguise of its passions, not even when its passions were of an irregular or abnormal character – or so Professor MacTaggart says on page 480 of's wee book on the subject.

MacBride Nooo. Though at P'm-pee-eye the passions, if promiscuous in their expression, appear to have been of an entirely normal nature.

MacFarlane But doubtless any irregular improprieties have been disguised by the modern authorities in the interest of the tourist traffic. Professor Hillsborough is quite certain that what modern psychiatry would term Ho Mo Sexu Aility was prevalent alike in the Greek and the Roman civilisations.

MacBride He attributes it, does he not, to the comparative seclusion of the womenfolk from the men, and a consequent relaxation of the normal taboos?

MacFarlane Something of that, ay. And he adds that a contributory effect may have been the custom of exercising in a nude state in the *palaestra*. It's a reasonable point, I think . . . though I am bound to say I noticed nothing of the kind at the University College of Dundee.

MacBride But there, of course, ye will have had plentiful access to feminine company in the evenings.

MacFarlane True. And in the gymnasium a small pair of shorts and a white singlet or sweater were always insisted upon; the singlet in the summer, the sweater in the winter, when the days tended to get a wee thing chilly . . . (*fade*)

Traveller And certainly Judy and Walter, Margery and Bill, have done their duty. Refreshed by a pleasant two-and-a-half-hour nap under the trees, they have arisen and passed an energetic final hour of discovery. This has incidentally included the thorough examination of a house, which, though they are unaware of the fact, they had already visited with the guide in the morning. And now, twilight falling round them, they are sauntering across the breezy space of the Forum, amicably, harmoniously, nostalgically, team-spiritedly.

The Four (*distantly, in exquisite harmony*)
　　　　Roll . . . out . . . the barrel,
　　　　We'll have . . . a barrel . . . of fun . . .

Traveller Dusk is creeping into every street of the city, and filling every
　　　　house. Through the darkening shades of the Villa of the Mysteries,
　　　　the veiled maiden still enters upon her eternal initiation. Still she
　　　　recoils from the face of the Silenus; still, half-naked under the
　　　　chastiser's whip, she weeps into her companion's lap . . . And in
　　　　the Street of Plenty, a lizard creeps into the house of the Priest
　　　　Amandus.

The Lizard In-out-in-out-in-out-in-out. Cold, all over back now. Cold.
　　　　Leaf near? Yes. Can wriggle? Just a bit. Stone, under belly.
　　　　Good. Cold. Sleep? In-out-in-out-in-out. Sleep? Sleep? Just a
　　　　bit. Now.

Traveller And in the most ancient quarter of the city, the Stabian quarter,
　　　　stands the Triangular Forum, with the Greek stumps of an
　　　　ancient temple in the midst of it.

Attilio (*softly*) The Friangular Torum . . .
　　　　The oldest ruins and the best. We will come here often.
　　　　I love the two theatres, and the promenade,
　　　　And those small oaks: they are sacred to Apollo.
　　　　And best of all my beloved Doric columns.
Francesca 　　　　　　　　　　　　　　　　　　　Those?
Attilio Yes, a whole long row. They were built by the Greeks
　　　　Ah, che bellezza . . . You can see them best from here, from the
　　　　　　　　　　　　　　　　　　　　　　　portico,
　　　　A whole long row of them vanishing away in the dusk.
　　　　Perspective . . . Come and stand close to me.
Francesca 　　　　　　　　　　　　　　　Attilio, do you see?
Attilio See what, Francesca . . . ?
Francesca 　　　　　　　　　　　By those ruined stumps in the trees . . .
Attilio The archaic temple . . . Yes. It is the old gentleman and lady.
Francesca They are still not speaking.
Attilio 　　　　　　　　　　But they are thinking a great deal.
　　　　They are very intelligent; they do not need to talk much.
Francesca But, look, Attilio . . .

170

Attilio (*in surprise*) Yes . . . !

Francesca   They *are* speaking.

Attilio She has turned to him.

Francesca   And put her hand on his arm.

Attilio Ah, Francesca, I wish I knew what they were saying. Yes, she is speaking . . .

        (*brief pause. No fade*)

Old lady It is time to go, now, my dear.

Old gentleman M'm? Yes, yes, dear, time to go.

Old lady What were you thinking about?

Old gentleman M'm? Oh, only . . . that young couple by the gate.

Old lady The boy and girl, yes.

Old gentleman Nice young people, they look.

Old lady They are beautiful, yes. A beautiful pair. And, oh so young, so very young.

Old gentleman I've seen the boy about here before, I think; haven't you?

Old lady Several times, yes. Not the girl.

Old gentleman No. I'm glad he's found such a charming companion. Perhaps we might have spoken to him . . . Ah, well. Time to go, I suppose, Flo, dear?

Old lady I told you it was.

Old gentleman Oh dear. We've only three more days.

Old lady But we shall come back again, I hope. I hope so.

Old gentleman So much of it's just the same as it was before the war, you know. Well, naturally – but I mean I've remembered a great deal of it, Flo. They're slower at the excavations now, of course, than they used to be; but better, of course; much better. I've remembered a great deal.

Old lady I know you have, my dearest. Are you tired?

Old gentleman Not a bit. Not the least bit. Are you?

Old lady No. But they'll be turning us out in a minute.

Old gentleman Yes, let's go . . . Those two are still there. D'you think we might say good night as we pass them?

Old lady Oh, yes, I think so . . . They are looking straight at us.

Old gentleman Afraid we must have been rather in the way. Hope not.

Old lady Oh, I *hope* not . . . Sh . . .

           (*after a brief pause*)

Old gentleman I . . . ah . . . Good *night*, good *night*.

Francesca⎫ (*with overpowering eagerness*) Good night, signore, good night,
Attilio⎭ signora, good night!

Old lady Good night, good night!

Old gentleman Good night . . . I . . . ah . . . here tomorrow?

Francesca⎫ Yes, yes, signore, yes, sir, yes!
Attilio⎭

Old gentleman Good. Good. We too.

Old lady Splendid.

Francesca⎫ *Ehi, bravi, signore, signora . . . !*
Attilio⎭

Old gentleman Good night.

        (*good nights as before, but a little more sedate. Tiny pause*)

Old gentleman Good. Nice young couple.

Old lady As bright as lamps . . .

Old gentleman Yes . . . May they remain so.

Old lady May they remain so . . . Come, my sweet.

    (*clarinet finale*)

Return to Naples

To David Spenser

Return to Naples was first broadcast in 1950. The version given here was first broadcast on 4 August 1953, with the following cast:

H.	*Derek Hart*
MOTHER	*Vivienne Chatterton*
FATHER	*Esmé Percy*
BRUNO	*David Spenser*
ALBERTO (as a boy)	*Anthony Valentine*
ALBERTO (as a young man)	*David Page*
LEO (as a boy)	*Colin Campbell*
LEO (as a young man)	*Robert Rietty*
SIMONE	*Glyn Dearman*
NARRATOR	*James McKechnie*

In the earlier version, the part of 'H.' was played by Cyril Cusack. The production, in both cases, was by Douglas Cleverdon.

Note: the Italian form of the name Henry is, of course, Enrico. In Neapolitan this becomes Errico, and is often truncated to Erric'. It rhymes with 'unique', and is never pronounced like the English name Eric.

(*In the opening catechism, Alberto is serious, brisk and business-like. He is a mature twelve*)

Alberto Erric' . . .

H. Alberto?

Alberto Is it large? Is it larger than ours?

H. Is what large?

Alberto Your piazza, in Birmingham. Is it larger than ours?

H. We have three piazzas in Birmingham.

Alberto And what are they called?

H. One is called Piazza Vittoria.

Alberto After the Queen?

H. Yes.

Alberto And the others?

H. Well, one is called Piazza Stephenson.

Alberto Piazza Stephenson. Who was he?

H. An engineer, I think.

Alberto You are not certain?

H. Not quite, no.

Alberto Ah, you should have asked. And the third?

H. The third is called Piazza Chamberlain.

Alberto Another engineer?

H. No. A political family.

Alberto (*pleased*) E, braviss'. And which is the largest?

H. The Piazza Vittoria, I think.

Alberto The Piazza Vittoria is *very* large?

H. It is fairly large. It has the Town Hall, modelled on the Parthenon, on one side, and the Council House, modelled on the classical Renaissance, on another, and on . . .

Alberto (*passionately*) Ah but what *splendour!* (*with curiosity*) There is *much* splendour in Birmingham, Erric', is there not?

H. (*after thought*) Yes. Yes, Alberto, there is much splendour in Birmingham.

Alberto (*rhapsodically*) E bello, che bello . . . !

(*fade on last word*)

Narrator But that was not yet in Naples, you remember; that was in Rome. That morning, as the train moved south into the early sunlight of the *campagna*, you had drifted into conversation with an elderly doctor. He invited you to breakfast when you got to Rome. You went. You met his wife. You ate. You drank. And you were told you might stay in their apartment instead of going to a hotel. You accepted. Then you were left to doze off the effects of the journey in the misty heat of the shuttered *salone*. You slept. You woke. And you saw Alberto for the first time: fat, white-clad, tiptoeing gingerly across the room on his eternal blisters . . . Later that day, he wrote a letter which you were directed to give to his mother in Naples. It began, *Carissima Mamma . . .*

(*cross-fade*)

Alberto 'Dearest Mamma, This young man, who will present my letter to you, is a very great friend of mine, whom I met this afternoon at the house of Doctor Cappocci . . . '

Narrator That afternoon you had walked together to the Porta Pia, his small fat hand had created a pool of sweat in the crook of your arm . . .

Alberto '. . . His name is Enrico. He is English, and is staying with Doctor Cappocci, and next week he is going to Capri. On the way, he will call on you in Naples. Please receive him into our home with the greatest kindness. Your most affectionate Alberto.'

Narrator That letter, which was never delivered, you kept for many years, together with Alberto's other gifts: the sprig of unpolished coral, the slab of marble pavement from Tarquinia, and the life of Admiral Gravina, which sixteen years later you have yet to read . . .

There was no need to deliver the letter of introduction, for in the end Alberto's father and brother came up to Rome to fetch you, and you all travelled to Naples together.

(*faint continental train noises in background*)

Father Ah! Naples, beautiful Naples! It is the most beautiful city in the world, Signor Errico, and we shall all be very happy there, there is always something to do; we shall go to Posillipo . . . and Aversa . . .

Alberto And Pompei . . .

Father And Ercolano . . .

Leo And the cinema . . .

Father (*his French has a strong Italian accent*) Tu seras très contant, très contant, très contant . . . (*he laughs*) You speak French?

H. *Oui, un peu* ... It is very kind of you to have me in Naples, *cavaliere.* I hope you didn't mind Alberto asking if ...

Father It is my duty, it is my privilege. *C'est mon privilège.* You have seen the beauties of Rome?

H. Many of them, yes.

Leo Have you seen the Colosseo?

H. Yes, Leo.

Leo And Saint Peter?

H. Yes.

Alberto We have seen the Forum, and the Vatican, and Ostia, and the Baths of Caracalla ...

Father Good. Very beautiful and instructive. And, Signor Errico ... (*very tenderly*) have you seen the Duce?

H. I'm afraid not, *cavaliere,* no.

Father (*loud lament*) Ah, you have not seen the Duce! *Tu n'as pas vu le Douche!* Aaaah!

Alberto But Papa, I have told him how the Duce speaks. (*dramatically*) Senatus Populusque Romanus ...

Leo Alberto, don't be so silly, the Duce doesn't talk in Latin.

Father (*emphatically*) When you return to Rome, you must not fail to see the Duce. And do you like postage stamps?

H. I like to look at them, yes ... I don't know anything about them ...

Leo Papa has seventy-two thousand postage stamps.

Father I will explain them to you, one by one. And now, until we get to Formia, I shall repose; we have travelled all morning, and I shall repose for a little. *Je vais me reposer.*

    (*slight pause*)

Leo Erric'.

H. Yes, Leo?

Leo Let us go into the corridor, shall we?

Alberto (*angrily*) No!

Leo (*also angrily*) Why not?

Alberto Errico is *my* friend, not yours. You can't take him into the corridor.

Leo And why not? He's my friend, too.

Alberto Papapapà. Leo wants to take Erric' into the corridor; tell him no. *I* shall take Erric' into the corridor, not Leo ...

Father All three, all three, all *three:* go into the corridor. Look at the scenery. I shall repose.

Leo (*resignedly*) All right, let's all go.

Alberto (*savagely under his breath*) You wait, Leo . . .

      (*train noise briefly up and down*)

Alberto (*brightly*) Beautiful, eh?

  H. Beautiful. What are those hills in the distance?

Alberto I . . . I forget the name.

  Leo Would you like to know what they are called, Erric'?

  H. Yes, very much.

  Leo (*smoothly*) Alberto. Go and ask Papa what the hills are called. Your *friend* wants to know.

Alberto Papa is asleep.

  Leo No, he isn't, not yet. You go and ask him.

Alberto (*distrustfully*) Well, don't you talk while I'm away.

  Leo (*aloofly*) Of course not.

Alberto (*receding*) Don't let him talk to you, will you, Erric'?

      (*the briefest pause. The following dialogue is furtive and hurried, though distinct*)

  Leo (*eagerly*) Erric'.

  H. Yes?

  Leo Erric', tell me; the English *girls* . . .

  H. Yes?

  Leo Are beautiful?

  H. Not all of them, no. Some are.

  Leo But they are all *blonde?*

  H. Not quite all.

  Leo (*anxiously*) But there are more blondes than blacks?

  H. Oh yes.

  Leo There are hundreds, thousands of blondes?

  H. There must be, altogether.

  Leo And there are among them some who are *very* blonde, as of platinum?

  H. Some, yes.

  Leo If you went down any street in London, you would be certain to see a very beautiful blonde?

  H. I think so.

  Leo (*relaxing in sensual exhaustion at the thought*) Ah, che bellezz' . . . I would give twenty-five to thirty lire for a beautiful blonde. (*anxiously*) Would that be too much? How much does one pay for them?

  H. I . . .

  Leo Sh! Here's Alberto.

Alberto (*ferociously, almost in tears*) You were talking! You promised...

  Leo We were talking about colours. And what are the hills called?

Alberto (*petulantly*) They're the Roman Apennines.

  Leo (*silkily*) I thought so.

Alberto You...

  H. (*on fade*) The Roman Apennines...

    (*very brief pause*)

Narrator Curious, isn't it, how you have now forgotten what you expected of Naples, that loveliest of names? Did you then feel apprehensive of it, as you have always felt at every later return to it? *Voilà donc la terrible cité.* M'm? You can't remember, can you? And on that first arrival, among the shouting, unshaven porters, you had no need to clutch your money or protect your virtue, had you? They were both protected for you, by those who cared only for your comfort and seemed undisturbed by the dark, noisy, unintelligible people around you... In the swaying *carrozza* you were jolted across and up the city to a little square where one Naples seemed to end and another to begin. You alighted, and you all groaned your way up the nine flights of stairs to that bright, faded apartment, high over the winding Corso.

Alberto (*loudly*) Mamma, Mamma, here we are, all of us, back again. Aah, Mamma!

Mother (*ecstatically*) Alberto! What a long while you have been away! Are you well? Aaah, Albert'! And where is Papa? And Leo, where is Leo?

 Alberto They are coming up with Errico's luggage. Mamma, this is Erric'. Errico, this is Mamma.

Mother Signorino. A great pleasure...

  H. It is very kind of you to allow me to come here.

Mother On the contrary, it is a pleasure. We are very glad, very glad indeed. Alberto has been a good boy?

Alberto I've been very good, very good indeed.

  H. A very good boy, yes.

Mother Alberto is always a good boy. And here is my eldest boy, Bruno, who is also a good boy.

 Bruno How do you do, Errico?

  H. How do you do, Bruno?

Mother It is Leo who is sometimes not a good boy; but he is good enough. We cannot always be good.

>(*noises of the others arriving in the background. Their actual words are not audible*)

Father Oh, the stairs, the stairs, they will kill me, they will kill me ...

Mother Where is Leo?

Leo Here I am. Where have the others got to?

Mother Are you both tired, was the train late ... ? (*etc.*)

>(*Bruno and H. speak rapidly and loudly*)

Bruno And you like Italy, Erric'?

H. Very much.

Bruno You like it better than England?

H. I don't know yet, but I think so.

Bruno England and Italy are the best countries in the world, aren't they?

H. I think so, yes. Of course, I like France too.

Bruno Oh no, France never. I like England, because you see, I am fair-haired, I am much fairer than *you*, and people mistake me for an English person, and when I read I wear glasses, and they think I am more English than ever. (*anxiously*) You do think I look English, Erric'?

H. Yes, I think you would pass for an Englishman.

Bruno (*handsomely*) E brav'. And you would pass for an Italian.

H. Never. Especially when I speak.

Bruno No, you must be careful not to speak. I will speak for you.

Alberto Errico, come and see your room!

Bruno Erric' ...

H. Yes, Bruno?

Bruno (*nobly*) We shall be more than friends, Erric', we shall be brothers! You see, since I am fair-haired, everybody thinks ...

Mother (*incisively*) Signorino Erric'!

>(*silence*)

H. (*a little confused by so many people*) S-signora?

Mother Have you sweated?

H. Have I ... ?

Mother Sweated. Have you sweated? It is very hot.

H. (*embarrassed*) I ... I don't think I have swe ... psp ... persp ...

Mother (*authoritatively*) Come here. Let me feel if you have sweated.

Father (*plaintively*) *I* have sweated. I have sweated very much, coming up the stairs. And I sweated in the train. I shall dry myself, and change my shirt.

Mother Yes, Erric', you have sweated on the chest and on the back. You

must change your shirt and vest and put on a pyjama, otherwise you will catch cold. Brun', take Erric' and give him a
towel . . .

Bruno   Come along, Erric'. Alberto has taken your luggage in.

H.   I don't think I need . . .

Mother   (calling) Albert' . . . !

Alberto   (distant) Yes, Mamma . . . ?

Mother   Alberto. Have you sweated? (her voice recedes on this line)

H.   Leo, I don't think I really need change my shirt, need I? I haven't
sweated very much.

Leo   No. I haven't either. (politely) But, of course, Mamma, being
very fat, is also very humid, and she thinks that perhaps everybody
else is very humid too.

H.   I see.

Father   Yes, you must dry yourself, and then I shall show you my
postage stamps.

Bruno   Papa has seventy-two thousand postage stamps.

Leo   Yes, I told him. Erric' isn't interested in postage stamps.

H.   I am, Leo. I don't know anything about them, but . . .

Father   (interrupting, generously) I shall show you them all. Je te les mon-
trerai tous; tous; tous . . . Les timbres-poste. (mystically) Somalia;
Owstralia . . .

H.   I shall look forward to it.

Father   West Indies, East Indies . . .

Mother   (suddenly) Signorino Erric'.

Father   Canadà.

H.   Signora?

Father   Tierra del Fuego . . .

Mother   You come from England.

Father   China, Japan . . .

H.   From England, yes.

Mother   Then tell me this.

Father   New Guinea, Sudamerica . . .

Mother   Pietro, be quiet, I wish to speak to Erric'.

Father   (quietly extinguishing himself) Madagascar . . .

Mother   Now tell me . . .

H.   Yes?

Mother   In England, do they have – much divorce?

H.   Not a great deal. Not so much as in America.

Mother   But there is divorce?

H. Oh yes, there is divorce. You . . . have to show sufficient reasons, of course . . .

Mother And what reasons?

H. Well, there can be various reasons.

Mother You have to have reasons?

H. Yes.

Mother You cannot say, I am tired of my husband, and they say, very well, you are divorced.

H. Oh no, it's much harder than that. It takes time.

Mother And reasons.

H. And reasons, yes.

Mother And what reasons?

H. Well . . . great cruelty, for example . . . or infidelity . . .

Mother Ah, one can divorce for infidelity?

H. (*increasingly embarrassed*) I think so. But of course it takes time; and some people who wish to divorce but haven't been unfaithful . . . they have to *pretend* to be unfaithful.

Mother They pretend?

H. Yes.

Mother How?

H. I . . . I don't exactly know how . . .

Mother But they pretend?

H. Yes.

Mother To be unfaithful?

H. Yes.

Mother Ah! (*a polite, conclusive sound*)
(*brief pause*)

H. I think I . . . *will* go and change my shirt . . . Excuse me.

Mother (*graciously*) *Prego.*
(*fade on last word*)

Narrator On that first visit, you slept, did you not, in that farthest room of all, a high blue chamber with lattices outside the window. From one window you looked on to a thousand roofs; pink, grey, russet, the gentle colours of that ungentle city. From the other, you could see Vesuvius, now dead, then living, the steady plume of smoke floating away over towards Sorrento . . .

Bruno You have many English colonies, Erric'.

H. Yes, Bruno.

Bruno You are a great Empire.

    Leo A great Empire; magnificent, strong.

    H. (*modestly*) We *are* a great Empire, yes.

Alberto Italy too will become a great Empire. We will divide the world. Italy can have Africa, eh? (*confidentially*) It is better so, we are used to a hot climate. And you can have India.

    Leo But they already have India.

Alberto (*generously*) Well, they can keep it. It is better to have a large Empire. The Duce says so.

    H. (*a little amused*) Not everyone else says so.

Bruno Do they say so in England?

    H. Not everyone, even there.

    Leo Do *you* say so?

    H. No.

Alberto Aren't you a fascist, Erric'?

    H. (*indignantly*) No, I'm not!

Alberto N–not a fascist?

    H. No! Why should I be?

Alberto A–a–are you a socialist?

    Leo⎫ Don't be silly, Alberto, how could he be?
Bruno⎭ Of course he isn't a socialist.

    H. Well, as a matter of fact, I *am* a socialist.
       (*pause*)

Alberto (*hurt and mystified*) But *why*, Erric'?

    H. (*uncomfortably*) Well, I believe in the equality of . . .

Alberto (*interrupting*) Are you a Bolshevik?

    H. Not exactly a Bolshevik, no. Though I think there's a lot . . .

Alberto And your Duce, Mr Ball, Ball, Ball – what is his name?

    H. Baldwin.

Alberto Baldwin. He is socialist too? He is like Stalin?

    H. No, not exactly.

Alberto He is fascist?

    H. No. He is what is called a conservative.

    Leo E pernacchi! I am sick of politics and duces and socialists. Alberto talks of nothing else.

Bruno What are you going to do when you leave the university, Erric'?

    H. I am going to be a writer.

Bruno Bravo. And you will be a great and famous writer like D'Annunzio?

    H. Perhaps.

    Leo You will write novels?

H. Yes.

Leo Hot novels of love and passion?

H. Yes.

Alberto Listen, Erric'. Will you write about us?

H. I shouldn't think so.

Alberto Why not? When I am in the Navy, I will direct a large fleet of cruisers, destroyers, and submarines. I will accomplish a victory, complete and magnificent, and the Duce will embrace me (*he makes the sound of two loud kisses*) and he will say, '*caro Alberto*' (*majestically, dropping his voice*) 'Senatus, Populusque Romanus'. You will write about that?

H. I will when it happens, yes.

Alberto (*nonchalantly*) Oh, it will happen, yes. Would you like to offer me a cigarette?

H. Yes, of course . . .

Alberto Thank you.

Narrator How far away from you, in those high clean rooms, the life of the city itself seemed to be. The noise, the squalor, the crowdedness, the narrow streets between what passed for wide ones. The cities of Hell must be built thus: on hillsides, where none can escape the upward or downward glance of his neighbour. High up, you seemed aloof from where, below, Naples stank and festered, but in two minutes you could plunge into a *vicolo* of descending noise and horror between high tenements, the bottom floors of which were, cave-like, open to the view. And always the same scene in the dark interior: the huge matrimonial bed, a single chair, a picture of a holy face. The washing hung across the street, tier on tier of it, people were up there, calling down. Their babies played round the legs of the patient, tethered donkeys. Past these you and your protective companions would go, day after day, down to the bay, to the boats and the bathing and the glorious inevitable weather; and back you would climb to the equally inevitable catechisms. How far did you ever penetrate, you who were their plaything, into them, who were also yours?

H. (*fade in*) And you have such beautiful names for your streets and piazzas.

Leo But so have you.

184

    H. Have we?

Father (*rapidly*) Yes, you have Lessister Squahre, Tráffalgar Squahre, Piccadilly Circle, Bairkelay Squahre.

Alberto Piazza Stephenson . . .

Mother Brookalyn Britch . . .

    Father That is in New York.

Mother Ah!

    H. But we have nothing like the via Partenope.

    Bruno Parthenope, the siren-nymph. You know that Ulysses discovered her on the beach where we bathed this morning, Erric'? She was very beautiful. Oh most beautiful. He stayed a very long time.

    H. She was blonde, no doubt?
        (*the boys laugh*)

Mother (*across the laugh*) Erric' . . . (*the laugh ends*) . . . Erric'.

    H. Signora.

Mother (*after a brief pause, a firm, sober statement*) I am the nymph Parthenope.
        (*brief pause*)

    H. Wh . . . what?

Mother I am the nymph Parthenope.

    H. You, signora?

Mother I. The explorer Ulysses appeared to me and told me so. 'You are the nymph Parthenope,' he said.

    H. Appeared to you?

Mother Ehi.

    H. When?

Mother (*shrugging, as if this were unimportant*) Ehi . . . about a fortnight ago.

    H. Where?

Mother At a séance.

    H. At a spiritualist séance?

Mother Yes.

Alberto Like they have at Doctor Cappocci's. Mamma believes in them: (*rapidly*) Bzz-bzz-bzz-boof, boof, boof. I don't.

Mother Alberto doesn't understand these things. Destiny. Fate. (*casually*) Very important.

    H. But aren't you a catholic, signora?

Mother Of course I am!

    Leo We are all catholics.

    H. But doesn't the Church say you mustn't go to séances?

Mother (*enigmatically*) Ehi.

    H. But it does say you mustn't?

Mother (*two tones higher*) Ehi.

    H. And yet you go?

Mother (*as at first*) Ehi.

    H. Oh.

    Leo And are you a catholic, Erric'?

    H. No.

Mother (*shocked*) Not a catholic?

    H. No.

Mother Then what *are* you?

    H. I'm a protestant.

Mother Ah . . . a protestant.

  Bruno Erric' is a protestant, Papa . . .

Father (*absently*) British Guiana, without filigree, 1912. What did you say?

  Bruno Erric' is a protestant.

Father (*interested*) Ah, you are a protestant. A Huguenot.

    H. No, *cavaliere*, not a Huguenot. They are French. I am an English protestant. We call ourselves the Church of England.

Mother And what do protestants believe? Do they believe in God?

    H. Yes, of course.

    Leo They believe in God, but not in Christ?

    H. Oh yes they believe in Christ. In fact many protestants believe more in Christ than . . . I mean that many . . .

    Leo (*interrupting*) They believe in Christ, but not in God?

    H. No, they believe in both; and in the Holy Ghost.

Mother Do they believe in the saints?

    H. Well, they believe in them, of course . . . but . . . not quite in the same . . .

Mother They don't venerate them?

    H. Well, they respect them . . .

Mother And they have divorce.

    H. Yes . . . there are many different kinds of protestant, of course. There are . . . many who might be said to . . . protest against the ordinary protestants . . .

Mother Why?

    H. For various reasons . . .

Mother And what are *they* called?

    H. They have many names. For example, there are Methodists, and Christadelphians, and Baptists . . .

186

Mother Baptists?

    H. Yes.

Mother They are catholics?

    H. No, they are not exactly catholics . . .

Mother What do they believe?

    H. They . . . believe in baptism.

Mother But we have baptism too! They must be catholics.

    Leo That is it! Protestants don't believe in baptism.

    H. Oh yes they do. I've been baptised myself.

Mother (*outraged and bewildered*) *But how can it be!* There is baptism, there is not baptism, it is here, it is there, it is, it is not . . . *e come si fa?*

    H. Well, baptists believe in . . . total immersion.

        (*a brief pause*)

Mother (*calmly*) Total immersion. They immerse themselves all.

    H. Yes, when they are grown up.

Mother Not as children?

    H. No, not as children.

Mother And not just the forehead?

    H. No, the whole body . . . I think.

Mother Ah, the whole body . . . They immerse themselves all.

    H. Entirely, yes.

Mother (*courteously*) Ah.

        (*pause*)

 Bruno And, Erric', (*rather slowly*) what sort of things do the others do? The others who protest against the protestants?

    H. Well, some of them believe that Christ was not divine.

 Bruno That he was not the son of God?

    H. Yes. I mean no. I mean that some of them believe he was only the son of God in the sense that we are all the sons of God.

 Bruno And in what sense is that?

    H. I . . . it is rather diffic . . .

Mother (*decisively, but politely*) Erric'.

    H. Signora?

Mother Become a catholic.

    H. Me?

Mother (*quietly and firmly*) Become a catholic. It is simpler. It is better. Become a catholic.

    H. I will think about it.

Mother Ah. You will think. Good.

        (*pause*)

Narrator Do you remember how such discussions would bear you all on their tide from room to room? Into Papa's study, for example, which was also a small laboratory, where under the ferocious bronze profile of Mussolini, test-tubes and retorts full of strange liquids would desultorily steam and change colour. Or into the dining-room, where a committee-meeting on some trivially urgent problem would spontaneously seat itself round the table, nibbling grapes. Or into the *salone*, where you would lounge, or sing, or dance. And for more intimate discussions, there would always be your own bedroom.

Bruno (*approaches warbling*) Errico, Errico, Errico . . .

Leo We're in here; what is it?

Bruno A letter for Erric'.

H. Thank you.

Bruno Papa says can he have the stamp?

H. Of course.

Alberto Open it, Erric'. Who is it from?

Leo From a beautiful *inglesina*?

Alberto A beautiful blonde?

H. Oh. It's from Elizabeth.

Alberto Elizabeth?

H. Elisabetta, a girl I play tennis with.

Leo Blonde?

H. Yes, very.

The others Aaaaaah . . . !

(*brief pause*)

Alberto (*politely and clearly*) Have you taken her?

H. Have I what?

Alberto Have you taken her?

Bruno (*faintly reproving*) Albert'.

H. Taken her where to?

Alberto No: taken her.

Leo (*helpfully*) Carnally.

Alberto In a bed, for example.

H. (*horrified*) Good God, no!

Alberto No? Ah, but you must.

Bruno (*as before*) Albert' . . .

Leo Yes, why haven't you, Erric'?

H. It . . . it never occurred to me.

188

     Leo (*satirically disbelieving*) Perhaps she won't allow it? There are some
        who won't allow it.

     H. But I never asked her . . . I mean . . .

 Alberto Ah, you must ask then . . . A blonde . . . You must ask.

     H. She might not want to.

 Alberto (*sagaciously*) Of course she wants to. They all want to.

  Bruno In England it is perhaps different . . .

     H. (*gratefully*) In England it *is* a little different, Bruno, yes.

  Bruno I understand England. I am fair-haired . . .

     H. And Elizabeth is a very modest girl.

 Alberto They are the best. You must ask her.

     H. (*uneasily*) I must read my letter.

    All Yes, yes, read it, Errico.

     Leo (*politely*) And tell us what she says . . .

Narrator They retreated, you recall, into a corner of the room, where they
        quietly communed with each other. As you read the letter, they
        gave you from time to time glances of supreme benevolence;
        perhaps they were even hoping she had written to ask *you*? She
        hadn't, in fact; but her letter was full of kindly feeling, hoping
        you were fit and eating well and not drinking too much and
        getting nice and brown and that Musso hadn't yet put you in jug.
        At home it had drizzled most of last week, though it had generally
        cleared up a bit in the evenings, and of course the hard courts
        hadn't been affected at all, in fact it had rather improved them . . .
        (*cross-fade to:*)

     Leo Don't be a fool, Alberto.

 Alberto Why? Why a fool? Who's a fool?

     Leo You are. You don't know what you're talking about.

 Alberto I do, I do, I do. I went to Posillipo with Annina last week.

     Leo You *couldn't*.

 Alberto I *can*, I tell you. I've been able to for two months. We went into
        the pinewoods in the afternoon, and she threw her arms round . . .
        (*quick cross-fade*)

Narrator What with all the rain, of course, Elizabeth had been reading
        quite a bit while you were away. She was halfway through *Sons
        and Lovers*, but in spite of what you had said, it did really strike
        her as sometimes leaving a nasty taste rather, didn't it you? Not
        all the way through, of course; but some of it. The Dramatic

Society was thinking of doing *A Cuckoo in the Nest* for Christmas,
though Bruce thought it was a bit too ambitious . . .
  (*cross-fade*)

    Leo Good news, Erric'?
    H. Well, it's a very nice letter.
 Alberto What does she say?
    Leo Does she say she loves you?
    H. Well, the letter ends 'Much love from Elizabeth'.
  Bruno *E bravo!*
 Alberto There you are! It will be easy.
    Leo You must ask her the minute you get back.
 Alberto (*wisely and slowly*) Yes. For clearly, Erric', you cannot go on as
you are.
  (*pause*)

Narrator And yet you were under the impression, weren't you, that your
life was one with theirs, that you had penetrated into it? 'We shall
be more than friends, we shall be brothers.' No, you were less
than brothers, even if you were more than friends. And sometimes you would feel how very far out of things you were. Do
you remember the typhonic rows that would suddenly blow up
in the distance, whose outer storm-circles you could only gape
at, during the ponderous hours of the afternoon rest?

  (*the following scene is played at the maximum speed compatible with
  clarity*)
 Mother Piet'! Piet'! Pietro!
 Father (*sleepily*) Eh? What is it? What do you want? I was reposing.
 Mother (*very rapidly*) It is dirty the floor in the passage, it is dirty the floor
in the bathroom, it is dirty the floor in the study . . . *E perchè?*
 Father Eh, beh . . . I was repos . . .
 Mother (*louder*) *E perchè?*
 Father Beh, perhaps Rosetta didn't clean it, clean them, this morning,
perhaps busy with something else. I was reposing – I must repose,
I have a bad head, I have to have my purge . . .
 Mother Rosetta cleaned everything before she left, the bedrooms, the
dining-room, the drawing-room, the bathroom, the vestibule,
the hall, the study, the kitchen; and now it is dirty, the floor in the
passage, it is dirty, the floor in the bathroom, it is dirty, the floor . . .
 Father (*a loud bellow*) I was reposing!

Mother Ehi! Reposing. (*a great cry*) *C'è sempre riposar'!* (*quietly and quickly*) And I? And I? And I? When do I repose? (*crescendo*) *Madonna mia,* when is there repose for me? I think, I worry, I make the kitchen, I go out, I go downstairs, I sweat, I sweat very much . . .

Father (*a protest*) Aaaaaah!

Mother I sweat.

Father Aaaaaaaaaaaaah!

Mother I sweat.

Father Ehi, we all sweat!

Mother I sweat every five minutes; I am bathed in sweat. (*with satirical sweetness*) And then I repose? Then I repose? Noh! *Non mai mi riposo io!* I sweat again, I buy the food, I come up, I keep the children clean, I scold Rosett' . . .

Father And I pay for Rosett'!

Mother You pay? You pay? You pay for Rosett'?

Father What does a little dirt matter, it is only a little dust, it is a very little, *poco, poco, poco.*

Mother È brutt'.

Father Noh!

Mother È brutt', è brutt'. È brutt', è brutt'. E bast'!

Father (*with sudden passion*) I will clean it myself. I will clean it now, I will suffer my headache, I will miss my purge, I will interrupt my repose for the sake of a little silence . . . *mamma mia,* for the sake of a little silence, I will clean it myself.

Mother (*calmly*) I have cleaned it already. Do you want Errico to go back to England and say, 'Ah, la signora napoletana, a very dirty house, one cannot eat, one cannot sleep. Dirt in the hall, in the bathroom, in the study, dirt, dirt, dirt, *and* filthy old postage stamps, used and filthy postage stamps, all over the table!'

Father You did not touch the stamps! *I francobolli!* Where are they? *I francobolli!*

(*his voice recedes as he goes to look. Hers recedes as she follows him*)

Mother (*derisively*) Francobolli, francobolli, sempre francobolli!

Father My postage stamps! My postage stamps! Where are they? Who has moved them? *I francobo* . . .

Mother And that is where the money goes to. Stamps, always stamps.

Father (*in loud distress*) They were on the table, my stamps of South Africa, and the English and Dutch and French Colonies, the colonies: Nyasaland, Congo della Francia, Congo del Belgio, the Congo, the Congo!

191

Mother Yes, the Congo, the Congo! It's a pity you can't go to the Congo, and stay there and dirty the hall and the bathroom and the study in the Congo!

Father Do not joke! It is not funny! Where are they? Has Rosetta been in here?

Mother In the Congo you could repose, you would like to repose and take your purge in the Congo.

Father Where are they?

Mother Yes. Get rid of the wife, the children, Bruno, Leo, Alberto, the maid, the apartment, go in the train, the aeroplane, the steamboat. Very nice. To the Congo: yes, one can have a good time in the Congo . . . *E buon divertimento* . . .

Father They are gone! Where have you put them? Do not joke. The stamps are very valuable; I have had them valued, they have cost me very much, they have cost me all I have, and now you and Rosetta have thrown them away . . . *I francobolli del Congo* . . .
(*sudden silence. Briefest pause*)

H. What is happening, Alberto?

Alberto (*placidly*) It is Papa and Mamma.

H. I hear it is. But what are they saying?

Alberto They reason together.

H. On what subject?

Alberto On various subjects.

H. Oh.
(*pause*)

Narrator You went to sleep among friends; only a thin wall and a door separated your high blue room from the room where the boys slept: crowded together a little, so that you might have a room to yourself. You slept among friends, and woke among them; and each day was a new day, different from the days before, unpredictable, but always golden, round and complete, a radiant bubble. You did not mind that it took hours to get to bed, each separate bubble floated away so reluctantly into the dark.

Bruno You have everything you want for the night, Erric'?

H. Yes, thank you, Bruno.

Bruno You have your night-vase?

H. Yes, thank you.

Bruno Good. Then good night, Erric'. Sleep well.

H. And you. Happy dreams.

Bruno Yes, and you. Dream of a beautiful blonde.
Alberto (*a little way off*) Good night, Erric'.
   H. Good night, Alberto.
Bruno What do you want, Leo? You ought to be in bed.
   Leo I want to ask Errico for a cigarette.
Mother (*calls*) Is Erric' in bed?
   H. (*calls*) Almost . . .
   Leo (*calls*) He is undressing . . .
Bruno Good night, Erric'.
   H. Good night, Bruno.

> (*the following scene must be played throughout with the utmost light-ness and delicacy of touch*)

   Leo Cigarettes?
   H. Over there.
   Leo Thank you . . . You?
   H. Thank you . . . (*sound of match*)
   Leo Did you like my cousin?
   H. Was that your cousin we met in via Roma?
   Leo Yes. Cousin Gianni.
   H. Yes, I did.
   Leo (*after a little pause, casually*) Did you know where he'd just been?
   H. No.
   Leo Can you guess?
   H. No . . . no, I can't.
   Leo He'd been to a little brothel.
   H. Oh.
> (*pause*)
   Leo Haven't you ever been to one?
   H. No.
   Leo Don't they have them in England?
   H. I think so . . . yes.
   Leo Mr Baldwin allows them?
   H. I don't imagine he's ever been consulted on the point.
   Leo No? Mussolini allows them in Italy.
   H. I know.
   Leo (*very casually*) Would you like to go to one?
   H. I don't know.
   Leo Wouldn't you like to go to one tomorrow afternoon?
   H. I don't think so.

Leo There are many beautiful girls.

  H. You've been?

Leo (*an ambiguous sound*) Ehi.

  H. Well, have you?

Leo Ehi.

  H. Shall we ask your mother if we can go?

Leo No!!

    (*brief pause*)

    (*still lightly*) Listen, Erric' . . .

  H. Yes?

Leo Don't you ever . . . make love in England?

  H. Sometimes.

Leo Don't you ever make love with other boys?

  H. No!

Leo Wouldn't you like to?

  H. No!

Leo Why not?

  H. I don't want to.

Bruno (*calls*) Leo . . .

  Leo (*irritably*) I'm coming.

  H. Go to bed now, Leo. I want to sleep.

Leo (*with a light sigh*) Ah, well . . . May I take another cigarette to
    smoke when I wake up?

  H. Yes, of course.

Leo You are sure you want me to go?

  H. I think so, Leo, yes.

Bruno (*calls*) Mamma's coming.

Mother (*fairly distant*) There is noise, noise, noise, how can we sleep?
    It is all right for you, you haven't to work, and there (*in the next
    room*) is always noise, noise, noise in the night, up till midnight.
    Ehi! Where is Leo?

Bruno (*next room*) Talking to Erric'.

  Leo Here, take this cigarette, Erric'. Smoke it for me.

  H. But I've *got* one . . .

Mother Talk, talk, talk, it is all he is good for . . . May I come in, Erric'?

  H. Please.

Mother Erric', you are smoking in bed. And why are you smoking two
    cigarettes?

  H. I . . . I . . .

Mother (*passionately*) Leo! Go to bed. You talk all night and . . .

194

Leo (*angrily*) I was only talking to Erric'.
Mother Dai! Va!
  (*briefest pause*)
  (*quietly, but matter-of-factly; she is anxious to get a point clear in her mind*)
  Erric'.
H. Signora.
Mother You have a sister.
H. Yes.
Mother You say she is married.
H. Yes.
Mother How long?
H. About four years.
Mother And she has made only one baby.
H. Yes.
Mother She can make more?
H. Yes. I suppose so.
Mother But only one, so far?
H. Only one, yes.
Mother After four years?
H. Yes.
Mother Ehi . . . It can be. (*to herself*) Four years . . . (*sighs, then gently*) Allora, Erric', buona nott'.
H. Buona notte.
Mother E buon ripos'.
H. Buon riposo.

Narrator How easily beings of a different race, with an unintelligible background and a language scarcely less so, can be teased into being . . . *characters* . . . They became a comic whole, completed when you left them and came home to England and began to arrange the pieces for the delectation and amusement of others. They were real indeed; but it was the reality that vanishes when we are not there in it. It was easy for you to compose them into a rounded whole, solid, complete . . . and, ever after, impenetrable.

So it was rather a shock, wasn't it, your brief glimpse of them *two years later?* For, so far from preserving your dream for you, for you to re-enter at will as you might re-enter the worlds of Proust or Dickens, they had substantially altered it. The new furniture was one thing: its modernity gleamed oddly among the more ancient pieces. But a bigger disconcertment was there, was there not?

Bruno (*loudly announcing*) And here, Errico, is the great surprise!
(*door. Murmurs of 'Here he is, Errico, what do you think of him?'* '*You didn't know about this*', *etc. Not, however, very distinct. Laughter*)

H. Good heavens . . . a *baby* . . . Are you *married*, Bruno?
(*they all laugh*)

Bruno Noooh . . . *Non hai capit'*? It is our new little brother, Simone.

H. Brother? But you never told me when you wrote. But of course you haven't written lately . . .

Leo Ah, we forgot to say.

Mother *Vedi*, Erric', after fourteen years I have put a new baby into the world. After fourteen years . . .

Father *Nouce avons fait un nouveau petit ainfaint.* (*he laughs*)

Alberto You like him, Erric'? Isn't he pretty?

H. Yes. How old is he?

Mother Six months.

Leo (*makes clucking noises to the baby*) Eh, eh, Simò . . .

H. Did you say his name was Simone?

Mother Simone Francesco Carlo Maurizio Antonio Cesare.

Father Simon - François - Charles - Maurice - Antoine - César. (*roars with laughter*)

H. Ah yes . . . *Ciao, Simone* . . . He is small, isn't he?

Mother But he will grow.

Alberto He will grow and be a good soldier for the Duce.

Mother No, he won't.

Father (*sentimentally*) And the Duce will be not only Duce of Italy, but Duce of the whole world. *Il ne sera pas le Douche seulemaint d'Italie, il sera le Douche de . . . de . . . de toulemonde.* (*he laughs*)

Mother Erric'.

H. Signora?

Mother Your sister . . .

H. Yes?

Mother She is married now how many years?

H. Six.

Mother And she has made only one baby.

H. Yes.

Mother Only one.
    H. Only one.
Mother *Ehi*, it is rather a few.
    H. Yes, it is not very many.
Mother *Ehi* . . . and I have made four.
  Father *Nouce avons fait un petit ainfaint après quarainte . . . nonon . . . après*
        quatorzezannées! Ehi . . . braviss' . . . !
        (*they all laugh slightly*)

Narrator Under the bronze chin of Mussolini, they clustered and clucked
        around the new baby. You felt that he had replaced you as a toy
for them. Why had he been born? You never dared, then or
later, to ask if his tardy arrival was a response to Mussolini's
exhortations to the men and women of Italy to breed him
soldiers. Could it have been so? A dull flush of success suffused
the country that summer. A conquest had been made; slowly,
bloodily and uncouthly, Abyssinia had been taken. But no, God
forbid that that was the reason. And was there not already an
uneasiness in their confidence? Perhaps. Perhaps not.

It seems to you now that on that day you were an intruder,
where you had formerly been a centre; but we do not easily
acknowledge the blows to our vanity, and you told yourself that
Naples (and Naples meant them) must be all or nothing. An afternoon call on the way to somewhere else was fatuous. Next time
it should be all or nothing . . .

And next time it was: but which, it was hard to tell. It was
1939, in a delayed spring. Albania had just been seized . . . On a
damp day in April you went once more through the well-known
streets; but they were oddly unfamiliar. Here and there had
sprung up smooth huge featureless modern buildings, which
seemed to say: whatever we make let us make it big, and let it be
all surface, let it have no features, for features betray human
idiosyncrasy and weakness. We will build in perfect cubes and
spheres and ellipsoids, buildings so big that all who enter shall
know their own smallness and despise their own separateness. All
shall be big. The letter-box at the new post-office shall be so wide
that in your sleep you shall dream you are posting yourself in it.
On. Up the via Roma and beyond, through the drizzle, past the
damp people – sad, they looked. And the old door opened. And

there they were, in the study ... You were old enough now to know that when it comes to it, we don't re-greet a familiar scene with the expected afflatus. But there it was, the retorts and the test-tubes, the great desk, the old armchairs; and you looked up at the wall for the belligerent bronze with the jutting chin ... and it had gone. But where? Pleasure was dulled by a second thought. They were calling in metal for arms.

Father (*spreading out the phrase*) Poor Italy! *Pauvre Italie!* Poor country! Eh–eh–eh ... What will become of her, Erric'? They give her an empire and they take away her food. Her bread you cannot eat, her coffee you cannot drink. Only the rich can have white bread. You think it is our fault? There is war here, there is war there; in a few minutes there will be war everywhere, and everywhere Italy will have been in it. *Partout, Italie.* In Abyssinia, in Spain, in Albania. Next we shall want Jugoslavia and Greece, if Hitler doesn't say no ...

Mother You will go to Capri again, Erric'?

H. I think so ... yes.

Mother Ah, you cannot stay away. You love it better than Italy ...

H. No, I don't.

Mother Yes, yes, better than Italy ...

Father And it is not Italy. You will go there and sit in the cafés. There will be notices in the cafés in German: never in Italian. *Jamais, jamais, jamais!* Capri is a German colony, and we shall all be a German colony. No Englishman ever comes here, no American, no French, no Swede: only German. *Pauvre Italie ...*

Narrator Outrageous it seems now, doesn't it, that you could have expected things to be as they had been five years before? You wanted still your former unexpected joy. You had stayed still, and could not bear that they had moved on, maturing faces, deepening voices. The days of that third long visit still formed visions like the first, only they did not now retreat reluctantly into the dark, they advanced cautiously out from it.

Mother And you have left the university, Erric'?

H. Yes.

Mother And what do you do for a living?

H. I write.

Mother Ah yes, you always said you would write.

198

Alberto (*young man's voice*) And now you are a great writer?

    H. No, Alberto. Not yet, I'm afraid.

Alberto But you will write a great novel?

    H. Yes. I shall write a great novel.

Bruno Only one?

    H. No, Bruno, a great number.

Mother (*absently*) Eh, braviss'. Simone, take your hands off the tablecloth.

    Leo (*still a young voice: but slightly more refined and self-conscious*) Yes, don't touch the bread with your filthy little paws.

Mother Leo! Don't speak to him like that! Don't you think he is a nice child, Erric'?

    H. Very, yes. He is fair-haired, like Bruno.

Bruno All the best people are fair-haired, aren't they, Simone?

Alberto Simone, tell Uncle Erric' how glad you are to see him. Go on, Simone, say you are glad.

    (*silence, then . . .*)

Simone (*beginning quietly and laboriously, and with steady crescendo*) Ki feh, ki fa . . . Erric' vagava, ga feh gafoo kikikikikikiki . . . e (*with great conviction*) Satch!

    (*the others laugh in a rather shocked way*)

    H. What did he say? Is he . . . speaking in the dialect?

Alberto (*giggling*) He said . . .

Mother (*hastily*) Albert', noh!

    H. But what did he say?

Simone (*loudly and gaily*) Erric' vagava (*rapidly*) ga feh gafoo kikikikikikiki e Satch!

    (*the others cannot help laughing again*)

Mother Simone, it is time for you to go and repose.

Simone (*a howl*) Nooooooooooooh! No vo' . . .

Mother⎫ Yes, take him, Bruno . . .

Bruno⎭ Come on, time for nice rest . . .

Simone (*receding*) Aaaah, nonononono! Lash, lash, lash! Aaaaaaaaaaaah, no vo', no vo' . . . ahhhhhhhhhh!

    Leo (*in the middle of Simone's cries*) Be quiet, you little beast!

Mother (*sharply*) Leo!

    H. (*door shuts*) You don't seem very fond of your little brother, Leo?

    Leo Oh . . . he's all right . . . but I can't tolerate the incessant noise.

Mother And do you think you never made a noise?

    Leo (*sulkily*) What has that got . . .

Alberto Erric'. Leo is very artistic now, very nervous.

199

Leo I shall be glad to get back to Rome.

H. Rome? What are you doing in Rome?

Leo (*aloofly*) I have to go there to pursue my histrionic studies.

H. Histrionic? (*pleased*) Are you going on the stage?

Leo I am going into films. (*tolerantly*) I *may* do a little stage-work.

H. A film-star, Leo? How wonderful!

Father Il va hêtre un grand comédien du shinema! (*laughs*) Un comédien!

Mother He gave us no rest till we let him. *E madonna mia*, the expense, Erric', the expense!

Leo (*coldly*) It's my career.

H. And shall you go to Hollywood, Leo?

Leo Eventually, I expect.

H. And what do you study at the . . . ?

Leo The Academy? Oh, mime . . . elocution . . . deportment . . . dancing.

H. Ballet dancing?

Leo (*coldly*) Ballroom dancing.

H. Well, it must all be very interesting, Leo.

Leo (*tolerantly*) Yes.

H. And you have a very beautiful face, Leo, and just the type for a film-star.

Leo (*judiciously*) Yes, that is true . . .

Alberto (*politely*) Especially if they ever want anybody to act the backside of a red-arsed monkey.

Mother⎫ Albert', how dare you speak like that!
Bruno⎬ Albert', Albert', you mustn't say such things!
Leo⎭ I'll *kick* your arse, you little beast!

Father (*a pathetic bleat*) Ne foh pas dire! . . .

Leo (*passionately*) I don't know how you expect me to go on, if I'm to hear Alberto's silly nonsense every time I come home.

Alberto I was only joking, Leo.

Leo Joking! . . . (*receding in tears*) Joking! . . . Enrico (*sic*) . . . Enrico is the only one of you who understands what it is to be an artist . . . (*door bangs*)

Mother Ehi . . . it is the same every day . . . Alberto teases . . . makes Leo unhappy . . .

Bruno Leo is very temperamental.

Mother Artistico, molto artist' . . . But you can understand him, Erric' . . . You are very serious, very religious. You are religious, aren't you, Erric' . . . ?

H. Well . . .

Mother (*anxiously*) You are a catholic, Erric'?

H. Well, no . . .

Alberto Erric' is a protestant, aren't you, Erric'?

Father *Un Huguenot.*

H. Well, I'm not even a protestant any longer . . .

Mother (*business-like*) Good, very good. Now you have stopped being a protestant, you can become a catholic, and that will be very good. You must become a catholic. It is better. It is simpler . . .

 (*fade. Brief pause*)

Alberto Erric', can I come in?

H. Yes, of course.

Alberto Erric'? Are you still a socialist?

H. Yes, Alberto. Do you mind?

Alberto It is a pity. It is better not to be.

H. Are you still a fascist?

Alberto (*unemphatically*) Of course I am. We are all fascists. It is best . . . (*with a mischievous giggle*) Albaneea . . . did that surprise you?

H. Of course it did.

Alberto (*gaily*) It surprised *us!*

H. It was wicked and brutal, Alberto; you know it was.

Alberto (*as if shrugging*) Who can say?

H. Your father says it will be Greece and Jugoslavia next.

Alberto (*dubiously*) No, it's finished now . . . now we have Albaneea . . . (*suddenly and happily*) Listen, Erric', you know how it rained all this morning . . . Well, when I was coming back from the college, I had my umbrella, and there, suddenly – suddenly, in via Roma, I saw a most beautiful girl wondering how to cross the road.

H. Blonde?

Alberto *Ehi*, blonde enough, yes. An Austrian girl, very aristocratic. And there was I with the umbrella, so I straightened my tie, and went up to her, and said, 'Permit me to accompany you across the road, it is too wet, and you see I have an umbrella.' And I held her arm and we went across the road together. Good, eh? Lucky.

H. Very. Perhaps you'll see her again next time it rains.

Alberto *Ehi*, I'm seeing her tomorrow afternoon! At three o'clock.

H. But you'll be at school.

Alberto Shhhhhh . . . (*fade*)

Narrator The same and not the same. They knew it too. The sight of you as they came into a room and found you there, would suggest the old days, and they would begin in the old way. But the years would not be squeezed out, the past would retreat, leaving, it sometimes seemed, not even a present. How surprising for all of you! . . . It seems appropriate, doesn't it, that so many of your interchanges should have been carried on in undertones, and during the afternoon siestas?

Leo Enrico . . . are you asleep?

H. No.

Leo Shall you come out this afternoon, or stay in?

H. Is it still raining?

Leo A little.

H. What do you propose to do?

Leo Some friends are coming for me at three. We're going to the cinema. (*a bit reluctantly*) Would you like to come?

H. I think I'll stay in. I can never get used to Greta Garbo speaking in Italian.

Leo (*relieved*) No, it's silly, isn't it? It's wet too. Better stay in.

H. Where's Alberto?

Leo In the next room, dressing. I don't know why he's putting his best suit on. Scenting himself, too . . . Shall I stay and talk to you till my friends come?

H. Yes, do. When do you go to Rome?

Leo Next week.

H. How do you pass the time when you're here in Naples?

Leo Oh, we walk a good deal. On Sundays I go with Papa and Mamma to see my fiancée.

H. Your fiancée, Leo? I didn't know you were engaged.

Leo Oh, it's not important.

H. Is she nice?

Leo (*indifferently*) She's a good girl.

H. But don't you take her out in the week?

Leo Oh no, I never see her alone.

H. Why not?

Leo One doesn't.

H. Don't you mind that?

Leo No.

H. Do you go out with other girls during the week?

Leo Of course I do.

H. Do you make love to them?

Leo Some of them . . . of course I do . . . Oh, the fiancée's a nice girl, but I don't especially want to see her.

H. Then why are you engaged to her?

Leo Our parents arranged it.

  (*long soft ring of doorbell*)

Leo There they are. I must go, Erric'. *Tante belle cose.* See you at supper. (*double kiss*) *Arrivederti, caro.*

H. *Ciao.*

  (*door. Next few speeches very quietly*)

  Oh, here's Alberto.

Alberto You going out?

Leo Going to the cinema . . . *Ciao.*

Alberto *Ciao.*

H. (*louder*) Hello, is that you, Alberto?

Alberto Sh . . . Papa and Mamma are reposing.

  (*door closing softly*)

H. Sorry.

Alberto I'm going out in a few minutes, Erric'.

H. Shall I come with you?

Alberto *Ehi*, I have to go and see that Austrian girl.

H. Oh yes, I'd forgotten that was today. I hope you have a good time.

Alberto (*casually*) Who can say?

H. Where is she staying?

Alberto Capodimonte.

H. When does she expect you?

Alberto Three o'clock.

H. It's nearly that now. You'll be late.

Alberto Oh, not very.

  (*pause*)

H. Why do you keep wandering about, Alberto? Are you looking for something?

Alberto No. *Ebbene* . . . I must go . . . Erric'?

H. M'm?

Alberto Erric', could you possibly lend me five lire?

H. Of course I can.

Alberto (*apologetically*) I'm sorry to ask. I shall have some money in a few days' time . . . You see, this Austrian girl may be very nice, in which case I ought to take her some flowers.

H. Of course . . .

203

Alberto Because that sometimes makes it easier.

H. Why didn't you ask before? Wouldn't you like ten lire?

Alberto (*radiantly*) Ah, thank you, Erric'. And I shan't be gone long. I'll be back in two hours.

H. I shall be looking at the book-shops by the museum.

Alberto I'll see you there. *Arrivederti*, and thank you Erric'. You are my oldest, dearest friend, now and forever. (*two loud kisses*) Thank you.

H. (*a little satirically*) Prrrrego.

Alberto (*giggles*) E ciao.

H. (*on fade*) Ciao, Alberto . . .

Narrator A bit lonely, eh? In spite of the endearments and the fraternal embraces. 'We shall be more than friends, Erric', we shall be brothers . . . ' But their experiences were no longer yours, you played no part in them. You saw only broken arcs, and what lay inside the circle it might be as well not to inquire . . . But there are always book-shops. Galsworthy, Virginia Woolf, Hugh Walpole, Aldous Huxley, even Freud . . . And in the book-shop a hand was laid on your arm.

Alberto Here I am, Erric'. Am I late?

H. No. I was looking at the books.

Alberto What are you reading? . . . (*reads out*) 'Three Contributions to the Theory of Sex'. (*roguishly*) E-e-eh! Bello, eh?

H. Enchanting. Did you have a nice time?

Alberto Ehi . . .

H. Did she give you tea?

Alberto A glass of sherry.

H. (*with attempted off-handedness*) And all went well?

Alberto (*with real off-handedness*) Quite well, yes. Twice.

H. Shall we go for a little walk?

Alberto A little one, yes.

　　　　(*fade on last line*)

Narrator Even the outbursts of anger you thought you had become wholly familiar with brought with them a new element. The trivial seemed to have deepened into the real.

Mother (*heard in distance, angrily; words not audible yet*) I have told him he must not take money from the purse without asking, (*door opens*) and I have told him not once but many times that he must not take money from the purse without asking; and now, without asking, he has taken money from the purse. Erric'!

H. Signora?

Mother (*passionately*) You write in England?

H. Yes.

Mother (*a tirade*) You write in the journals, you are famous, you write! Very well, I will tell you what to write! Write in all the journals in England that your friend the signora in Naples complains and is always complaining, and that she cannot stop complaining because there is always something to complain of!

Bruno (*protesting*) *Ehi,* Mamma!

Mother '*Ehi,* Mamma.' Always '*ehi,* Mamma!' The boys they are ungrateful and deceitful, and I complain, and it is '*ehi,* Mamma'. The husband he never speaks, and I complain, '*ehi,* Mamma'. The baby will not eat, and I complain, '*ehi,* Mamma'. Write it, write it, write it in all the journals in England, la Signora Dusolina Maria Rosaria Emilia Caterina complains and complains and complains! (*suddenly switching off her passion at its height, she says quietly and gently*) Erric'.

H. (*breathless*) Yes?

Mother Your sister.

H. Yes?

Mother Is married how many years?

H. Nine.

Mother Nine. And only one child.

H. Only one.

Mother (*loudly*) Ebbene, Erric'! (*more quickly*) Write. Write to your sister and say: *Clever girl.* Only one child; and the poor signora in Naples has *four* children, all boys, (*slight crescendo*) and she complains and complains, because they are all bad and there is always something to complain of. (*quietly*) And Alberto.

Alberto Mamma?

Mother Please leave your great-uncle Carlo's war-medals alone.

Alberto Yes, Mamma.

Mother And turn on the wireless.

Alberto Yes, Mamma.

Mother Good.

(*door shuts firmly*)

Bruno (*placidly*) Mamma . . . is very nervous.

Alberto And sometimes . . . she complains.

(radio noises up and out. Next dialogue is subdued and wearied)

Mother (*fade in*) Ah, thank goodness they have all gone out, and we can have a few minutes' peace, Erric'. Come and sit here. I have sent Rosett' out too. It is better. One cannot speak one's mind.

H. Why not?

Mother Servants – they listen. And sometimes they tell tales.

H. What kind of tales?

Mother Oh, if one says it is a pity there will be a war . . . if one says it was foolish about Albania or that Abyssinia is a disappointment, or we have lost too many men in Spain . . . *ehi*, there is so much to say.

H. But doesn't everyone think these things?

Mother Except for some of the young ones. There are many fanatics, of course. They think it is glorious and heroic to make war. Is it?

H. No, I don't think so.

Mother But there will be one?

H. I think so.

Mother And you are not frightened?

H. I am very frightened. Aren't Bruno and Leo?

Mother Perhaps. Alberto is too young to understand.

H. He loves the Duce.

Mother Ah, the Duce. There is *some* justice, isn't there, Erric', in asking for a seat on what-is-it . . . the Suez Canal Board?

H. Well, in England I suppose most of us don't like to think of the Duce getting *anything* he asks for. It is like Hitler; everything is a step to something else.

Mother Perhaps so, perhaps you are right. At first the Duce was so good . . .

H. You don't like him any more?

Mother He makes mistakes, he has his faults. Who else is there? We have to have a leader in Italy. Before the Duce nobody ever did anything . . .

H. But you don't want him any more? Three years ago the *cavaliere* said Mussolini was not only the leader of Italy but of the whole world.

Mother Well, everybody said it. It seemed so.

H. But you don't believe it, signora? Do you?

Mother Ah, what can one believe? Except that there will be war.

H. And if there is war . . .

206

Mother Ah, if there is war, what? Bombs, everything destroyed, all of us killed.

H. And Italy will have a revolution.

Mother Ah, you all want us to have that, don't you?

H. (*after a brief pause*) If there is a war, it will last a long time, and all that we shall know of each other is that we are on opposite sides.

Mother Perhaps you will come in on our side?

H. No, we shan't do that, *cara*.

Mother (*gently*) What then, Erric'?

H. (*wearily*) Oh God, if there is a war, we shall be enemies. We shall try to conquer each other.

Narrator The fruitless political discussions of those approaching the edge of despair. Discussions of the weather were of equal use. The weather would come, whatever you said. In that third visit, you had travelled from top to toe of Italy for the first time. Returning from Messina you came back into the Bay. The great temples of Paestum had stood outlined against a rainy sunset; it darkened and you drove through the cliff from Salerno into the Bay itself. You knew you would probably never see it again. Soon there would be a war. Later the train bore you northwards again. And again you wondered if it would be forever. 'Believe, obey, fight,' said the black letters on the white walls. 'Every attack will be repulsed with the maximum precision . . . '

On a summer day a year later you opened a newspaper in the piazza in Birmingham, the Piazza Stephenson, and learned that at last you and they were enemies. Did they at that moment think of you?

In the years that followed, Italy would sometimes invade your sleep. You would dream you had been allowed there for one day only. It was war, therefore it was a fugitive day, you must hurry back before dawn. Your friends did not appear.

News of Naples – but never of *them* – came and went. Towards the end, a pall of smoke stood for ten days over their city. For ten days, no light, no water, almost no food. This you read. They were enemies. Then, it seemed, they were enemies no more, they were allies. Good. It proved as little as any war ever proved. Only one thing you knew, but in fact you had always known it: if they were still alive, if their house still stood, one day you would be welcomed there again. They would not mind that there had been a war. Then you wrote, then you heard, and they were safe and you would see them again, and they would see you. When were you coming?

And the day approached when you were to see them again. Rome floated up to you, tilted against the diamond light of her early evening, received you, delayed you, but eventually you went.

And here was Naples, after so many years. It was 1947, Roosevelt, Hitler, Chamberlain, Mussolini were dead, and anonymous millions with them. And the crowded, sweating tram that trundled up the via Roma was still numbered seven, and you remembered you had once liked noise. And as you climbed the final stairs there came back through the mists of memory the names on the doors you had always had to climb past before you reached theirs.

H. Ciccarelli . . . Calise . . . Guida . . . Lembo . . . Pavese . . . And here it still is.
   (*long single ring on doorbell. Pause. Door*)

   (*Leo is now acted by a man*)
Leo (*surprised and pleased*) Errico!
H. Leo! *Eccomi.*
Leo After eight years. Welcome. We thought you were coming tomorrow.
H. I always precede expectation, Leo.
Leo No, usually you were three weeks late.
H. I am a reformed character.
Leo Sit down. We mustn't make too much noise. Papa is reposing. I will tell Alberto.
H. Is he too reposing?
Leo Yes, but he won't mind . . . Oh, he's coming. Look who's here, Alberto.
Alberto (*loudly*) Errico! Dear Errico! *E come va?*
Leo Shhhhh! Papa . . .
Alberto (*in a whisper*) Ah, yes, Erric'; papa is reposing. *Come stai?*
H. Bene. *E tu?*
Alberto *Non c'è male.* How good it is to see you. We expected you every day when the Eighth Army was here.

208

(conversation gradually returns to normal pitch)

H. I wasn't brave enough for that, Alberto.

Alberto But you were in the army, you wrote?

H. Only modestly, and only for a short time.

Leo But you were a colonel?

H. Indeed I wasn't. I was a humble private.

Leo No, Erric', we don't believe you; you were at least a major.

H. I wasn't. I assure you I wasn't. Not even a corporal.

Alberto He's joking, Leo. He was really a brigadier.

H. Where is your mother? And Simone? And Bruno?

Alberto Mamma and Simone have gone to the beach . . .

Leo Shhhh . . .

Alberto And Bruno is in Amalfi.

Leo You knew he was married, and has a baby?

H. No, I didn't. Good old Bruno.

Alberto *(incisively)* Have you sweated, Erric'?

H. I have rather, yes. It was those stairs. I'm not so young as I was.

Leo We none of us are.

H. And are you married, Alberto?

Alberto No, but I am engaged to a beautiful schoolmistress.

H. Blonde?

Alberto No. I never liked blondes. She is lovely, Erric'; very intelligent. I will show you her letters.

H. Thank you. And are you married, Leo?

Leo Never, Erric'. Free Love – that's what I believe in. And now you must excuse me. I shall see you at supper.

H. *(raising voice)* Are you going away, Leo?

Leo Shhh. *(Papa.)* Yes. I have to get back to the Comune. *Ciao, (caro).*

H. Ciao. *(after he has gone)* Why does he have to go to the Comune?

Alberto He works there. In Income Tax.

H. But he was training to be a film-star.

Alberto *Ehi,* the war stopped that.

H. Can't he start again?

Alberto It would cost too much money. We are poor now, Erric'. Didn't you guess?

H. I half guessed, yes. But Leo has taken his doctorate?

Alberto Yes.

H. Then why is he only an Income Tax Inspector?

Alberto Oh, you must have a doctorate for a government job.

H. What is he a doctor of?

Alberto Natural Sciences.

    H. But that's nothing to do with Income Tax.

Alberto No, but it's a degree, that is what they ask. I am taking my doctorate next month. Russian, Polish, and Philosophy. Have you studied philosophy, Erric'? Do you know Berkeley? Adam Smith?

    H. Only by name.

Alberto Very great English philosophers. Yes, I shall be Doctor of Philosophy and Slavonic Languages.

    H. And what shall you do then?

Alberto I shall try to get a job in a bank. It is a useful degree to have. They respect it.

    H. And what was Bruno's degree?

Alberto History.

    H. And he teaches history in Amalfi?

Alberto No, no, he is a veterinary surgeon.

    H. Does he like that?

Alberto No. He too wants to be in a bank. And you, Erric': you are a great writer now?

    H. No, not yet.

Alberto Not yet? Haven't you written your great novel?

    H. No, Alberto.

Alberto But haven't you started it?

    H. No.

Alberto But in your letter you said you wrote?

    H. I write journalism.

Alberto *Ehi, bravo,* Erric'. Permit me to ask, where did you buy those trousers? They are the same as mine.

    H. In Rome.

Alberto How much did you pay for them?

    (doorbell)

    Ah, excuse me, Erric', that may be Mamma and Simone.

    (distant voices of Mother, Alberto and Simone, words indistinguishable)

Mother *(off)* The stairs, the stairs . . .

Alberto *(off)* Erric' is here.

Mother *(off)* Already? He said tomorrow . . .

Simone *(off)* Erric'? *Bravo!*

Mother *(approaching)* But he said that he was coming tomorrow; where is he? Erric', Erric', where are you?

Alberto (*hastening after*) Mamma, Papa is reposing.

Mother (*impatiently*) He is always reposing. And Erric'! After so many years, unfaithful Erric'! Only two letters, not even a postcard.

   H. Well, *cara*, there was a war.

      (*double kiss*)

Mother Ah, the war, the war, don't talk to me about the war. The aeroplanes, German, American . . . bombabombabom. A nightmare. But here we are, we have survived. And how are you, Erric'! You are fatter; you see I am not so fat, I have shrunk.

   H. Very much, yes.

Alberto Mamma has only half her former weight.

   H. Well, perhaps that is better?

Mother *Ehi*, perhaps it is. I am still not a thin one.

Alberto You see Erric's trousers, Mamma? They are the same as mine. I had those before the war, Erric'. They cost twenty-five lire; how much did yours cost?

   H. Three thousand: and mine don't seem to be so good.

Mother Ah, here is Simone . . .

Simone (*aged eleven, a little shyly*) Good evening, Errico. How are you?

   H. Very well, thank you; and you?

Simone (*delicately*) OK, thank you. You have never seen me before, have you, Errico?

Alberto (*loudly*) Of course he's seen you.

Mother Sh! Papa . . .

   H. Of course I've seen you. I saw you when you were three.

Simone (*delighted*) Ah?

Alberto And two and a half years before that, when you were still at Mamma's breast.

Simone (*radiant*) At Mamma's breast? Mamma, is that true? Errico saw me at your breast when I was little?

Mother (*indignantly*) Of course. I have always been able to suckle my own children, thank God. Bruno, Leo, Alberto, you, all of you. *Ehi*.

   H. Yes, I remember you very well, Simone.

Simone Why I haven't very much hair on my head, is because Mamma has cut it off on account of the heat.

   H. Ah, yes?

Simone We have just come from the Sea-Garden.

   H. What is that?

Mother It is the bathing beach at Mergellina. You must go there with Simone tomorrow.

Simone Yes, we will go together! OK?

Mother You will like it, Erric', because it is a nice beach, without eccentricity.

   H. Why, are some of the other beaches eccentric?

Mother Some of them, yes, very eccentric.

   H. In . . . in what way?

Mother They have diving-boards.

   H. Oh . . .

Mother And now I will make you some coffee. Go and put the water on, Alberto.

     (*pause*)

Mother You have seen how much poverty there is in Italy, Erric'?

   H. Some of it, yes.

Mother Is it the same in England?

   H. No. We can't buy such big meals in England, but we can all afford to buy what there is.

Mother You are rationed?

   H. Yes, so are you, aren't you, for some things?

Mother Yes, but nobody takes any notice of the ration cards. (*sighs*) Aaaah! And Rosetta – you remember Rosetta?

   H. The maid?

Mother She has left us. She became very rich, and went away.

   H. Rosetta rich? How?

Mother She became a bad girl and made a lot of money from American soldiers, then she went in the black market and made a fortune from *pasta*. Now she has a flat below us, much better than this. And she has become a communist. And very fat. (*indignantly*) Much fatter than I am. And now I have to open my own door myself.

Alberto I have put the water on, Mamma.

Mother I will go and make the coffee. But it is not good coffee, Erric', it is very bad. We cannot afford good coffee, we are poor. Only Rosetta can afford real coffee.

Alberto (*rather loudly*) Ah, you have heard about Rosetta, Erric'? She has become a communist.

Mother (*with bitter regret*) And fat.

Simone (*rather loudly*) And a prostitute.

Mother Shhhhh . . . Simone . . . Papa is reposing.

Simone Sorry . . . (*whispers*) A prostitute, Errico.

Mother Yes, indeed. And now I will make the coffee.

Alberto You are not communist, Erric'? You are still socialist?

    H. Yes.

Alberto Bravo. So am I.

Simone So am I . . . Erric', why did you not come with the Eighth Army? We expected you.

    H. I wasn't in it, Simone.

Simone But you were a soldier?

    H. For a time.

Simone You were a major-general, were you not?

    H. (*protesting*) No, Simone, I was only . . .

Simone Shhhhhhhhhhhhh! Papa is reposing . . .

    (*fade*)

Narrator Would you rather not go on? Would you rather not forget what seemed silently to be happening under the flow of discontinuous conversation? Was it that humiliation of the spirit that comes when we see again a once-loved face and try in vain to find in it what once we loved? Or had the war incarcerated all of you in your separate selves? You had seen, each of you, so much unseen by the others, thought for so long in ways the others could not follow . . . there was nothing left in common, it seemed. They felt it too, you were sure. It was more than boredom . . . it was bafflement and sadness . . . After a few days you fled, promising to return; and you were faithless. The letter of thanks, the old jokes in the letter . . . and nothing more. Returning from Capri, you could not face them, you could not face their courtesy. And whenever you thought of them thereafter, guilt and uneasiness smouldered in your mind. The defection was yours, not theirs. You were unwilling to understand. 1939 had almost been the end. This was really the end. Never again.

    (*pause*)

Then, idly, in an idle time, you decided you would go back. Three more years had passed. You felt more than hesitation, and only a little less than dread. To see them again would be something more than a mere return; joined with the hope of rediscovering something lost was the fear that it might never be found again at all. Boldness was pointless . . . since you felt so shy. What could you do? . . . Yes. You would go there first, and learn their city, that city you had known only through them, never of itself. That might be a way . . . So you went, and waited; vaguely, they knew you were on your way; you wondered how they would take it that you had stayed in a hotel. For a long time you circled the place before entering it. It was a formidable prospect. Only one thing seemed certain: the time of day you must go – in the relenting cool of the evening. So, on a June evening, you went. You went on foot, you climbed the familiar stairs, past the familiar names . . .

H. Ciccarelli . . . Calise . . . Guida . . . Lembo . . . Pavese . . . and here it still is . . . as sixteen years ago . . .
    (bell)

Narrator No answer. A mild hope stirred in you, that they might be out.
    (bell, door)
    But the door opened. It was Papa, awake.

H. *Cavaliere . . . eccomi.*

Father Aaah, you have come . . . *vouce êtes venu,* hahahahahahaha! You have come. *(two loud kisses)* Come in, come in, come in, come in.

H. You had my letter?

Father Only yesterday. We have been away with Bruno in Amalfi. Have you been here long?

H. Only a little while.

Father My wife and Simone are out at the cinema. They will be back and there will be much jubilation . . . But please excuse me a moment. I have a business guest in the next room. I will get rid of him in a few minutes, a very few minutes. Sit. Sit. Smoke. *Fume. Fumez.* Read. You have cigarettes?

H. Yes.

Father A book, a book. Yes, here is a book. *Crime and Punishment.* Hahahahahaha! And here is a better book, the Yvert-Tellier catalogue of postage stamps, very up-to-date, *très à la mode.* It will please you . . .

H. Thank you.

Father You are comfortable? Please forgive me. And Erric' . . .

H. Yes?

Father It is good to see you . . . *Pardon.* I will be back.

Narrator You sat there a long while. The business guest was not easy to get rid of. The cooling evening stole in like a benediction. You waited. From time to time, you went on to the balcony and looked out of the window. The tiny garden in the courtyard far below lay already in shadow. In the building opposite, halfway up in a lighted room with open windows, there was music. The young were dancing there. You saw them. Brown and smiling faces, lithe, enchanted forms, sweet, untarnished names. You waited, patiently now, your apprehension receding . . .

(bell)

The doorbell. You must not answer it, surely? Not you? Papa would answer it? Could he not hear it?

(bell. Longer)

No. You must answer it. Go on.

Simone (behind door) Ehi, Papa, Papa! Open the door! It is me and Mamma.

(door)

Mother⎱ Erric'!
Simone⎰

H. Eccomi.

Simone⎱ Good old Erric'! We didn't expect you so soon.
Mother⎰ Where have you been? We thought you would be in Rome.

H. I . . .

Mother False. False, false, false. Faithless Erric', who never came to say goodbye, who ran away . . .

H. But I wrote and explained . . .

Simone⎱ (laughing) Ehi, explanations . . . ! Lies, all lies and deceptions.
Mother⎰ We know what happened.

H. What?

Mother You ran away to Rome with a young American woman from Capri.

Simone A miglionaria.

H. (laughs) What nonsense!

Mother Always the same. Young women from Capri.

H. It's not true, it's not true!

Simone It is! True, true, true, true, true!

Mother (accusingly) You have just come from Capri?

H. No.

Mother You are going there?

H. Perhaps.

Simone⎱ Aaaaah!
Mother⎰

Mother Faithless, faithless. You have sweated?

H. No.

Mother I have sweated. But only a little. You are thinner.

215

H. A little.

Mother And I, you see, have re-expanded. *Ehi*. Faithless. Nevertheless, it is good to see you. I shall make you some coffee. Where is Papa?

H. He is rep . . . I mean, he has a business guest.

Mother *Ehi*. (*receding*) I shall go and make you some coffee . . .

Simone Erric', it is *good* to see you.

H. It is good to see *you*. Where are Alberto and Leo?

Simone Didn't you know? They are married, and each has a baby.

H. Good heavens. Alberto has married his beautiful schoolmistress?

Simone Oh no. The next but one after her.

H. Ah. And Leo . . . who believed in Free Love?

Simone Yes. He got married before Alberto. It is always the way.

Mother (*returning*) Yes, it is always the way. The sons, they marry, they go away, and leave the house empty: Mamma and Papa all alone.

Simone (*protesting*) But Mamma, you always say that. *I* am still here.

Mother Yes, you are still here . . . I am boiling the water. I am tired. I must sit down. You see how empty it is, Erric'. Only the three of us here. And Simone, always reading. He is like you, very serious, always a student.

H. And what do you read, Simone?

Simone I am a great admirer of the Russian novelists. Gorky. Tolstoy. Dostoievsky. Cronin. I am reading *Crime and Punishment*.

H. You are very young to read Dostoievsky.

Simone No. I am fourteen. And the Russian novelists are very good, you know. (*slowly and sweetly*) 'Bravo, bravo, Karamazov!'

H. 'Bravo, bravo, Karamazov!'

Mother (*absently*) *Ehi*. Bravo, bravo, Karamazov . . .
      (*rapid fade on last line*)

Narrator Why is it that when, by rare accident, an occasion is made easy and happy for us, it seems easier and happier than we have ever deserved? And here were happiness and ease, however come by. This place was an unexpected haven, it had provided no ordeal. *Che strano* . . . The world lay outside: the swarming streets, the tiny children who would spend the night, their heads on their knees, sleeping on the doorsteps, Capri, Rome, and the non-stop flights, the piazza Stephenson, the empty lawns and cliffs of England, the Atlantic. The world lay outside . . . All the next day as you wound your way in and out through the crash and roar of the city the vision of those still, high rooms remained, and you wondered what there had been to fear. Was it that further encounter with the years' onslaught there, which you knew you had yet to make? You made it two days later.

(*bell. Door*)

Bruno Errico! (*his voice is deeper; he is now thirty-three*)

H. (*has not recognised him*) Oh, good evening, sir, I thought – Why, it's Bruno!

Bruno (*laughs*) Eh, Erric' . . . After all these years! Come in, come in! You didn't recognise me!

H. Of course I did; but I thought you were in Amalfi . . . It was a surprise.

Bruno Ah, I am older, Erric'. But I am still fair-haired. Look!

H. (*laughs*) Yes . . .

Bruno And I still sometimes wear glasses, and then people take me for an Englishman.

H. And you've a family too.

Bruno (*modestly*) A little one. I came specially from Amalfi to see you.

H. Ah, dear Bruno. How kind.
    (*behind last line and the next few lines, Mother and Simone are heard in background, indistinctly*)

Mother Who is that, is it Erric'?

Simone Yes, I think so, Bruno went to the door.

Mother Late, always late, he always comes late.

Simone No, Mamma, it is quite early.

Alberto (*approaches bellowing*) Errico! *E come stai, come stai?*

H. Alberto!

Alberto Yes, I know what you are looking at. I am very fat. It is from drinking too much beer. I don't like wine, I have to drink beer. But Erric'! It is really you! (*embrace*)

H. Ehi.

Leo (*advancing*) Alberto, don't suffocate Erric'.

H. Leo! You here as well! How wonderful.

Father (*bleats*) *Tous ainsaimble! Nous sommes tous ainsaimble!* Haha! All together!

Alberto Leo, you see, is still very slim.

Bruno It is Leo's nature to be very slim.

Alberto It is not my nature to be so. Nor Mamma's.

Mother (*contentedly*) Yes, I have re-expanded, thank God.

Simone I am slim, too. Look at my legs! (*slaps them resoundingly*) They are
slim. Leo says they are scraggy.

H. Well, you all look very well.

Leo Così-così.

Father Yes, they look very well because they have beautiful wives.

Alberto Like you, Papa.

Father (*hoots*) *Comme moi, comme moi:* like me!

Mother (*not pleased*) Ah, but even if you have a beautiful mamma, it does
not prevent you from wanting a wife as well. Ah, Erric', one
brings them up, one cleans them, one educates them, and then:
poof! they desert one. It is Fate, it is Destiny. You are religious,
Erric'?

Leo But Mamma, we never desert you: we come back every day, one
or other of us.

Mother Yes, and after an hour or so you go away again.

Father They have to get back to their beautiful wives.

Mother (*sadly*) *Ehi*, beautiful wives . . . But a wife is never the same as a
mother, is she, Erric'?

H. No, but I understand that that is sometimes considered an
advantage.

(*the sons laugh*)

Bruno and Leo⎫ Eh, bravo, Erric'. Bravo!
Father⎭ *Ne foh pas dire!*

Mother What did he say?

Alberto He said it was a good thing.

Simone He said it was a great advantage.

Mother Aaaaaaaah! Errico, Erric'. False, false!

Simone (*politely*) The Oedipus complex. Bravo Karamazov.

Mother Who *is* this Karamazov?

H. I hoped you would bring your wives with you.

Alberto (*regretfully*) Ah no, that was not possible.

Leo (*maturely*) They have things to see to.

H. Well, you all look very happily married.

Mother Not so happy as at home.

Bruno It is not so bad. Leo has a very beautiful wife.

Leo Alberto's wife is very beautiful too.

Alberto (*firmly*) No. Beautiful she is not. But she is very good to me.
You see, Erric', one gets one's darning, and pressing, and washing
done, buttons put on, shoes . . .

Leo (*seriously*) And that is a very great consideration, Erric'.

218

Alberto But of course, it is not the same as being a bachelor.

Leo Oh, no.

Alberto Everywhere you go it's 'Alberto, don't look, don't look, who are you looking at over there?'

Bruno Yes, dear Errico, there is such a thing as jealousy.

H. So I have heard.

Alberto And there *was* such a thing as liberty.

Simone Mamma, today I was with Alberto in the street, and do you know what he said as we passed a young lady?

Alberto (*hastily*) I didn't say anything.

Mother What did he say?

Simone He said, in American . . .

Alberto Simone!

Simone He said, 'Ello baby.

         (*the others laugh*)

Mother (*with the laugh: a sad lament*) Aaaah!

Alberto I didn't.

Simone 'Ello baby. I shall tell Carlotta.

Alberto And see what you get.

Simone 'Ello baby.

Bruno You must see the real babies, Errico.

Leo I shall call my next one after you. Enrico, or Enrichetta.

Alberto Ah, Errico, my baby! You must see him, my baby! He's wonderful! I could play with him *forever!*

Simone (*politely*) If only he didn't make pee-pee all over one's legs.

Leo And do you think *you* never made . . .

Father *Ne foh pas dire!*

Mother Yes, you can enjoy your babies now, but you will find they will grow up and leave you all. Fate, Destiny . . .

Leo *Ehi*, Mamma . . .

Mother *Ehi*, Mamma . . . Do not get married, Erric'.

Father Yes, he must. We will find him a nice wife in Naples.

H. Thank you.

Alberto No. Don't get married, Erric': have a great career instead. I lost my career when the demo-christians got in at the elections. But you know many famous people, writers, ambassadors, statesmen . . . you will have a great career.

H. I really don't know any ambassadors or statesmen . . .

Alberto Do you know any Jewish rabbis?

H. Any *what?*

Alberto Jewish rabbis. Because, Erric', if you did, I could get a better job at the bank.

Father Yes, that is true.

H. (*mystified*) I really don't see how.

Alberto My employer is a Jew, you see. I am not, so it is difficult for me to advance in my career at the bank. Now, a colleague of mine who is a Jew persuaded a rabbi in Palermo to write a letter of recommendation to the manager of the bank, and in consequence my friend is now well advanced; so that if you knew a rabbi in England . . .

Leo Or even a rich Jewish business-man . . .

Alberto Yes, or a rich Jewish business-man, you could ask him to write . . .

H. But Alberto, think: can you imagine anyone going up to a rich Jewish gentleman in London and saying: 'Listen, you are a Jew. Now I know a friend employed 2,000 miles away by another Jew, in Naples. I have been wondering, etcetera, etcetera . . .'
(*they all laugh*)

Alberto (*also laughing*) Yes, I am sorry, it was ridiculous.

Mother Alberto is always a baby. As if such a thing would be possible . . . But, Erric'.

H. Yes?

Mother You can help Bruno.

H. How?

Bruno Yes, Mamma, how?

Mother You said that you knew ambassadors, statesmen . . .

H. I didn't. Alberto said so. I don't know any . . .

Leo But you once said you knew the Italian ambassador in London.

H. No, Leo. I said I once met a previous ambassador.

Mother Where?

H. At an art exhibition in London.

Mother And you had a long conversation?

H. No, I merely said how do you do, when a friend presented me to him.

Mother A friend?

H. Yes.

Mother Your friend is a friend of the previous ambassador?

H. Yes. He's not a very close friend of mine, and I haven't seen him for three years.

Mother It is very good. It is very simple. It will save Bruno.

H. I . . . I . . . I . . . what am I to do?

Mother (*lucidly*) This is what you will do. When you get back to your hotel tonight, write a letter to your friend, and tell him to write as soon as possible to the previous ambassador and ask him to have the very great courtesy to write to the present ambassador, requesting him to write, at his convenience, to the manager of the Commercial Bank of Milan a strong letter of recommendation for Bruno, who is now employed as a veterinary surgeon at Amalfi, and who is desirous of becoming a cashier in the Naples branch of the Commercial Bank of Milan. It is simple.

   All (*dispersedly*) E bene! Benissimo. Excellent. Oh Mamma, how splendid! (*and Father: C'est très bien, très bien*). And Bruno can come home.

   H. But the present ambassador doesn't know Bruno.

   All Ehi, that doesn't matter, that isn't the point (*etc.*).

Mother The present ambassador knows the previous ambassador, who knows your friend. Your friend knows you, and eleven years ago you used to see Bruno every day.

Alberto It is quite simple, Erric'.

Mother And Bruno is very unhappy at Amalfi.

   H. Yes, I see . . . Are you, Bruno?

Mother (*interposing*) Yes, very unhappy.

  Bruno (*reluctantly*) Yes, Erric' . . . I am rather unhappy at Amalfi. But it is not impor . . .

   Leo He cannot get such a job without a very sound recommendation such as you could get from the ambassador.

Alberto And your friend would be pleased to help, if you said how unhappy Bruno was.

Mother And if you have not seen him for several years, it would be a very good excuse for writing to him again. You see, Erric'?

   H. (*doubtfully*) Yes, I see . . .

  Bruno (*very slowly and hesitantly*) I . . . I know it is difficult, Erric'. But perhaps if you said I was fair-haired, and looked like an Englishman when I put my glasses on, somebody might . . .
     (*fade*)

Narrator 'Great wealth in the hands of a few; petitioners at the gate.' . . . You could not get those words of Yeats's out of your mind, could you? Outside of these rooms, you all, it seemed, had a separate life, precarious and vulnerable; disappointments, hopes deferred or forever abandoned could not help showing themselves momentarily in their faces and voices; did they show at all in yours? But in these rooms, they could be put aside, if only for a hundred minutes. Something had rebuilt itself here, at least for you. This was the small good place . . . But wait . . .

Leo You are looking thoughtful and studious, Erric'. Why?

H. M'm? I was only thinking how often you had let the false Errico return here.

Alberto Who said you were false?

Bruno False, never.

Simone The faithless Errico!

Mother *Basta*, Simone.

H. Well, if I promise to be really faithful in future will you let me come here oftener?

Father Of course, of course, *quand vous voulez, monsieur*. It is a privilege.

Mother You must always come here. You have always been faithful, Erric'. (*casually*) The true heart is always faithful even in absence; it is not a matter of postcards and letters.

H. (*enigmatically*) Well.

Alberto Why not come here straightaway?

H. Perhaps I could come the night before I go back to England?

Mother But come tomorrow.

H. (*incautiously*) No, tomorrow I'm going to Ca . . . (*stops*)

Simone
Bruno Aaaaah!

H. . . . pri.

Mother Where you will meet another American young woman.

H. No, no, no!

Simone 'Ello baby.

Mother Well, you will come on your way back.

H. And shall I have the room with the blue walls I stayed in when I first came?

Mother Of course, of course.

Simone And Erric'.

H. Yes?

Simone When you come *next* year it will be even better!

H. It can't be better than it has been.

Several Yes, yes, next year it will be better. You will like it much better (*etc.*).

H. How?

Simone Why, because when you come next year we won't be here.

    H. (*mystified, suspecting a joke*) Do you mean you'll run away when you hear I'm coming?

Simone No! You will come too.

    H. I ... Whatever is the child talking about?

Alberto Haven't they told you, Erric'?

 Father He does not know, he does not know! (*he laughs*)

Simone We are *leaving* here, Erric'.

    H. Leaving? ... (*a long pause*) Good God.

      (*the others laugh*)

Mother Yes; *e madonna mia*, how glad I shall be to be elsewhere, Erric'. We are going into a little ground-floor apartment at Bagnoli. Oh, not far away, but quieter and nearer the sea. No more stairs to climb, no more sweating ...

 Bruno We are all getting old, Erric'. I am thirty-three.

Alberto And I am getting so fat. Nine flights of stairs. Terrible. The heart.

    H. I was just beginning to find them easier. I only had to stop twice on the way up today.

Mother I stop six times. I sweat.

   Leo I stop three.

 Bruno I stop three also. Very tiring.

Simone I stop once.

 Father (*triumphantly*) And I! I never stop at all. Because I never go down, and so I do not have to come up.

      (*the others laugh a little*)

   Leo Errico still looks rather sad.

Mother Why?

    H. Ehi ...

Mother Di; di, Erric'?

    H. Well ... it is just that I regret the thought that soon I shall have seen these walls for the last time.

Alberto The walls? These are dreadful walls. The walls are much better at Bagnoli.

 Bruno Yes, they have very good walls at Bagnoli.

Mother (*loudly*) That is not what Erric' means. He is better than the rest of you, he is the only faithful one, the rest of you all go away with your beautiful wives, yes, all of you, but Erric' is the only faithful one, the only one who ...

      (*her sons drown her voice*)

   Sons (*laughing*) *Ehi*, Mamma, *basta! Dai, dai!*

223

Mother Come here, Erric', you are the only true one, I shall embrace you. Yes!

    (*loud kisses while the others laugh*)

Simone (*across the laugh*) But Erric'! Erric'!

    H. Yes, Simone?

Simone We haven't told you the best thing of all about the apartment at Bagnoli.

Several Ah, yes!

Simone At Bagnoli the new apartment will have ... (*almost religiously*) central heating!

Several Aaaaaah!

  Father (*triumphantly*) Chauffage centrale! Tous conforts modernes!

    H. Well, on that warming thought I must leave you.

   Leo We will walk back with you, shall we, Alberto?

Alberto Yes, I'll get my jacket.

 Father Ah yes, you go home, to sleep, to repose.

Mother Good night, Erric'. You will come again as soon as you can. And you will come many times before you go. And the night before you go home you will not stay at the hotel, you will come here and stay in your old room, where you slept the very first time you came and have never slept since; and for dinner I have thought of a little menu for you: you shall have ham and melon, an omelette and potatoes, a beefsteak, a tomato salad, a cake, and some peaches: because I know you find spaghetti too heavy. You will like that?

    H. Immensely.

Mother Then good night.

    H. Good night.

    (*general good nights*)

Narrator Once it had seemed farewell for ever; but now such a farewell would never be said. 'You will visit us many times.' After the harbour and the sombre castle, after the via Roma and the pink and green of the Piazza Dante, after the Museum and the hard upward climb, after the fresh haphazard of the little provincial square, where one Naples ended and another began; this was their ambience. Here they were, in those familiar rooms, which would soon know you and them no longer. Once on an evening when time was all your own, you were drawn to go past and go on – and as you passed, a shutter in your mind opened for a second upon a glimpse of *them, with you absent,* high up in their high rooms, silent, three, four or five of them, silent, or whispering from room to room, and thus also answering. They would wait, while you pursued your way down the merciful winding Corso, with the cries of evening children softening upon the breeze and dying and dying down to the moment of silence in the hillside garden where, among the roses and oleanders and the great towering pines, Leopardi lies in peace at last, by the side of Virgil.

(*softly*)

Look back: the city is a city regained ... Go back: where one Naples ends and another begins ... Ascend. The stairs seem daily less hard to climb ... Past the eternal names: Ciccarelli ... Calise ... Guida ... Lembo ... Pavese ... And there it still is ...

(*fade. Bell. Pause. The door opens*)

Simone (*dwelling on the word*) Erric'.

H. Eccomi.

The Great Desire I Had

Tranio, since for the great desire I had
To see faire Padua, nurserie of Arts . . .

To Marjorie Westbury

The Great Desire I Had was first broadcast in 1952. The version given here was first broadcast on 23 November 1955, with the following cast:

WILLIAM SHAKESPEARE	*Marius Goring*
ISABELLA ANDREINI	*Irene Worth*
FRANCESCO ANDREINI	*Patrick Troughton*
THOMAS SHEWIN	*Alan McClelland*
GIULIO PASQUATI	*Carleton Hobbs*
OTTAVIO	*David Spenser*
ORAZIO	*Jeremy Spenser*
SILVIA RONCAGLI	*Marjorie Westbury*
A VERONESE GENTLEMAN	*Ivan Samson*
A FLOWER-SELLER	*Patricia Field*
A BOY	*Marjorie Westbury*
VINCENZO, DUKE OF MANTUA	*Hugh Burden*
NARRATOR	*James McKechnie*

In the earlier version the parts of Isabella and Francesco Andreini were played by Flora Robson and John Phillips; Thomas Shewin was played by Frank Duncan; Vincenzo by Neville Hartley. The production of both versions was by Douglas Cleverdon. The music for the boy's song was by Donald Swann.

Narrator This is the air ... That is the glorious sun ... Westward from Venice the blind bronze eyes of Verrocchio's horseman, high-mounted in the square of St John and St Paul, glare toward the domes of Padua. In Padua, city of learning, the eyes of the horseman of Donatello, in the square of St Anthony, glare eastward back. The servitors of violence. Between them plies the peaceful river, the Brenta, charged with boats, the red sail floating above the fields, slowly, slowly, from Venice and the lagoons to Padua's water-gate ... And there are the Euganean hills ... there are Este, and castled Montagnana ... there is a covered boat, small, sturdy, bearing stone, nosing its way to Vicenza, city of building ...

And westward still, there lies Verona, city of merchants, gripped by a noble river bearing wealth and plenty downward from Germany. Verona: in the safe-keeping of Venice, safely kept; in Verona's harbour the ships of the Adriatic whore ... And downward, southward ... There is Mantua, islanded upon her lake, city of painters, of rare Italian masters. And of the masters' masters also: Gonzaga is the duke's name. Many boats here also, sliding smoothly round the city, smooth-sliding down the Mincio to the Po, to troubled waters. And eastward down the river, and down the river to Ferrara, Ferrara, city of comedy, town of the good Ariosto ... This is the air ... that is the glorious sun. But Ariosto is dead, and it is the blessed moon that shines so bright: shines on Ferrara, and on a theatre therein.

     (knocking at a door. Pasquati is in a state of fretful indignation)

Pasquati No ... ! No, Orazio! Nobody, *nobody* must come into the dressing-room, I mustn't see anyone, I can't see anyone. My poor stomach is revolving over and over ... *no one*, Orazio! And where is Ottavio? Who *is* it? ... Worn out, and people pestering me everywhere, oh, but *everywhere* ...

     (inaudible colloquy at door, behind Pasquati)

Shakespeare Good evening. Signor Ottavio is expecting me, I think.

Orazio He's just changing, sir. Do you mind waiting a few moments?

Pasquati Who is it? What do they want of me? I mustn't see anyone. Bring them in. Oh dear. Who is it?

Orazio It's an English gentleman, come to call for Ottavio.

229

Pasquati (*despairingly*) Bring them in, no matter, let them all come in, all of them . . .

Orazio There is only one of him . . .

Pasquati Let them all come in . . . (*a fierce whisper to himself*) Oh, stomach, stomach!

Orazio Do come in, sir.

Shakespeare I hope I haven't come at an inconv . . .

Pasquati (*disconcertingly melodious*) Good eve-ning . . . Wel-come . . . The name?

Shakespeare My . . . my name is William Shakespeare.

Pasquati Again?

Shakespeare William Shakespeare.

Pasquati And mine, Mr Williams, is Giulio Pasquati. Again? Giulio Pasquati.

Orazio I will tell Ottavio, sir. He is just behind the screen there, putting his clothes on.

Ottavio (*off*) I will be with you in a minute, Guglielmo. I'm not decent at the moment.

Pasquati Not decent. Putting his clothes on. Welcome, Mr Williams. A chair for you, a little chair. Yes. Now tell me, tell me from start to finish, what you thought of us, all of us, one and all.

Shakespeare I thought that everyone was . . .

Pasquati Good, good. I was not at my best tonight, no, no. The stomach, the stomach.

Shakespeare I'm sorry.

Pasquati I shall purge myself tonight, all by myself, alone. I long for solitude, I must have it. (*intimately*) The desperate agony of it. But no, you have no such troubles, Mr Williams, you are English, easy-going, phlegmatic. Orazio, give Mr Williams an egg, some chicken, grapes.

Shakespeare No, thank you, I . . .

Ottavio (*off*) We are going out to supper, Giulio.

Pasquati Supper. Tell me, Mr Williams, you will know, you are a traveller, you saw my performance tonight . . . ?

Shakespeare Yes, and may I . . . ?

Pasquati Do I play the part of the poor old *pantalone* too dramatically, I sometimes wonder? Too much drama? I ask myself that question. Do I? Sometimes, as I stand in the wings, waiting to go on, I put that very question to myself, I hear the audience, and I say to myself, 'Mr Williams, what is laughter?' . . . How pasty I look.

Oh, *look* at my face. You can tell I'm not well. What play did we act tonight, Mr Williams?

Shakespeare 'The Supposes.'

Pasquati (*gloomily*) I thought as much. And was there an element of tragedy in my performance tonight? Yes? The audience roared with laughter, I heard them – but were they also a-weeping?

Shakespeare No ... not obtrusively.

Pasquati Good-good. I hate display, hate it, hate it ... And what does my looking-glass say to me? It says, 'No colour in those cheeks'. Too ill, too ill to go on, if the truth were known.

Shakespeare And of course in life itself, a character like ...

Pasquati (*loudly*) Ah! That is it! Life! *Life itself!* Ottavio! What are you doing behind that screen?

Ottavio I'm putting my shirt on. I can hear you. I'm listening. Go on.

Pasquati Did you hear what Mr Williams said?

Ottavio Yes.

Pasquati Did *you* hear, Orazio?

Orazio Yes, certainly I heard.

Pasquati '*Life itself*', he said. Let that be a lesson to you, Orazio.

Orazio It always has been, Giulio.

Pasquati As you say so justly, Life, sir. We Italians, we go on, we go on, we ask questions, difficult questions, passionate questions. But Nature gives no answer, none. And then, a brave Englishman comes all the way across the Alps – frozen with snow, terribly cold – and he tells us the answer. Phlegm. The English phlegm. We hear so much about it. How profound it is when we meet it. *Pro-found.* It may of course be my bladder. Who can say? Who knows what we really *mean* by a bladder? The King of France once said to me, 'Dear Giulio Pasquati', he said ...

Ottavio (*approaching*) I'm sorry to keep you waiting, Guglielmo. I'm so glad you came. Did you enjoy it?

Shakespeare Very much. I ...

Ottavio You could follow it?

Shakespeare Most of it, yes, easily. I took the precaution of reading it this afternoon; and of course we have a beautiful translation of it.

Orazio Ariosto: in *English*?

Shakespeare Yes, it was translated years ago. Many of our plays are translations.

Pasquati Translations: *Hic ibat Simois:* here ran Simois, the name of a river. *Je vous félicite, mon beau monsieur:* I congratulate you, my fine

231

sir . . . Ah yes, the noble art of translation, God's greatest gift. Towel, towel, towel, where are you?

Ottavio Did you find the play very different here? It was written here in Ferrara, you know . . . oh, eighty years ago, I suppose.

Shakespeare Well, it was much better acted here, I think.

Ottavio Oh, we are only a modest little company. The best of us aren't here, of course.

Pasquati (sharply) What was that?

Ottavio The best of our players are in France at the moment.

Orazio And you mustn't judge us by these old plays where the script is all written down. They give us no scope.

Pasquati Scope. Mr Williams said I was like life itself, a compliment I shall always cherish . . . from a true friend of the theatre.

Ottavio Well, he should be a true friend of the theatre. He's an actor.

Pasquati Mirror, mirror! T't, t't, t't! Two new wrinkles, just here. Where were they three weeks ago? Who knows? *All* men are actors. The whole world is a stage. We all play many parts on it before our final scene. Take the case of myself, for example. I began as a dear little baby, my first entrance.

Ottavio I hope you weren't as late for it as you usually are.

Pasquati My first entrance, and my first exit. What contraries rule our lives, Mr Williams! Mirror, mirror! . . . (to himself) My mother had a very narrow pelvis.

Shakespeare But of course what I had most looked forward to, was, I am afraid, the simple excitement of seeing *women* on the stage.

Ottavio (laughing) Yes, all English visitors make straight for that.

Shakespeare I was sorry there was so little of the heroine.

Orazio There was quite enough of *her*, thank you.

Shakespeare They are . . . I suppose . . . honest women?

Ottavio I wouldn't vouch for the chastity of all of them. You know what the life of the stage is like.

Pasquati St-rumpets.

Ottavio You would like to have women on the English stage?

Shakespeare I hardly know. I think so, yes. You can scarcely imagine how strange the idea would be. We would have to change our first conception of the parts completely. I have, as you know, written several plays myself.

Ottavio A very boring job, *that* is, I should think, isn't it?

Shakespeare (disconcerted) Well . . . it keeps me going . . . when I'm not acting.

Pasquati All the world's a stage; and all the men and women actors and actresses, respectively.

Ottavio Do be quiet, Giulio, and get your breeches on; that's how you get your stomach-trouble.

Orazio We have to look after him. There they are, on the chair.

Pasquati Breeches, yes. Let me hide my shrunk shranks. Shunk shanks.

(*he continues struggling vaguely with this difficult phrase in the background*)

Shakespeare All the women's parts in my plays are done by boys, or youths. I've never found anything strange about that till tonight.

Ottavio Well, I believe it still happens in Italy, here and there. When I was a boy, down in Rome, I acted women's parts myself. But it would seem very old-fashioned now, up here.

Shakespeare Old-fashioned: yes, I'm sure it is. Still, when *we* write women's parts, we write them with boys in mind. And some of them are very talented, especially at ranting and moaning. But I wonder if, after tonight, I shall ever feel the same again.

Orazio It must be very agreeable to rant and moan on the stage.

Shakespeare And to write speeches, parts, plays, for real women; that I would dearly love to try.

Pasquati Ah! You are a lover of women, Mr Williams?

Shakespeare Well ... of course.

Pasquati Orazio. Go down to the women's dressing-room and see if Rosalba is still availa ...

Shakespeare No, I didn't mean ...

Ottavio Don't be silly, Giulio; Mr Shakespeare was talking about women on the stage.

Orazio (*laughs*)

Pasquati Who enacted my part in England, Mr Williams? Did *he* touch it here and there with melancholy?

Shakespeare It's interesting that you should ask that. The English translator has in fact written in a long pathetic speech for the *pantalone* at the point when he learns that his daughter is Dulipo's mistress.

Pasquati A pathetic speech in the middle of a c-homedy?

Shakespeare Y ... es.

Pasquati (*politely*) How ridiculous.

Shakespeare No, somehow it is not ridiculous when you hear it. It is as if a cloud passed for the moment over the whole thing – a kind of warning.

233

Pasquati How disconcerting. You have come to Italy to study the arts of the theatre, Mr Williams?

Shakespeare No, I have come here partly to escape from them. I . . . I mean that of course I hope to see many plays, and I have even promised to work a little at a play with an English friend of mine. But I have really come to Italy in the hope that here I can at last set to work on a different project I have been . . . *trying* to work at for many years.

Pasquati Its name?

Shakespeare I hope that at last I can make some headway with an epic poem on the Siege of Troy.

Pasquati There's one already, you know, dear friend.

Shakespeare Yes, I am aware of that. But perhaps it is one of those subjects that each age must try to do again.

Pasquati Restlessness. The canker of modern life.

Ottavio You have begun it, Guglielmo?

Shakespeare I have . . . picked at it, Ottavio. But (*half-laughing*) begun it . . . no, not quite.

Ottavio But . . . any minute now?

Shakespeare (*gratefully*) Any minute now.

Pasquati You are a poet, Mr Williams?

Orazio Of course he is. One can tell at once.

Pasquati (*amiably*) Recite your works.

Shakespeare (*embarrassed*) Oh no . . . not now . . .

Orazio Was it you who translated our play into English?

Shakespeare No, that was another poet. He is dead now.

Pasquati Recite *his* works.

Shakespeare Well, I don't know them all.

Pasquati Recite four of them.

Shakespeare (*abashed*) I . . . don't think I could.

Pasquati Recite three of them.

Shakespeare Well . . . I . . .

Pasquati Two of them.

Shakespeare I . . .

Pasquati One.

(*pause*)

Shakespeare Well, I . . . might recite one, if you insist.

Pasquati Do so. You wish to gargle? Or a glass of wine?

Shakespeare No . . . no, thank you . . . I . . . I have no wish to drink just now.

Pasquati Is that how the poem begins?

234

Shakespeare (*in increasing distress*) No . . . I . . .

    Pasquati (*firmly*) Mr Williams. Without further ado – *begin*.

    Orazio Yes, please.

    Ottavio It will be very interesting for us.

Shakespeare Well, it . . . goes like this:

> *Sing lullaby, as women do,*
> *Wherewith to bring their babes to rest.*

    Pasquati Yes, well that's a very interesting poem, Mr Williams. I am glad to have heard it. Rather brief, I would have said, but . . .

Shakespeare Oh, there is more of it. I . . .

    Pasquati Oh! Then utter it, my dear sir, utter it! Continue, without pausing, or stint.

Shakespeare

> *And lullaby can I sing too,*
> *As womanly as can the best.*
> *With lullaby they still the child,*
> *And if I be not much beguil'd,*
> *Full many wanton babes have I*
> *Which must be still'd with lullaby.*
>
> *First lullaby my youthful years,*
> *It is now time to go to bed,*
> *For crooked age and hoary hairs*
> *Have won the haven within my head,*
> *With lullaby then youth be still,*
> *With lullaby content thy will,*
> *Since courage quails, and comes behind,*
> *Go sleep, and so beguile thy mind.*

(*no fade. Brief pause. Narrator begins incisively, as before*)

Narrator Ferrara. The good Ariosto dead. And dying the House of Este. But the Pope will put out a hand, and catch it as it falls, dying. And Tasso, from Ferrara long departed and gone to Mantua. To Mantua, and thence away, preparing for death, for the last climb up the Roman hill, in the stormy, delaying spring. And the spring, hidden in the hills above Verona. And Verona is where he would come to, is it not? – our beloved the author, to see what it was he ought to say of it. Flowers all over the walls and the balconies, and he from the north, a new spring advancing also. And the blossoming lion of Venice on the walls of Verona, city

235

of merchants. Verona, the bright Verona morning, the bright, bright flesh everywhere about him . . .

(bells intermittently behind this. Keep distant, but not woolly)

Shakespeare The bright, bright flesh everywhere about me . . . Let me, oh God, do nothing more than praise it . . . *(pause)* How curious, that jealousy vanished the moment I got here. Perhaps here, if I stayed here forever, it would vanish forever . . . No. I think not. The bright anonymous flesh would take to itself a name: one name, as yet unknown. Let me not think of it, sweet passers-by, whose tongue I thought I knew . . . not counting on the dialect you all speak in. Bless you, oh casual exilers, who banish me from your talk, unknowing that one day I shall banish others hereabout. I shall banish Valentine, shall I not . . . to Mantua; and I shall banish Romeo to Mantua also – at greater length, and in choicer language, so ready, so beautiful, so intolerably glib. And who am I, that I speak of banishment so often? I who last night, by the dribbling candle in the inn, read Ovid, sweet voluptuous Ovid, who died in *real* exile, exile not voluntary, never to return, none to caress him, out on the frosty rocks, beyond the Pontic. Every memory ending in the night of departure, every memory of pleasure finishing there, in the last, strained glance from his wife. And the star Lucifer rising over them. *Uxor amans flentem flens acrius ipsa tenebat.* 'My loving wife held me as I wept, and wept more bitterly' . . . If only Anne had ever wept, dear brave Anne.

Woman *(suddenly and angrily)* Bunches of flowers! Big bunches of flowers! Buy a beautiful bunch of flowers! Buy . . . *(sweetly)* such a beautiful bunch of cyclamens for your lady, sir, fresh this morning. *(angry again)* Look at the beautiful . . .

Man *(peremptorily: an aristocrat)* Get out of the way.

Woman . . . flowers, may-your-poxy-guts-turn-purple, beautiful flowers, the best in Verona, buy a . . . Ah, young sir, you will buy a bunch of cyclamens for your lady, beautiful young sir?

Shakespeare But . . . where should I put them?

Woman Take them to your lady.

Shakespeare But I have no lady here.

Woman There are thousands of ladies in Verona; they will all come to you if they see you with flowers. Look, what a beautiful bunch!

Shakespeare I . . .

Woman You are Dutch?

Shakespeare English.

Woman There, sir, then of course you want a bunch of flowers to put in your chamber, a beautiful . . .

Gentleman (*officiously*) Excuse me, sir, is this woman molesting you? Take no notice of her. Get away, you nasty baggage, we know all about you.

Woman (*violently*) And I know all about you! Who are you to interfere with me, you spotty old stinkard!

Gentleman (*also angry*) Don't address me in that way, you slut!

Woman Who are you, to stop me in the lawful pursuit of my trade, you dirty . . .

Gentleman Be silent!

Woman I won't be silent! I was selling the gentleman a nice bunch of flowers . . .

Gentleman I warn you!

Woman You great slack-twisted . . .

Gentleman Silence!

Woman Empty-gutted . . .

Gentleman Silence!

Woman Daughter-fiddling maphrodite, you!

Gentleman I will set the watch on you! Come, my dear sir, come this way, take no notice . . . I shall remember you!

Woman And I shall remember you, you lousy-teated, clap-chapped, slip-slopping hog's rump!

(*her voice recedes behind the others*)

Gentleman (*quivering with rage*) Come this way, sir, let us proceed in the direction of the river. What an impression to create on a visitor! I beg you not to judge Verona from such encounters as that, sir. You are from foreign parts?

Shakespeare From England, yes.

Gentleman An admirable country, I am told. And *we* are admirable, too, at our best, sir. Don't judge us from this morning. We are doing our best to put an end to things like that. Furtive trafficking at street-corners . . .

Shakespeare She was only trying to sell me a bunch of cyclamens.

Gentleman Cyclamens! Ha! Is that what she called them?

Shakespeare Well, they *were* cyclamens.

Gentleman A blind, my dear sir.

Shakespeare For . . . what?

Gentleman Aphrodisiacs.

237

Shakespeare Oh . . . I see.

Gentleman A terrible traffic, rotting the life of the city. They are brought from Holland, of course, and circulated by clandestine agents. We have so far found no way of arresting it. It is one of the few remaining blots on this fair city, now that we have succeeded in getting the theatre abolished.

Shakespeare The theatre?

Gentleman I would have had the building itself plucked down, if I had had my way. It is being used as a granary – a dangerous compromise, if you ask my opinion.

Shakespeare Nature replacing art, in fact.

Gentleman Art? There is no art in the lewd tumbling of mountebanks. And we have our fair share of art already. Fine buildings, fine pictures.

Shakespeare Yes, the castle is beautiful. And the cloisters at . . .

Gentleman But wait, my dear sir, wait! Have you seen the new sewer? Ah, there's a work of art for you, sir, there's a miracle. Across the river there . . . I do beg you to get up early one morning and see it at sunrise, before the heat of the day sets in, of course.

Shakespeare Indeed.

Gentleman And we are putting up any number of new buildings in the northern quarter, fine splendid places all of them. Verona, sir, is coming into her own. I think you will find that we can furnish you with the best game of tennis south of the Alps.

Small boy (*approaching, bowling a hoop*) Whang, whang, whang, whang, whang, whang. (*terrified*) Oh, sorry, sir, no, I'm sorry sir, I didn't . . .

Gentleman What do you think you're doing, confound . . .

Small boy No, no, no, sir: I . . . don't sir, no, no, no!

Gentleman Take . . .

Small boy Noooooooh . . . (*bursts into triumphant laughter*) Missed! Missed! Missed me, silly old cheese-bag! (*roars with mirth*) Couldn't catch a mushroom!

Gentleman Come down from that wall! Come here!

Small boy Melons!

Gentleman Get down!

Small boy Get up! (*laughs and bursts into loud, teasing song*)
> Oh Teresa, oh Teresa,
> Oh what a girl is she!
> She'll do whatever you ask her to
> With you or him or me.

Gentleman Will you get down!

Small boy And now it's two in the morning,
And I hope nobody will pass,
For she's taken my Sunday breeches off,
And she's kissing me on the . . .
Oh Teresa, Oh Teresa,
She's a girl to know . . .

(recedes gleefully)

Gentleman Forgive me, sir! The chief magistrate shall close this street to such urchins, I promise you. I shall see . . .

Shakespeare Oh, it doesn't matter in the least to me . . .

Gentleman Let us sit down here. They will bring us some refreshment. *(calls)* Drawer! Drawer! It *does* matter, indeed, sir, it matters. You are an Englishman, unused to such displays.

Shakespeare Oh, London too has its moments.

Gentleman You are from London, yes, I guessed it . . . A flask of dry red wine, quickly.

Waiter Yes, sir.

Shakespeare Thank you.

Gentleman I pride myself that I can tell everything about a man from the cut of his clothes: his nation, his character, his mode of life, his profession, everything.

Shakespeare The art of the English tailor is to disguise his customer's profession, not to disclose it.

Gentleman Haha, you can't deceive me. No, no. Silk, isn't it?

Shakespeare Only the facings, I'm afraid. The rest is . . .

Gentleman I am not referring to your doublet, my dear sir. I mean you are *in* silk, are you not? That is the nature of your merchandise. That is why you are here.

Shakespeare No, I am not precisely a silk-merchant . . .

Gentleman Oh. Jewellery, perhaps?

Shakespeare I see my tailor has been even more successful than usual in disguising me.

Gentleman Disguising you?

Shakespeare Shall we put it like that?

(the drinks arrive)

Waiter The wine, sir.

Shakespeare Thank you . . .

Gentleman But if you are not here on . . .

Shakespeare I have a definite purpose in coming here, certainly. But perhaps

239

I had better not disclose it . . . at the moment.

Gentleman You have . . . connections in Verona?

Shakespeare Well, it might be said I was connected with it, in an obscure way, but only by a mere private cryptography.

Gentleman Oh.

(*pause*)

You will be here for long?

Shakespeare No, only for a day or two. I merely wanted to take a glance at Verona before meeting a young colleague of mine in Padua.

Gentleman A Paduan?

Shakespeare No. Another Englishman. We have a little work to do together. It may be a good place to start in.

Gentleman Oh.

Shakespeare I am afraid I bore you?

Gentleman By no means. Your work in Padua . . . will be . . . exacting?

Shakespeare Oh, it will be only a question of watching and observing and making notes. And perhaps making the acquaintance of a few Italians engaged in similar pursuits.

Gentleman Indeed.

Shakespeare I hope I am not being over-evasive? I am secretive by nature: an English habit, I fear.

Gentleman Not at all. Forgive me one moment; I believe the master of this place has a much better red wine than this. I will . . .

Shakespeare I find this excell . . .

Gentleman I shall return immediately.

Shakespeare (*to himself, ironically*) What strange, unwanted encounters force themselves upon us out of the vast unknown. I would rather have talked to the flower-woman; I could have spoken Anne's name: she would certainly have asked me sooner or later if I was married, they all do. I would rather have played games with that little boy, and taken down the words of his charming song: some pretty mountaineering ballad, no doubt. I could have told him about Judith and Hamnet. Instead I meet a . . . theatre-hater. One person out of a thousand, perhaps. I was even content to be alone thinking about my poem, in this strange town, which says so little to me. Troy, my own Troy, had you tall towers like these? Did Scamander flow as fast as the Adige? Can I make the small men and women of the people, who stand, terrified and obscure, behind the heroes' backs, can I make them as real as that woman who dabbles her bed-linen in and out of the river? (*mutters,*

almost desperately) I must . . . otherwise . . . Oh God, so far, I can
see no more than the large, vague brightnesses every man can
see. The brave pavilions, Priam's six-gated city: Dardan and
Timbria, Helias, Chetas, Troien, and Antenorides . . .

 (*the gentleman begins to speak in the distance at 'brave pavilions'*)

Gentleman (*off*) There he is. That's the one. At once.

Guard (*off*) Yes sir. Follow me, the rest of you.

 (*these words of the gentleman and the guard have not been distinguishable behind Shakespeare. Then, sharply, after 'Antenorides'*)

Guard Stand up.

Shakespeare (*absently*) M'm?

Guard You are English?

Shakespeare (*politely*) How pleasant not to be thought Dutch for once. Yes,
I'm with a gentleman of this city. He seems to have . . . ah, there
he is . . .

Guard I advise you not to talk. Stand up.

Shakespeare But . . .

Guard I do not advise a struggle or other violence, flight or attempted
flight, or interference with a military officer in the performance
of his duty.

Shakespeare I wouldn't dream . . .

Guard You are under arrest in the name of the republic.

Shakespeare Arrest? Whatever for? I am sure that your fellow-citizen will
tell you . . .

Guard I am permitted to divulge for your information that the im-
mediate charges are loitering with intent, consorting with disorderly female vagrant, trafficking in drugs, espionage, imper-
sonation, and utilisation of secret cypher.

Shakespeare (*politely*) Great God in heaven: what a misspent morning.

Guard Profanity will be of no avail.

Shakespeare No. It rarely is, I find. Lead on.

 (*without pause fife breaks cheerfully in with the small boy's song.
Play through once, and sink to faint drone behind speech*)

Narrator To see fair Padua, nursery of arts. In Padua, the sharp sun stings
the domes and bounces back. The great bronze horseman stares
through the golden light and may not flinch: Gattamelata, they
call you. And the city is spread before you. Under the arcades
moves one named Galileo, and dangerous knowledges burn
already within him; and another passes him named William

Harvey, circulating warmly through the heart of the city. The boats glide in from Venice, covered with arching hatches; 'and there is very pleasant company, so a man beware to give no offence'. Down by the water-gate in a sunny corner our beloved, the author, is pleasant company also, and also gives no offence, here in the bright day of Padua.

(*loud delighted roar of laughter from Thomas. Shakespeare's mirth is only a little less*)

Thomas　But how long did they keep you there, Will?

Shakespeare　For three whole days, dear Thomas.

Thomas　In a cell?

Shakespeare　In a cell. And entirely alone.

Thomas　I cannot tell you how sorry I am.

Shakespeare　So I observe.

Thomas　Ah, but truly I am.

Shakespeare　I was greatly sustained by the thought of the distress it would cause you, when I told you.

Thomas　But what did you do when you got out?

Shakespeare　I went straight down the principal street to the corner and bought a large bunch of cyclamens. Later in the day I presented them to a small boy whom I met driving a hoop near the river. He in his turn regaled me with a few local songs, and the next morning I left for Padua. You will forgive me for arriving a day late.
(*Thomas laughs again*)
Thomas, dear worldly youth, you know the ways of this fair land so much better than I do. Are my adventures in any way exceptional, or are they the custom of the country?

Thomas　I will see it does not happen again. I will protect you. Have some more of this excellent restorative wine.

Shakespeare　Thank you. Has Padua changed since you last saw it?

Thomas　Very little. I shall enjoy showing you round. Some of my friends are still at the University.

Shakespeare　Acting tragical Seneca, no doubt, in their spare time?

Thomas　*All* of the time, when they're not acting comical Plautus.

Shakespeare　My stomach turns over at the thought. You haven't, I suppose, seen any Italian plays in your travels?

Thomas　I have seen the improvisers once or twice.

Shakespeare　Have you seen the *Gelosi*?

242

Thomas They are in France, I heard.

Shakespeare No, I think they are back. At any rate, I am to meet them in Venice at the end of the month; I met several of those who had stayed behind, when I went to Ferrara.

Thomas Were they improvising, or acting?

Shakespeare They were doing Ariosto's *Suppositi*.

Thomas Oh, Gascoigne's old thing.

Shakespeare Gascoigne's old thing; which I must urge you to refer to with a great deal more respect than you employ at the moment. You will be spending a good deal of time during the next fortnight, eagerly scanning its admirable pages.

Thomas Why?

Shakespeare In preparation for the little joint effort we had planned to do – should the fatigues of our travels fail to exhaust us.

Thomas (*pleased*) Aaaah! Have some more drink. I hoped you would mention it first.

Shakespeare As was fitting.

Thomas As was fitting.

Shakespeare (*politely*) Your legs being younger than mine.

Thomas (*politely*) And you with your interesting prison experiences behind you.

Shakespeare I was about to revert to those. When I tell you how I passed the hours of my solitude, you will be very surprised.

Thomas But tolerant withal, I trust. What did you do?

Shakespeare I worked.

Thomas Worked!

Shakespeare I found prison highly stimulating. My mind to me a kingdom was, such perfect joy therein I found. I felt that if only they would keep me in prison long enough, I might settle down there and truly start my epic on the Siege of Troy.

Thomas William, dear. Don't say you actually *began* it?

Shakespeare Alas, dear Thomas, alas for our hopes. The prime need of the epic poet, without which there would have been no Homer, no Virgil, no Ariosto, no Tasso, no Spenser, is an unlimited quantity of paper.

Thomas Which was denied you.

Shakespeare Which was denied me. I was forced to confine myself to mental creation: I composed four sonnets, two of which I have forgotten; I added seventeen new stanzas to a poem on *The Rape of Lucrece*, and finally I turned to the drama.

Thomas (*with a very slight belch*) That great art. And what did you do with it?

243

Shakespeare I outlined a little diversion for solo performer to be called *The One Gentleman of Verona*, which I abandoned when the plot became too complicated. Finally I contented myself with trying to decide, what is the worst play in the world? When I had decided – it was no easy matter, there was a rich assortment of possible choices – I made a vow that *that* should be the play we would rewrite. Can you guess which it is?

Thomas My mind misgives. Can it be . . . *The Taming of a Shrew*?

Shakespeare What sympathy! What exquisite concordance of two minds! Of course it was. You need have no fears in uttering its title in future, however. I have changed it.

Thomas To what?

Shakespeare To *The Taming of* The *Shrew.* (*complacently*) It was the high point of my prison achievement.

Thomas Happy the man to whom simple emendation can bring such content.

Shakespeare It is you who are simple, dear Thomas. Consider, for example – please pass the bottle, will you? Thank you – consider the phrase, 'the skinning of a rabbit'. A common daily action towards an anonymous small creature. But suppose you yourself, dear Thomas, were the possessor of a *private* rabbit, a rabbit of some concern to yourself, the only one you knew, the only one any of your devoted friends knew. Sooner or later you would kill this rabbit, your healthy young appetite triumphing, as so often, over the claims of affection . . .

Thomas Do get *on!*

Shakespeare Think. Think carefully. How momentous would be the great operation of removing the poor creature's fur. It would be no casual exploit; no, it would not be one of several hundred rabbits that might be skinned that day. It would be skinning *the* rabbit. Think of that for a moment: you would be skinning poor Bunny, the only rabbit in the world.

Thomas Rabbits I can scarcely abide, let me mention it briefly in passing.

Shakespeare No matter. The skinning of the rabbit. Alter 'The taming of a shrew' to 'The Taming of The Shrew'. What happens? The Shrew becomes for a moment the most important such person in the world. The Shrew: the one woman like that the people about her know. She is herself as interesting as the operation of taming, where previously she was not. We wonder why she was shrewish, among others not so afflicted. We wonder what she will be like when tamed. She becomes in fact the faint shadow of a *woman*, whom we can substantiate as we may. Or rather as *I* may – for need I say that I have appropriated that delicate and interesting little task to myself?

Thomas As was fitting.

Shakespeare As was fitting.

Thomas Do you imagine they will permit any alteration of the title?

Shakespeare Possibly not. But it will permit us to write our play.

Thomas Did I hear once more that charming word 'us'?

Shakespeare To you, dear Thomas, I shall allot the intricate delights of the underplot. You will delete all those cribs and imitations of Marlowe, substituting for them a ravishing, elegant, witty concentration on the matter under treatment. Allow yourself a full play of poetic fancy once every eight lines.

Thomas Thank you . . .

Shakespeare Scenes where the two plots combine we will consider together. I will scrutinise your contributions at half-past four every afternoon, correcting here an error of taste, there a faulty scansion . . .

Thomas And lightly adding sublime master-touches as needed?

Shakespeare As needed.

Thomas Are we keeping the induction? They will never let us cut Christopher Sly, will they?

Shakespeare I have no wish to. We shall re-do it, of course. Or rather *I* shall, with my warm kindly feeling, ever sympathetic to the humours of honest simple folk.

Thomas Honest simple *English* folk, dear Will.

Shakespeare English, yes. I knew I had left something out: in fact, that is the point. When the play within the play starts, I want us . . . I want us to surprise everyone with a sudden transportation away from the cold lumpy winter of Warwickshire to the warm smooth ease of Italy. Our abysmal predecessors called the scene Athens for some unascertainable reason. We will move it all to Italy, in fact we will move it to this very city, to Padua. And we will make it *seem* like Padua, we will make it glow like Padua. Does it occur to you how little of Italy we put in our plays when we call this place Naples, that one Rome, that other one Milan? We must do better than that. It will be something new, a subtle colouring of the sky, a richness of excitement, a strangeness of the air that makes the impossible accident credible . . .

Thomas It might be . . . wonderful, if we can do it . . .

Shakespeare *You* shall do it, Thomas.

Thomas I?

Shakespeare You. Even though *I* have thought of it, now it has gone into your mind too, do you think you could bear to let me produce a botched picture of a place you know far better? I would be ashamed, and you distressed. Of course you shall do it . . .

Thomas My legs being younger than yours.

Shakespeare And I with my long prison experience to recover from. Go: get my books.

Thomas (*as he retreats*) Save a little of that drink for me . . .

Shakespeare (*to himself*) How pleasant he is . . . Yes, it will work . . . though it will be a mistake in any case. I vowed I would never work thus. And now I, who dream of a vast work of solitude, a poem of dazzling richness with Hector and Achilles so close to the reader that he could all but smell their flesh . . . I am back at the old job. I am writing one half of a little popular comedy, and apparently by choice . . . Still, at least it is comedy, which may be shared; it ends in happiness, which can be, indifferently, shared or solitary. Indeed a solitary happiness multiplies us into more people than we are, our heart becomes the underplot to our brain, and our sensuality sings and dances interludes in our day. So, two or three or four people may make a comedy together. Nevertheless, it was a mistake. Already I regret that I shall never know what I might have found in those parts of my comedy to which I have denied myself first access.

If this were tragedy we would not be together. That will not be shared, one is alone with it, as one is alone with it in life. Not, I suspect, that it ever happens in life. We confuse it with grief and loss and exile, with the breaking of the heart and the death or departure of the beloved . . . which are only minor ailments. But even in those we are alone, and it is better for us so. If this were tragedy we would not be together . . .

Thomas The books, the books!

Shakespeare Ah, here you are. What energy . . !

Thomas How splendid this will be. I will work nine hours a day. All I wish is that you had chosen a tragedy instead.

Shakespeare Do you, indeed?

Thomas Another time perhaps.

246

Shakespeare (*banteringly but firmly*) Thomas, dear open-hearted youth, I trust you do not think that our little collaboration is going to establish a precedent?

Thomas Never in the world.

Shakespeare Good. Now, first of all, let us rebaptise all the characters with Italian names.

Thomas The hero almost has one already. He is called Ferando.

Shakespeare If we do not change his name, his sordid ghost will dog us everywhere. In any case I have already altered it to Petruccio.

Thomas But dare you possibly alter Kate? The audiences are so used to her under that name, they will certainly never come if she is altered.

Shakespeare Wise child. I have thought of that. We shall call her Caterina. 'Kate' shall be Petruccio's repeated insult to her. That will make everybody happy.

Thomas Ingenious and resourceful.

Shakespeare 'Kate' shall be his insult; Caterina shall be his occasional reward to her. The last time he addresses her by her proper name must bring tears to the eyes of the spectator.

Thomas It still is a comedy we are writing, may I briefly ask?

Shakespeare (*mockingly sententious*) Dear Mr Shewin, all comedy is touched with sadness, if you do but look deep enough.

Thomas (*politely*) Hurrah.

Shakespeare And Caterina's final speech in response to him, when she reproaches the other wives: we shall scrap that deplorable little sermon on the page before you; I shall put in its place the ennobled heart of a girl who has just become a woman. And by her speech, Petruccio is chastened also, as they all are.

Thomas And which of our handsome little lads have you in mind for this girl who has just become an ennobled woman?

Shakespeare Oh . . . ! I had almost forgotten those . . . bloody boys. (*Thomas laughs*) Thomas. Have you ever seen this woman they all talk about so much, Isabella Andreini?

Thomas The divine Isabella. Yes, a number of times. I have met her too.

Shakespeare What is she . . . like?

Thomas As an actress?

Shakespeare As a woman. As everything.

Thomas (*lightly*) Oh, she is probably the greatest woman in Italy.

Shakespeare Beautiful?

Thomas Not entirely. Yet she gives you the illusion of beauty, not only on the stage, but off it too. Wherever she is, she moves and speaks like an angel. She has a curious radiance, so that everyone who comes into her presence seems also to partake of it. One ... postpones one's crimes on her account.

Shakespeare Oh ... You haven't seen her for some time, I gather?

Thomas No. But you will find I am quite right. It is well known that the members of the *Gelosi* company under Isabella and her husband are much better behaved in their private lives than the usual run of actors. It is as though they were all part of a happy court under a virtuous king and queen.

Shakespeare There is none of the jealousy there is among us? About casting, I mean ...

Thomas How can there –

Shakespeare Oh, yes, I forgot. They all write their own parts – the very thing we spend our lives trying to prevent our actors from doing. It must be disgusting.

Thomas It is not disgusting when you see it, because they are all so brilliant and alive.

Shakespeare Have you met old Pasquati?

Thomas Yes. Mad as a hatter.

Shakespeare I met him in Ferrara. But, you know, he isn't an actor at all, as we conceive an actor. His mask, or his act, or whatever you call it, has taken an absolute possession of his mind.

Thomas Yes, bless his ancient heart. If two coherent thoughts ever presented themselves to him, he would burst into tears.

Shakespeare I shall think of Isabella all the time I am rehabilitating poor Kate.

Thomas Much better to remember little Robin Goffe.

Shakespeare Robin Goffe ... yes. (*sighs*) God help me, I once had to act opposite him, when someone else was sick. His mother only lets him shave every second Thursday. This was a second Wednesday. (*between his teeth*) It was like embracing a gorse-bush.
(*fade*)

Narrator This is the air ... That is the glorious sun ... On the light lagoon a million ripples kiss and dissolve and interchange; it is Venice. The gondolas slide on the fluttering water, a million glances of light sustaining them. A million flames of coolness dance from the sea to her bright palaces. She awaits complacently, the Adriatic whore, her centuries of lovers; they will die in her arms and their flowery hearses will float down the Great Canal. The ceilings and halls are frescoed with falling gods, and over them all dances

the light from off the sea. Useless our eyes where so many have
stared before, of poet, of painter, of sculptor. Their traffic stands
in our way. So does another: of pantaloon, magnifico and
pedant; parasite, braggart, zany and lover: their women are
with them, lingering on every bridge. The hooded gondolas bear
them in secret to the Giudecca, in secret to the Cannaregio; in
secret. And he, our beloved the author, he is there with them.
Will they give him birth once more? Will he be their heir . . .
will he be their glorious son?

(*babble of laughter and chatter*)

Silvia Yes, read it, Isabella, do read it.
Francesco Yes, let us hear Guglielmo's poem.
Shakespeare It will be a great honour for me, Donna Isabella.
Pasquati Declamation, the art of speaking out. One should eat anchovies
beforehand, always. Did you know that, Mr Williams?
Shakespeare No, I'd never heard that.
Silvia Let's all sit down. Quiet, everyone.
Ottavio I'll bring up some more chairs.
Orazio I shall sit by you, Silvia.
Silvia Quiet, everyone. Do sit down, Giulio.
(*noise of chairs and dresses*)
Pasquati Very few people ask *me* to declaim in these times, Mr Williams,
almost no one.
Shakespeare Oh, I am sure that's not true . . .
Pasquati Oh yes, my good friend. I am a forgotten man. And afflicted
with maladies, as you can perceive. (*with relish*) I have a *great*
variety of them.
Silvia Hush, Giulio.
Orazio Donna Isabella's going to read.
Ottavio We must all be quiet.
Pasquati (*loudly*) Hush, yes; hush-hush-hush.
(*pause*) A silence.
(*pause*)

Isabella Fie, fie, unknit that threatening, unkind brow,
And dart not scornful glances from those eyes,
To wound thy Lord, thy King, thy Governor.
It blots thy beauty, as frosts do bite the meads,
Confounds thy fame, as whirlwinds shake fair buds,

249

And in no sense is meet or amiable.
A woman mov'd is like a fountain troubled,
Muddy, ill-seeming, thick, bereft of beauty,
And while it is so, none so dry or thirsty
Will deign to sip, or touch one drop of it.
Thy husband is thy Lord, thy life, thy keeper,
Thy head, thy sovereign: one that cares for thee,
And for thy maintenance. Commits his body
To painful labour, both by sea and land,
To watch the night in storms, the day in cold,
Whilst thou ly'st warm at home, secure and safe,
And craves no other tribute at thy hands,
But love, fair looks, and true obedience;
Too little payment for so great a debt.
Such duties as the subject owes the Prince,
Even such a woman oweth to her husband:
And when she is froward, peevish, sullen, sour,
And not obedient to his honest will,
What is she but a foul contending Rebel,
And graceless Traitor to her loving Lord?
I am asham'd that women are so simple,
To offer war, where they should kneel for peace:
Or seek for rule, supremacy and sway,
When they are bound to serve, love, and obey.
Why are our bodies soft, and weak, and smooth,
Unapt to toil and trouble in the world,
But that our soft conditions, and our hearts,
Should well agree with our external parts?
Come, come, you froward and unable worms,
My mind hath been as big as one of yours,
My heart as great, my reason haply more,
To bandy word for word, and frown for frown;
But now I see our lances are but straws:
Our strength as weak, our weakness past compare,
That seeming to be most, which we indeed least are.
Then vail your stomachs, for it is no boot,
And place your hands below your husband's foot,
In token of which duty, if he please,
My hand is ready, may it do him ease.
  (*applause*)

Thomas Thank you, Donna Isabella. It was beautiful.

Shakespeare Thank you, Donna Isabella, from the bottom of my heart. It sounds better than I ever dreamed it might.

Isabella (*approaching*) I hope I did no injustice to it in my reading, Doctor Shakespeare. It is beautifully written. May I copy it out into my book, and keep it?

Shakespeare I will copy it for you.

Francesco (*approaching*) I think that I had better copy it out. I shall learn it, and recite it to Isabella whenever the occasion arises.
     (*laughter*)

Silvia (*approaching*) It was lovely, Signor Guglielmo. It brought tears to my eyes.

Shakespeare Ah, Signorina Silvia, that was the way it was read.

Silvia⎫ No, no, it was beautiful.
Francesco⎬ A charming piece of writing.
Ottavio⎭ Bravo, Guglielmo.

Silvia And it was full of wisdom and good sense, and charming conceits. I would like a copy of it too.

Ottavio I will give it to you as a wedding-present, Silvia.

Orazio I will give it to you well before then, Silvia.

Silvia In that case I shall get Signor Guglielmo to write a riposte to it.

Thomas No. That is the point. There must be *no* riposte to it.
     (*they laugh*)

Pasquati Riposte: a French word. A fine collection of words, Mr Williams. I would like to declaim them myself.

Silvia Giulio . . .

Isabella Let us all go and sit on the balcony. It is not every day that we are in Venice. Come, Doctor Shakespeare. Orazio and Ottavio, bring a few more chairs.

Orazio Yes, Donna Isabella.

Ottavio I'll take this one. How many are we?

Pasquati I have a cold in my left eye. I must be very careful of draughts, very careful indeed. I . . . I . . . what was the *substance* of it all, Mr Williams?

Shakespeare Substance?

Pasquati Of the discourse, the address, the writing that dear Isabella read to us. What did it all mean? (*cheerfully*) And what do I mean when I say 'What did it mean?' What does *anything* mean?

Shakespeare I . . .

251

Pasquati What *is* meaning? Did you write it *by* yourself, or is it from some commonplace book? I remember very well the poem you insisted on reciting to us in Ferrara: a long poem about going to sleep.

Orazio And you went to sleep during it.

Pasquati (*hurt*) But the poem *said*, 'Go to sleep'. I recall it quite distinctly. It began, 'I have no wish to drink just now'. I am very cross with you, Orazio. And you told us all about your native land, Mr Williams. *Flat.*

Shakespeare F-flat?

Pasquati As flat as a halfpenny. Canals, and great windmills, windmills going round and round like this, all through the night, creaking, creaking . . .

Silvia Giulio . . .

Pasquati Creaking, creaking! Holland.

Silvia Signor Guglielmo is an Englishman, Giulio, you know he is.

Pasquati An Englishman?

Shakespeare That, I am afraid, *is* true, Signor Pasquati: I do come from England.

Pasquati (*after a tiny pause*) Oh no, no, no. No. I think you will find it's Holland you come from. (*to himself*) Holland, a nordic land . . .

Isabella Do come and sit here, Doctor Shakespeare.

Pasquati (*to himself*) . . . Surrounded by icebergs.

Francesco Come and watch the gondolas.

Shakespeare Thank you.

Francesco Have you written a great number of these moral essays, Guglielmo?

Isabella Yes, I was about to ask the same. I would like to have a whole book of them to keep by my bedside.

Francesco There are many such subjects you might treat in the same way. And the completed volume could make a whole dignified and well-phrased treatment of all the problems of married life.

Silvia A thing I wanted to ask, if I may, Signor Guglielmo, is why you treated the subject in verse?

Thomas (*disturbed*) But, Silvia, didn't I . . .

Shakespeare Hush, Thomas, hush . . .

Isabella Yes, I wondered that. Though of course the verse was very beautiful, as Virgil is beautiful. 'A woman moved is like a fountain troubled.' But would you not have found greater liberty if you had treated the topic in prose?

Francesco There were several points in it that could have been enlarged on at some length if you had employed prose.

Isabella And prose would have enabled you to include illustrative references and anecdotes from the ancients.

Pasquati The ancients: Aristotle: Julius Caesar. My left eye is terribly painful.

Isabella I know that you won't think what we say is intended as adverse criticism, Signor Guglielmo.

Shakespeare No, certainly not; but I thought Thomas had perhaps explained...

Thomas I am so sorry, Donna Isabella. I thought I had explained. What you have just read is a speech . . . from a play.

(*pause*)

Isabella A *play*?

Shakespeare A comedy. (*pause*) A comic play.

Thomas Which William and I are writing together.

Pasquati A severe inflammation of the left eye. It should be better by about next Tuesday.

(*pause*)

Silvia But how could it come from a *play*?

(*pause*)

Shakespeare Well, it . . . does come from a play.

Isabella (*golden-voiced*) I see, Doctor Shakespeare . . . (*humbly*) Oh, what a foolish, incompetent creature you must think me. Of course it is the heroine's great *tirade*. It should have been delivered dramatically. Where is the copy?

Shakespeare Here it is. But I was perfectly satisfied, Donna Isabella, with the way . . .

Isabella Thomas, you should certainly have told me. Oh, I see it all, I see it, I see it, I see it perfectly. It must be the dramatic speech, at the culmination of a long and arduous interchange, yes, yes, yes. How intolerably stupid of me. (*pause: almost to herself*) I know just what you mean, just what you mean.

Francesco Perhaps you'd like to run through it again, Isabella?

Isabella (*absently*) Hush, my dear. (*to herself, pondering*) Yes, that might be it. Fie, fie . . . Wait a moment . . . (*after a pause: to the others*) Yes, of course. The *points* to be made in the first half are obviously: Fie, fie . . . eyes . . . and whirlwinds. (*to herself*) Whirlwinds might be especially good. One would have to repeat it several times, naturally. It's a good word. (*resolutely*) Yes, of course. (*pause: then suddenly and boldly*) Fie!

    (*pause*)

Fie, fie, fie!

(*rapidly in a low voice*) Unnnnn-knit that threatening unkind brow and dart not.

    (*pause*)

Scornful glances.

    (*pause*)

(*a touch of menace*) from those eyes. To wound thy king thy lord thy governor, fie, fie, fie, fie, fie! I think one's almost bound to bring that in again at that point, don't you? Fie, fie, fie, fie, fie, fie!

    (*brief pause*)

(*sternly*) It blots thy beauty.

As frosts do bite the meads.

(It would be more effective to repeat the word *blots*, I think, rather than say *bite*.)

It blots thy beauty.

As frosts do blot the meads.

Confounds thy fame as:

    (*pause: a virtuoso passage follows*)

Whirlwinds, whirlwinds (whirlwinds?), WHIRLWINDS!

    (*pause*)

(*plaintively*) Shake fair buds. Shake . . . fair . . . buds. (*thoughtfully*) Yes, yes, I see now what you mean.

Silvia   That was splendid.

Ottavio   Excellent.

Orazio   It's wonderful.

Isabella   One could even *sing* some passages . . . Come and see, Silvia darling. It's perfectly simple, and I am so very stupid . . .

Silvia   Yes, that would naturally explain the punctuation.

Francesco   May I look too? Very interesting. Ye-es . . .

Pasquati   The drama. My eye is so painful.

Ottavio   Why are you holding your handkerchief to the wrong one?

Orazio   It is the left one that is inflamed, Giulio.

Pasquati   I don't want to get the good one infected. And I am very cross with you, Orazio. Sleep, indeed!

Isabella   Forgive me. Forgive us all, Signor Guglielmo.

Francesco   We Italians are a very stupid race.

Isabella But, Doctor Shakespeare, though I assure you I'm not being in any way critical, there is a practical difficulty about the ending of the speech: (*reads*)

> And place your hands below your husband's foot:
> In token of which duty, if he please,
> My hand is ready, may it do him ease.

Now you know, an actress would find it very difficult to shout those last three lines as she rushed off the stage.

Shakespeare I ... I hadn't quite ... envisaged her as rushing off the stage at that moment.

Isabella You see, it is very important when writing a long *tirade* of this nature to remember that the last few lines must be so written that they can be *shouted from the wings, after the exit.*

Francesco Of course, if the speech is well delivered, the end should in fact be inaudible in a sudden burst of applause from the spectators. But one can't always take that for granted.

Silvia You could, of course, cut the last three lines.

Isabella Let me see. Yes, yes, yes: and end there. That would be excellent. 'And vail your stomachs, for it is no boot!' That would be a perfect exit-line.

Pasquati (*gloomily: to himself*) Boot. Stomachs.

Francesco And do you seriously intend to try writing for the theatre one day, Guglielmo?

Shakespeare I ... well ...

Thomas I am sure I have explained, Francesco ... and Isabella, that William is already a writer for the theatre, and also an actor in it ...

Shakespeare (*who has, in fact, been enjoying himself*) No, no, please, Thomas, all that is quite unimportant ...

Silvia You are also an actor, Signor Guglielmo, as well as an essayist?

Shakespeare I ... I ... (*helplessly*) Yes, I am.

Ottavio I've told you he is, Silvia.

Silvia But do you mean you have written this speech to be delivered by yourself in some play?

Shakespeare Not exactly, no. Perhaps I had better explain –

Silvia But surely ...

Francesco Dear Guglielmo ...

Isabella How can ... If you are on the stage ...
(*etc.*)

Thomas Do let him speak! (*silence, though not a sudden one*) I did warn

255

you, William, that if you came to Italy, even your flow of words would occasionally find difficulty in making headway.

The Italians (*together, very pleased:*)

Francesco Yes, it's quite true. We all talk too much.

Isabella I love talking.

Orazio Silvia can never stop talking.

Isabella Once I start I want to go on.

Ottavio There is always so much to say.

(*etc.*)

Francesco We must let Guglielmo explain what he was about to explain. We are all listening, Guglielmo.

Shakespeare I . . . I . . .

(*long pause*)

Pasquati A profound silence.

The others (*softly, swishingly*) Hush . . .

Shakespeare It is all very simple. Thomas and I are collaborating in rewriting an old comedy which we hope to give after the plague dies down in London. It is a very crude old play, extremely popular, but utterly lacking in style, or consistency, or anything recognisable as . . . human life. That for us is its attraction. We have deliberately chosen the lowest thing we could find. We wish to bring new life and elegance to it. But since coming to Italy I have been haunted by a fatal defect of the English theatre, which is the limitation placed upon it by the prohibition of women on our stage. Our women's parts are accordingly written with no real thought of womanhood in our minds. Our women will be acted by boys. A further thing that has haunted me has been Thomas's glowing eulogies of Donna Isabella. Even before I met her, it had become a secret longing that my words might one day be spoken by her.

Isabella Ah, signore . . .

Shakespeare I thought that Thomas had explained all this when he gave Donna Isabella that isolated speech and asked her to read it to us.

Francesco
Isabella Ah, yes, yes, yes. That is it.

Thomas In self-defence I must say that I did *try* to explain . . .

Isabella But yes, dear Thomas, I snatched the paper from you and began to read. It is always the same. I cannot resist the sight of poetry, either printed or in the poet's own hand; I have to read it, and all conversation around me sinks into nothingness. You do believe me, dear Guglielmo? Ah, there! I have called you Guglielmo . . .

Shakespeare I do believe you . . . Isabella.
    (*slight laughter*)
Pasquati (*sharply*) Mr Williams!
Shakespeare Giul – Signor Pasquati?
Pasquati (*pained*) Do I understand that the speech you have written will be
    declaimed by a b-hoy?
Shakespeare I am afraid so.
Pasquati (*deeply shocked*) Great God in Heaven!
Orazio Oh don't be silly, Giulio, I acted women's parts in Rome when I
    was a boy. Women aren't allowed to act in any of the Papal States.
Ottavio I once acted women's parts too.
Pasquati Papal States. Mr Williams. When I was a boy of thirteen they
    wanted to do just the same to me. I refused to allow it.
Shakespeare Do what, Pasquati?
Pasquati That operation. It has to be done. Can't manage without.
Shakespeare⎫ Oh, but, I don't think we are thinking . . .
Thomas⎭ No, no, no, Giulio, it isn't what . . .
Pasquati (*ignoring them*) When I was a boy of thirteen, I had a very pure
    voice, very pure indeed. I sang like an angel. (*sings an arpeggio:
    alto*) A-a-a-ah! The priests said to me, 'Wouldn't you like to
    keep that nice voice, Giulio?' 'How?' I said. A-a-a-ah! 'No,' I
    said, 'thank you very much; I wouldn't.' And I didn't. (*bass*)
    A-a-a-ah! (*gravely*) I am very shocked indeed to think that such
    cruel mutilations are still carried out in Holland, Mr Williams.
Shakespeare I think you misunderstood me, Signor Pasquati: we never make
    any efforts to arrest the young lads' natural development. When
    they are old enough, if their talents have not deserted them, they
    begin to take young men's parts.
Pasquati (*alto*) A-a-a-ah! 'No,' I said, 'thank you very much; I wouldn't.'
Orazio And he didn't.
Pasquati I am very cross with you, Orazio.
Ottavio (*bass*) A-a-a-ah!
    (*Orazio and Ottavio laugh*)
Isabella That will do, Ottavio, behave yourself.
Francesco I think I understand perfectly well your aims, Guglielmo; and
    we are all sympathetic to them. But you will realise that – with-
    out any offence – it all seems to us a little, how shall I say – a little
    primitive.
Thomas (*shocked*) Primitive?
Silvia Yes, I thought that.

257   I

Francesco I mean that what you have outlined to us represents the theatre in an early stage of development, a stage it has to outgrow. It is the stage our Italian theatre passed through thirty years ago when an author, an actual writer, in fact, was responsible for the words spoken by the actors.

Isabella It must have been intolerable.

Francesco No one knew any better. And of course, many of those old pieces have survived. They are acted today, and they are often the crude basis in plot and so forth for our own improvisations.

Isabella Though I trust we manage to disguise the fact.

Francesco Of course, the old plays also provide admirable academic exercises with which the young are enabled to learn their trade. It sometimes takes years before an actor can be trusted to go on and make up his own part . . .

Silvia If he is not a creator, of course, he cannot do it at all. In which case he is not an actor, but a mere interpreter of other people's words.

Shakespeare (*baffled*) I . . . see . . .

Pasquati (*alto*) A-a-a-ah!

Thomas But, Silvia, do you never falter? Do you never forget what you must do, or feel at a loss for words?
(*they all laugh*)

Silvia They are laughing at me.

Francesco We usually have to send one of the zanies on to stop Silvia's prolific flow of invention. I don't think I have ever known a member of the *Gelosi* at a loss for words.

Isabella And surely there must be infinitely greater danger if the script is already written and the actor forgets the words?

Shakespeare I would not have thought so. We do have prompters.

Thomas Well, I do remember one remarkable occasion in London. So do you, William. We were acting a comedy of low life in London. During some bustling scene of merriment, our attention was attracted to the gallery at the back of the stage. On to it our leading actor had emerged, his head resplendent with a high-plumed helmet. Under the impression that we were enacting a classical tragedy, he began to declaim a long monologue announcing the death of Hector.

Shakespeare (*sadly*) Yes. It began with the words:
> Women of Troy, deck Ilium's towers with black!
> Women of Troy, alack, alack, alack!

Pasquati (*suddenly and loudly*) But, oh, what a lovely piece of poetry! Do say it again. Women of Troy . . .

Shakespeare   *Deck Ilium's towers with black!*
           Women of Troy, alack, alack, alack!

Pasquati Isn't that lovely? Isn't it lovely, Isabella? Is that from the epic you are writing, Mr Williams? Well done! And, oh dear, oh dear, it has begun to make my poor eye feel distinctly better. What wonderful power this Dutch poetry has.

Francesco Thomas's story illustrates what we have been saying. The theatre in your stage of development, Guglielmo, must necessarily be precarious . . . the work of enterprising dilettanti. Splendid and courageous, of course, in its way, but . . .

Isabella I see you are looking rather downcast, Guglielmo.

Shakespeare Oh, no, no, my dear . . . I shall think very carefully over all you have told us, Donna Isabella.

Francesco And remain profoundly unconvinced.

Shakespeare No, no, no.

Francesco It is very difficult to shake an Englishman's convictions.

Shakespeare No, no, you have deeply shaken them already. When I see you again tomorrow acting Captain Spavento at the theatre you will shake them further. When I see you next week in Mantua you will shake them again. By the time I am back in England I shall have no convictions left.

Silvia Signor Guglielmo, you are laughing at us.

Thomas No, he is not!
Shakespeare No, no, no!

Isabella Guglielmo, it is very easy, I know, for English travellers to think that our comedy is artificial and exaggerated, that my husband's Captain Spavento, for example, is only a ridiculous artificiality, because it makes you all laugh so much. But do you think it is founded on nothing? That it is merely a vast blowing-up of the old braggart soldier?

Shakespeare No, Isabella, I know it is far more than that.

Isabella Everybody laughs when Francesco rants about the base Phrygian Turks and the anthropophagi, and all the slaughterous deeds he has done . . .

Francesco Hush, my dear, it is only meant to be funny . . .

Isabella But Francesco *knows* about those things. He fought against the Turks as a child, as a soldier in the Tuscan galleys; he was taken into slavery by them and sold to whoever asked for him. Ask him one day to tell you how he escaped from the Turks after eight years of cruel and ignominious suffering.

Francesco Isabella . . .

Isabella He would talk about those things for hours on end, seriously and truthfully, long before the idea of making fun of them on the stage occurred to him. You see only what he has made of them, something to laugh at. I laugh too, but I also see buried beneath it, beneath all the rant and the fantasy, the young man who made me fall in love with him as he told me of them.

Francesco I was only trying them out on you, my darling, to see if they went down well.

(*the others laugh*)

Isabella Ah, you are taking Guglielmo's side!

Shakespeare Then I shall desert him and come over to yours, Isabella.

Isabella Let me see if I can put everything into its place. You and Thomas are writing plays. And some time or other, without doubt, plays have to be written. Otherwise it is just possible there might be no theatre. Now, dear Guglielmo, do not be discouraged. What you are doing is splendid pioneer work. Be content to regard it as that. It will be the better for it. I think I must have read or seen every play that has ever been written. These plays are often carefully composed, and are full of good feeling and observation; the plot and the intrigue are finely phrased, the jokes are well placed – but what is missing?

Pasquati The epic touch! Women of Troy, alack, alack, alack!

Isabella What is missing, Guglielmo, is *something to act.* The characters whom the author invents are often no more exceptional than the people one meets in life itself. And that is fatal. Think of those of our dramatists who used to be famous for their fidelity to nature in drawing people of humble life, who could draw a faithful servant with every pathetic trait perfectly observed. But what do they offer the actor? I have known a grocer who could imitate to perfection the walk and talk of the parish priest; he would have been the perfect actor for such drama. But where could there possibly be any delight for a *real* actor in that? Where would be the creation in the actor's life? It would have been usurped by the writer. Do not ever give in to the temptation of believing that *the play itself* is of major importance, dear Guglielmo, or you will be lost.

Francesco The theatre, after all, is not in any way the province of the serious writer.

(*pause*)

Silvia (*sympathetically*) Have you never thought of trying your hand at any other form of literary activity, Guglielmo?

Thomas Of course he has. There is his magnificent epic on the Siege of Troy we are all waiting for.

Isabella Ah, now that would be worthwhile!

Francesco That would be splendid. You are writing an epic, Guglielmo?

Shakespeare I am not exactly writing it . . . though a little of it is written. But I am hoping, here in Italy, to . . . begin it.

Ottavio 'Any minute now.'

Shakespeare (*laughs*) 'Any minute now.'

Silvia⎫ Splendid.
Francesco⎭ Excellent.

Isabella That indeed is news worth hearing, Guglielmo. It shows you are a writer with a purpose. Because surely you cannot seriously imagine anyone writing a *play* of any importance in itself. How petty the old-fashioned little comedies of Ariosto are, beside his *Orlando*! Can one even imagine a writer who could compose a play and make it fit to put beside Tasso's *Jerusalem*, or Dante's *Divine Comedy*? I would walk barefoot to Jerusalem to meet such a man. Ah, find me a dramatist whose words and people are comparable with *theirs*, and I will unlearn all I have ever learnt, and learn again from the beginning – on my hands and knees, in prayer and fasting, dear Guglielmo. But can you imagine a 'dramatist' who could stand beside Dante?

Shakespeare No, I cannot.

Isabella Can you, Thomas?

(*pause*)

Thomas I will answer that question in a written communication, dear Isabella.

(*they all laugh affectionately at him*)

Isabella Thomas is the perfect Englishman. He makes a joke of everything.

Shakespeare I am afraid he does. Thomas, behave yourself.

Isabella He is young and frivolous. You must teach him to be serious.

Silvia Only don't make him too serious. That would spoil him.

Pasquati Phlegm. The English phlegm. And what is underneath it? The English sense of humour. It makes one's flesh creep.

(*several of them laugh*)

Francesco I think we have all talked enough. Let us recover ourselves by watching the gondolas for five whole minutes in absolute silence.

Shakespeare Silence. Here we sit, and I watch them. Francesco leans on the balcony, noble head bent to the contemplation of the water. Isabella watches a gondola cross the canal below us; as it reaches the palace steps opposite, she smiles a little as though at the solution of some simple problem. The dark heads of Orazio and Ottavio are close together, pondering my manuscript. Ottavio looks briefly down towards the lagoon as a thought strikes him. His gaze falls again to my words, on one of which Orazio lays a questioning finger. Silvia regards the intriguers painted on her fan. And dear old Giulio seems offended that with his good eye he is unable to see how his bad one is looking.

What things might I not make with them, these glittering people, who have carried artistry to the point where it has killed the art that gave it birth? What other things, in a proper place, might I not make of what they have built on that destruction, and of the separate images each has so curiously chosen to make of himself? . . . Oh, Italy, sweet land, where every gesture and every tone of the voice have that in them which strokes the heart and sets itself forever in the recollection, your gestures and voices have done such delectable murder here . . . And Isabella suddenly said she would unlearn all she had learnt . . . if she saw cause . . . Good God, there could be cause enough, if one were free to work, ardently, laboriously, cunningly, perséverantly, at *that!* If one could only . . . but no, no, no, my ardour, my labour, my cunning and my perséverance, such as they are, shall be for Troy . . . and Troy only.

(*pause*)

Narrator Gonzaga is the Duke's name. Here is Mantua, islanded upon her lake. The waters running round her walls, and the boats sliding smoothly on the lakes, smooth-sliding up the Mincio from the Po, bearing riches, bearing homage, bearing exiles to the dusky streets, bearing rare Italian masters to the tawny palaces. Gonzaga is the Duke's name, a true friend of the theatre, a good master to the Italian masters. It is Mantua, where at sunset a stifling air steals into the palace and loiters against the walls, against the cool faces of the Duke's ancestors, painted there by the precise hand of Mantegna ...

(*thunder*)

And in a distant room, another stifling air caresses the passionate coarse paint of Giulio Romano: the walls of Troy, and a hundred torn bodies blazing with scarlet blood, under the chariots and the rearing chargers; Sinon, and the scaffolded, expectant horse; lascivious Helen slipping into the waiting boat; Laocoön and his well-serpented sons. Achilles, Hector, Priam, Andromache, Hecuba.

(*murmur of conversation. Occasional notes of musical instruments*)

Isabella Ah, Guglielmo, what a comfort to have you here. And isn't it wonderful to have the Trojan room for a green-room?

Shakespeare (*with some reserve*) Yes. It is beautiful.

Isabella And the Siege of Troy all over the walls, specially for you.

Shakespeare Yes.

Thomas It is destiny, you see, Will. Destiny.

Isabella You are coming in to the comedy? We begin in five minutes.

Shakespeare Yes, certainly.

Isabella Did you hear them practising the thunder for the shipwreck?

Shakespeare I thought it was real thunder.

Isabella (*laughs*) Oh, no ...

Francesco Isn't it disappointing that we shan't have Duke Vincenzo with us? We had so much looked forward to it.

Shakespeare Where is he?

Isabella Who knows? You can never depend on Vincenzo. He is always disappearing to Innsbruck, or Rome, or Vienna: so mysterious, so unpredictable ...

Silvia I have only ever seen him once.

Ottavio I've *never* seen him.

Pasquati I know the dear Duke intimately. (Though what do we mean by intimacy? Who can say?) He once helped me to cure a little fluid on the right knee. *This* knee.

Shakespeare (*mildly*) He once murdered a young countryman of mine in the streets of this city.

Isabella Ah, you must not hold that against him. It was long ago.

Shakespeare I don't. But I am rather relieved that I shall not have to meet him.

Isabella But you and Vincenzo would like each other. He is a great patron of poets. He would be interested in your work.

    Pasquati It was *this* knee. Just here. Acute discomfort it caused me.

    Orazio (*from the door*) Five minutes!

    Francesco Come, everyone.

          (*the buzz of conversation rises and falls as the actors go out. Remarks heard:*)

    Silvia I hope those rocks are safe.

    Francesco I don't want you to come on until I go down on to one knee.

    Pasquati My voice is giving way, if it's of any interest to anyone . . .

    Ottavio Orazio, when I trip you up, after Isabella's exit . . .

          (*etc.*)

          (*long fade on this conversation*)

    Shakespeare (*alone*) And they leave me with the Troy of Giulio Romano! So that I, who for ten years have dreamt of my own Troy, of my Achilles, my Hector, my Andromache, may twitch in envy at another's, done in paint, sprawling triumphantly over four walls and a ceiling; that the shouting colours may mock me with their fixed and confident accomplishment, may laugh at my emptied skull, and deride my inoperant talent which can neither begin a new thing nor end an old one . . .

          (*pause*)

    This room is haunted. Here in this very room Tasso must have stood, whom three years ago I could have met here, exiled within these walls. No, I forget, it was not exile, it was refuge, refuge, where the shouting walls mocked him as they mock me. Oh, Tasso, Torquato, what did you think, when you wandered in here, destitute of power, desolate and lonely, watched on all sides, in a corrupted castle, a prince disinherited of your gift, incapable of action, a book forever in your hand, reading the words of others, words, words, words, wandering in bereavement through the halls of smiling murderers . . . ? At least I escape *those* . . .

          (*Vincenzo speaks from the other end of the room. His voice should at first have a slight echo. Shakespeare is irritated at the interruption*)

    Vincenzo What are you doing in here?

    Shakespeare I beg your pardon?

    Vincenzo What are you doing in here?

    Shakespeare If it comes to that, what are you?

    Vincenzo I said what are you doing in this room?

Shakespeare I asked you the same.
Vincenzo Is it your business to ask me questions?
Shakespeare I hope not. Is it yours to ask me?
Vincenzo If I choose to.
Shakespeare Indeed! Who are you?
Vincenzo Never mind who I am. Who are you?
Shakespeare I am very cautious about revealing my identity, as are you, apparently.
Vincenzo You choose to be impudent.
Shakespeare I try to fit my manners to my company.
Vincenzo You mean *I* am impudent?
Shakespeare It was your word: not mine. Discourteous, shall we say, and let it rest at that? In any case, I know who you are.
Vincenzo Oh, do you?
Shakespeare One of the palace guards, sent to see that I don't run off with the actors' belongings. I am perfectly safe.
Vincenzo Are you English?
Shakespeare Does it matter?
Vincenzo Not in the least.
Shakespeare Good.
Vincenzo Why are you not at the play?
Shakespeare Because I am in here.
Vincenzo The entertainments of Mantua are not good enough for you, I suppose?
Shakespeare Are they good enough for you?
Vincenzo I asked *you*.
Shakespeare Have you seen this piece before?
Vincenzo Have you?
Shakespeare Several times. Or others like it.
Vincenzo Well?
Shakespeare Do you know what happens in it?
Vincenzo What?
Shakespeare A shipwreck, complete with ship, sea, thunder, and lightning; sailors and lordlings cast up on a magic island; a magician ruling it; a satyr attempting to rape the magician's daughter; a disguised prince falling in love with her; three drunken clowns trying to steal the magician's book and rod; and in case this should not be enough, a pretty little echo scene, and a disappearing banquet. Did you ever in your life hear of such . . . *trash?*
Vincenzo Trash?

Shakespeare Oh, for God's sake, sit down, man, and stop talking.
    (*pause*)
Vincenzo Thank you.
    (*pause*)
Shakespeare Do you come from Mantua?
Vincenzo Yes. I was born here.
Shakespeare Have you spent all your life here?
Vincenzo Not all. Most of it.
Shakespeare Are you contented here?
Vincenzo I can put up with it.
Shakespeare Do you never find the air of the place . . . oppressive?
Vincenzo The breezes from off the marshes, you mean? I think people make too much of them. I'm a military man, of course. Such things don't trouble me.
Shakespeare Oh, not only that . . . The air that seems to breathe through this palace, I mean.
Vincenzo Why, what's wrong with that?
Shakespeare (*absently*) Ah, of course, if you are used to it, I suppose . . .
Vincenzo But what's wrong about it?
Shakespeare The air seems dense with . . . quiet corruption.
Vincenzo I don't think I follow you.
Shakespeare (*after a very brief pause*) Are the Gonzagas popular down in the town? (*pause*) The . . . lords of the place. The dukes. (*pause*) Are they?
Vincenzo I was just considering. Yes, I would say they were very popular.
Shakespeare Even the present Duke?
Vincenzo Vincenzo . . . ?
Shakespeare Yes.
Vincenzo (*thoughtfully*) I don't think many people hold much grudge against him. He's no better than he ought to be, I suppose.
Shakespeare (*slowly*) The present Duke, Vincenzo Gonzaga, ran a rapier through a young Scotchman in this city some years ago, in a carefully-planned nocturnal encounter.
Vincenzo People still talk about that in England, do they?
Shakespeare Here also. They refer to him as the admirable Critonio. His real name was Crichton.
Vincenzo I rather fancy there were two sides to that murder.
Shakespeare There are to most murders. Crichton's was the unsurviving one.
Vincenzo What else have you heard?
    (*thunder in the distance, and out*)

266

Shakespeare And last May, Rodolfo Gonzaga got rid of his uncle at Castel-
goffredo by the novel expedient of pouring poison into his ear
while he slept.

Vincenzo Ah, now, that is not quite right. He didn't do it himself. He got his
barber to do it. I used to know him – the barber, I mean. He came
from Mantua.

Shakespeare (*a little apprehensively*) Is he still here?

Vincenzo (*lightly*) Oh, no, he was torn to pieces in the streets. You seem to
be a close student of local history. Have you been here long?

Shakespeare Not long. I came with the actors from Venice.

Vincenzo You don't seem to think very well of them.

Shakespeare On the contrary, I am dazzled by them.

Vincenzo Then what's the matter?

Shakespeare The matter?

Vincenzo Are you ill?

Shakespeare You might call it ill.

Vincenzo What's the trouble?

Shakespeare Impotence.

Vincenzo (*suddenly sympathetic*) Oh, now, that's very bad, really bad. I'm
very sorry to hear that. No wonder you were looking rather
down. I wonder if you've tried . . .

Shakespeare Mental impotence, man. Not the other kind.
   (*pause*)

Vincenzo Oh . . . you must be a writer, I gather?

Shakespeare Yes.

Vincenzo And you find you can't work.

Shakespeare Yes.

Vincenzo What is it you can't do?

Shakespeare (*a little amused*) Would you really like to know?

Vincenzo Yes. I have a few minutes to spare.

Shakespeare Thank you. For the last ten years, I have been planning an epic
poem, of some ten or fifteen thousand lines, on the subject which
you see so vividly depicted on the walls around us – the Siege of
Troy. I have often begun it, or thought I had begun it; I have even
written short fragments of it here and there. I have never been
free to keep at it for very long; my professional duties as an actor
and purveyor of written entertainments and other things have
occupied my time and often exhausted me. In a week's time I shall
be thirty; at some time during every day, every single day that
passes, it comes into my mind, and says, 'I am the Siege of Troy.

You have still not written me.' This has gone on so long that it is no longer the idea of writing it that ravishes me, but the thought of its being finished and done with. It has already turned a good deal of my life to frustration and emptiness . . . Do you understand?

Vincenzo *(after thought)* Yes.

Shakespeare Well?

(long pause)

Vincenzo *(quietly)* Well, I should give it up.

Shakespeare You see, it is not as if . . .
    (another pause)
    You would *what?*

Vincenzo Give it up. That's what I should do. I should give it up.

Shakespeare Give it up?

Vincenzo Yes. If it's so extremely difficult, it can't be worth it. If *I* can't do a thing, I find after a time it isn't meant for me, and I give it up, and do something else instead. The trouble with you fellows is you take no exercise.

Shakespeare How ridiculous. Give it up, indeed!

Vincenzo Well, that's my advice, for what it's worth. Give it up. Isn't there anything else you want to do?

Shakespeare Hundreds of things.

Vincenzo Which you can't do because the Siege of Troy stands in the way?

Shakespeare Yes.

Vincenzo Well, push it out of the way. Do something else. Try something shorter. Does it have to be all that length?

Shakespeare My good man, *all* epics are long. How can one throw away ten years' thought just like that?

Vincenzo Better than having to throw away fifteen in five years' time: which you *would* be doing, I take leave to think, unless one of these Italian dukes ran you through before. Abandon it. And a year from now you'll scarcely think about it. Ten years from now you'll roar with laughter at the very thought of the Siege of Troy.

Shakespeare *(coldly)* The Siege of Troy is not a theme for mirth. And if I did give it up, where do you suppose I would be tomorrow?

Vincenzo *(thoughtfully, after a pause)* I tell you what: why not write a *little* epic?

Shakespeare A what?

Vincenzo A *little* piece about the siege of Troy. Just to satisfy your conscience. Just give yourself, say, one solid afternoon's work on it,
and after that give it up for good. In any case, I'm sure people
will be far readier to read fifty lines about the Siege of Troy than
they will fifteen thousand. I know I would.

Shakespeare (*patiently*) And what do you suppose I should do with my fifty
lines of unparalleled concentration on this far from minor topic,
may I ask?

Vincenzo Oh, it would always come in useful.

Shakespeare Perhaps you could advise me further, and tell me how to set
about this little half-holiday task?

Vincenzo Well, it's not for me to say. I'm not a writing man myself.
Personally, I should just go very carefully round these walls with
a piece of paper and pencil, and describe these paintings. When
I'd done that I should stop. You needn't show it to anybody,
after all.

Shakespeare I assure you I should be much disinclined to.

Vincenzo I don't see why you should be so sarcastic. You asked for my
advice, and I gave it. You can't say it wasn't well-meant. I was
only doing my very best to try and help you . . .

Shakespeare (*distressed*) Oh, please, please, please, do forgive me, my dear good
fellow – what-did-you-say-your-name-was?

Vincenzo Vincenzo.

Shakespeare Vincenzo, yes. Please don't think I'm ungrateful; it's simply that
I'm in a distracted mood, and hardly fit to address a decent
person . . .

Vincenzo Oh, never you mind about that, Signor – I-didn't-quite-catch-
the-name?

Shakespeare (*a little absently*) Shakespeare. But everyone calls me Guglielmo.

Vincenzo The same name as the Duke's late father.

Shakespeare Yes, yes, indeed. (*without thought*) And yours is Vincenzo, the
same as the Duke himself. Life is full of these little coincidences,
my dear Vincenzo, full of them.

Vincenzo (*politely*) I don't know where we should be without them. And
now I must be off.

Shakespeare Look, Vincenzo, don't be offended with me. I would be so
grateful if you would accept this little gift . . .
 (*clink of coins*)

Vincenzo Oh, no, I couldn't . . . well, thank you, Guglielmo.

Shakespeare Good night, Vincenzo.

Vincenzo Good night.
Shakespeare Good night.
　　　　(*door*)

Great Heaven, what a country!...(*in satirical fascination*) 'Give
it up'...'Write a *little* epic'...'Just go very carefully round
these walls with a piece of paper and pencil and say what's here'
...'It would always come in useful'...'One solid afternoon's
work, and after that, give it...'
　　　　(*long pause*)
(*an amazed whisper*) And I could. (*pause*) I could. I could (*smiles*)
give it up. How simple that would be. And how simple my life
would be. I could...I should be able to...How simple life
would be. How very free; simple and free...and happy.
Happy. (*pause*) And I will. Even though it kills me...And it will
not kill me...Waking tomorrow...no Siege of Troy. And the
next day, and the next. And then. Yes, then. There will be Italy.
And there will be England again. And Venice and Padua and
Verona and Mantua will not be with me. And yes, and yes, I
know that then they will cease to be silent. They will open their
mouths and speak to me when I am gone, when I have left them,
and I shall know what they say: when the fore-looking images I
once had of them and cannot now recall, and the backward
glances I cannot yet bestow...have met and coupled...behind
my back...without my asking. Patience, oh God. And no Siege
of Troy. Not even the *little* epic. (*he giggles*) 'But personally I
would take a piece of paper and pencil, and go *very* caref...'
(*quietly*) God bless my soul. Why not? Of course. Why did I
never think? (*rapidly*) Carefully round the walls, with Giulio
Romano. 'To this well-painted piece has Lucrece come.' A little
epic for my poor Lucretia. (*a long, happy and increasing laugh, and
he begins to sing gaily*) 'Oh, Teresa, oh, Teresa, oh, what a girl is
she. She'll do whatever you ask her to, for you...'
　　　　(*the door opens and the noise of the crowd swells. The actors enter.
　　　　Confusion and merriment, against which the following lines are very
　　　　distinctly heard*)

Thomas William, where have you been? What are you doing in here?
Shakespeare What's the matter? Hasn't the play begun yet?
Thomas (*approaching*) No, the Duke Vincenzo has come home!

270

Shakespeare Has he? I'm so glad – they all seemed so disapp . . . *Who* has come home?

Isabella (*approaching*) Our dear Duke Vincenzo's here. He has returned unexpectedly from Vienna. We have delayed the opening for half an hour at his request.

Silvia (*approaching*) Isn't it wonderful, Guglielmo? The Duke has returned. Oh, how exciting!

Isabella Our visit has not been wasted. Isn't it delightful?

Shakespeare D-delightful. Yes.

Pasquati Delightful isn't the word. What *is* the word? The dear Duke, an intimate friend of mine, Mr Williams. Such an expert on medicines. As good as those lovely lines of yours: Women of Troy, deck Ilium's towers with black!

Shakespeare (*mechanically*) Women of Troy, alack, alack, alack!

Francesco Don't look so dazed, Guglielmo. Have you been overworking?

Shakespeare No, not exactly.

Francesco Good.

Shakespeare (*suddenly*) Thomas . . .

Thomas Yes, dear Will?

Shakespeare Thomas, (*with genuine curiosity*) have you ever *given a duke a tip?*

Thomas No. Have you?

Shakespeare (*laughs*)

Isabella Guglielmo, what are you laughing about?

Shakespeare Isabella, five minutes ago, in this very room . . .

Ottavio (*calls*) The Duke is coming! He's coming in here, to see us, before the play!

(*evvivas have begun in the outer room. They increase*)

Isabella My hair! My dress! Silvia!

Silvia My dress! My head-dress! Ottavio!

Thomas William, what is the matter? I've never seen you look so happy.

Shakespeare Thomas, dear transcendent child of the morning, if I get through the next five minutes alive, I shall be the happiest man on earth!

Full cast (*the shouts of welcome have grown, as the Duke enters*) Evviva, Vincenzo! Evviva Vincenzo! Vincenzo! Vincenzo! Vincenzo! Evviva! Evviva! Evviva!

Vincenzo

To Douglas and Nest Cleverdon

Vincenzo was first broadcast on 29 March 1955, with the following cast:

IPPOLITA	*Rachel Gurney*
BARBARA SANSEVERINO	*Margaretta Scott*
ELENA	*Molly Lawson*
VINCENZO GONZAGA	*Hugh Burden*
THE DUKE OF MANTUA	*Newton Blick*
THE DUCHESS OF MANTUA	*Mary O'Farrell*
MARCELLO DONATI	*Robert Marsden*
MARGHERITA FARNESE	*Gwen Cherrell*
RANUCCIO FARNESE (as a boy)	*Glyn Dearman*
RANUCCIO FARNESE (as a man)	*Derek Hart*
OLIVO	*Neville Hartley*
CARLO BORROMEO	*Carleton Hobbs*
FRANCESCO DE' MEDICI	*Norman Shelley*
BIANCA CAPPELLO	*Gladys Young*
A FLORENTINE MOTHER	*Cecile Chevreau*
ELEONORA DE' MEDICI	*Barbara Lott*
SILVIO	*Denise Bryer*
AGNESE DEL CARRETTO	*Barbara Couper*
ADRIANA BASILE	*Marjorie Westbury*
GIANFRANCESCO SANVITALE	*Frank Duncan*

The date: 1580 to 1612

This production was by Douglas Cleverdon. The music was arranged and conducted by Denis Stevens from the work of Mantuan composers of the period. The performers were:

April Cantelo (soprano)
Desmond Dupré (lute)
Charles Sparks (harpsichord and organ)
The Ambrosian Singers
An instrumental ensemble led by Neville Marriner

(In the gardens of Colorno, three young women are singing an impassioned canzonetta)

Ippolita The place: I remember it: it was Colorno, halfway between Mantua and Parma: the rose-gardens: the rose-gardens of the palace of Barbara Sanseverino, the Countess of Sala. And the year was fifteen hundred and eighty.

(during the latter part of the song, a loud sob has been heard)

Barbara Hush, Elena.

Elena (another, louder sob)

Barbara Elena!

Elena (after only a slight effort at control, wails) No, no! Tell them to stop!

Barbara (sharply) Elena!

Elena (weeping) I can't bear it, I can't bear it! Stop! Stop, I tell you, you horrid heartless creatures! I can't bear it . . .

(the singers, who have gone on unconcerned hitherto, break raggedly off. They are heard murmuring: 'What ever is the matter? What offensive behaviour! How very ill-bred.' etc.)

Elena I can't bear it! Tell them to go away. Oh, heaven help me!

(lark heard in distance)

Barbara (quietly, after a pause) My dears, will you very kindly take your music and sing it to us from behind the further box-hedge, down the steps? We will rejoin you in a few minutes. Are you going also, Ippolita?

(brief pause)

Ippolita No. No, I think I shall stay.

Barbara (sharply) Now: Elena?

Elena I shall never survive it, never, never. Oh, *why* has he gone away? Why has he left me? Why has he gone off with Giulia? Why hasn't he come back? Why does he make me suffer like this? What has happened to everything? Why can't we be happy together as we used to be? Oh . . .

Barbara (after a pause) Do you wish me to answer those questions in the order in which you have asked them? Or am I to use my discretion, and select a few here and –

Elena (violently) What is it that has put an end to our happiness? Why can't he come back, and take me in his arms again?

Barbara Well, perhaps he will, dear, if you are patient, and a trifle more

275

composed in demeanour. He lays great store by that in his . . . friendships. Doesn't he, Ippolita?

Ippolita I have frequently heard him say so: in those very words.

Elena You hold your tongue!

Barbara Elena!

Ippolita I beg your pardon!

Elena I won't be spoken to by you, you adulterous strumpet!

Barbara Elena, I have told you before that I will not have my guests refer to each other in such terms.

Elena How else should they refer to each other? (*in renewed grief*) Oh, and to think he's run off with Giulia! My best friend!

Barbara Well, you must be glad it is not with one of your enemies. You would find that much harder to bear. And I hope you and Giulia will *remain* friends.

Elena Never! Never!

Ippolita Elena: let me set your mind at rest. He has not gone away with Giulia.

Elena N-not . . . ?

Ippolita Certainly he has not.

Barbara There.

Elena Oh, *why* didn't you tell me this before? Why have you let me go on suffering like this? Oh, how unjust I have been! To everyone. Please, please forgive me, both of you, oh please . . .

(*polite parenthetic murmurs from the others*)

He told me he would never leave me. I ought to have known.

Ippolita You ought indeed. (*pause*) It is Isabella he has run off with. If you insist on the expression.

Elena Isab . . . ! No! No! No! I shall go mad!

Barbara No one goes mad, Elena. Not quite mad. Ever.

Elena Oh, God! To think . . . Isabella! He . . . may even be . . . *with her*, at this very moment.

Barbara Not at five o'clock in the afternoon, I imagine, dear. If I understand you aright.

Ippolita (*murmur*) Oh yes, sometimes.

Barbara (*murmur*) Indeed?

Ippolita (*murmur*) Occasionally.

Barbara (*murmur*) Well well: I never knew.

Ippolita (*murmur*) Oh yes.

Elena (*loudly, on a sob*) Sunlight . . .

Barbara Yes, Elena?

Elena . . . Sunlight used to stream from his breast.

Barbara It does from many gentlemen's breasts, dear. That is why the world is such a bright place. And I scarcely think you should make such detailed observations in front of Ippolita.

Elena Ippolita? She's shameless.

Ippolita Yes, Elena, I am shameless. So now we have two things in common.

Elena Never mind. I shall triumph over all of you.

Barbara I hope so, my sweet. In what way?

Elena I shall have his child.

Barbara (*sharply*) Elena!

Elena I shall have his child. I know I shall. Something of him will be mine forever. I shall triumph.

Barbara (*coolly*) Well, if you call that triumph . . . Ippolita is in the same condition. Do you feel triumphant, Ippolita?

Elena (*horrified*) Ippolita isn't . . . ! (*she breaks off, as she realises that Ippolita, in fact, is*) Oh, oh, oh! This place is nothing but a filthy brothel!

Barbara Well, you appear to have found your way about in it.

Elena I'll run away. I'll wait till he comes back, and then I'll run away! And I won't *let* them sing like that when I'm so unhappy!

    (*beginning to run away down the garden*)

I'll tear their eyes out! Stop that singing! Stop it, I tell you, you cruel baggages . . .

    (*she is out of hearing. A brief silence*)

Barbara (*calmly*) I abominate this particular aspect of passion. (*sighs*) I'm sorry, Ippolita, my dearest. I hope she hasn't distressed you?

Ippolita Not at all.

Barbara And she cannot possibly know about a baby yet, the idea!

Ippolita I shall not mind, even if it is so.

Barbara Truly?

Ippolita Truly.

Barbara Oh, Ippolita, my jewel, how well you behave. That's why he loves you.

Ippolita Yes.

Barbara Oh, I do not mean for that alone. And I love you too. You are lovely, and I love you, and everyone will always love you. And I must run after that little trollop and see that she does no damage to the pictures. It has happened before now. They go straight for the St Sebastian. I will come back. Or will you come with me?

Ippolita No, Barbara dear. I would not be much help. I will stay and look at the roses.

Barbara Bless you, my darling. You are like a rose yourself.

(*she goes*)

(*a distant, single lark is occasionally heard during Ippolita's meditation*)

Ippolita So I stayed and looked at the roses and was like a rose myself. Oh, roses; roses of Colorno. In the windless summer air, millions of them, calm and unshaken. And in the distance, blooming beyond the roses, the road and the river to Mantua ... Mantua: Mantua, his city ... Poor Elena. It was then, with the soft full blooms of yellow and red about me, as I cupped my hands gently over this one or that, that I knew how many kinds of jealousy can be felt at one and the same time ... How often? Where? And what had he called her? He never believed in real names; we were unreal to him until he had found his own names for us. Me, he called Andromeda. (If I could only mislay jealousy, if I could lose mistrust ...) It was silent in those labyrinths of roses, save for a single lark, high and far away ... And what miles of green to the horizon! And the hills and the castles on them! And the roads: that way to Mantua, where perhaps I would never go; that other way to Reggio and my husband and children, where I would go again so soon; that way to Florence, where *he* would go, to marry his chosen bride. He said 'I will always come back, Andromeda, I will always come back.' Oh, roses of Colorno, million-petalled. The roads, and the wayside inns, slumbering in the heat. And now, in one of them ... which way? That way, towards Parma? That way, towards ...

Vincenzo Andromeda.

Ippolita (*on an intake of breath*) Vincenzo.

Vincenzo Andromeda.

Ippolita And it was he ... There, preposterously, he stood between two of the great rose-trees, unsmiling. He had taken off his shirt because of the heat, and held it in one hand, dragging on the grass. (They should not appear so before us, even when they are not yet men; and he was not quite nineteen.)

Vincenzo Andromeda.

Ippolita On his white breast – oh, Elena! – a gold medallion caught the

sun, and (*a remote trace of tears in her voice*) lost it as he came towards
me, arms outstretched.

Vincenzo (*as they embrace*) Andromeda . . .

Ippolita You frightened me, my loved one.

Vincenzo Good.

Ippolita Where have you come from?

Vincenzo Only across the river. I went to Viadana.

Ippolita Have they any better news for you?

Vincenzo No. My father has still sent no money. All the servants are
grumbling. I've already borrowed all they have, poor devils. He
probably suspects I am here.

Ippolita I hope not.

Vincenzo Oh, my father doesn't know about you. It's our dear hostess
he fears. He thinks Barbara's a witch, the evil eye, the great
seduceress. (*tonelessly*) I would like to kill someone. Quietly. Like
that. Now.

Ippolita Why, my love?

Vincenzo Well, I never have, have I, so far? And to make him notice me.
To scandalise dull Mantua; and to make him treat me as a prince,
not as a schoolboy. And, oh-God-above, to make him give me
some more money, if only to keep me quiet. Which it might do,
after all. Come and sit on the grass.

(*brief pause*)

Ippolita Vincenzo.

Vincenzo M'm?

Ippolita Elena says she's expecting a baby.

Vincenzo (*absently*) Is she? Well, she should know, presumably.

Ippolita Darling. You are being disingenuous.

Vincenzo About what?

Ippolita Look at me, darling.

Vincenzo You dazzle sight, my Andromeda. Well?

Ippolita Elena said, here, a few minutes ago: 'I shall have his child.'
Meaning yours.

Vincenzo (*laughs lightly*) She must be confusing me with someone else.
These easy-going times. Which *is* Elena? Aren't there several of
them?

Ippolita The one you danced with last night.

Vincenzo (*reflects*) Oh, yes. Elena. The girl with the bosom. Is that the
one?

Ippolita (*modestly*) Dearest, we all have bosoms.

Vincenzo Yes, but you do cover them up on public occasions, most of you. Is that the one?

Ippolita (*laughs*) Yes. Do you mean it's not true?

Vincenzo What? Of course it's not true. Look at me. Don't you believe me?

Ippolita Yes.

Vincenzo Would you like it to be true?

Ippolita *No!*

Vincenzo Would you be jealous?

Ippolita I . . . hope not, Vincenzo. I don't think so.

Vincenzo You callous girl, so wicked.

Ippolita I love you beyond jealousy.

Vincenzo That is too far.

Ippolita I love you farther than that.

Vincenzo (*flatly*) I want to make love to you.

Ippolita I love you from here to Parma.

Vincenzo I love you from here to Mantua. I want to make love to you.

Ippolita No. I love you from here to Padua.

Vincenzo I love you from here to Florence. I want to make . . .

Ippolita *Not* Florence.

Vincenzo Why not Florence? I love *you* from . . .

Ippolita You know why not Florence.

Vincenzo I do not. Why?

      (*pause*)

Ippolita (*pretending to sulk*) Eleonora de' Medici.

Vincenzo (*laughs: then says*) Eleonora de' Medici is no more, Andromeda.

Ippolita Do you mean she is dead?

Vincenzo I mean she is no more to me, to us, to them. They have broken it off.

Ippolita The Medici?

Vincenzo The Medici be damned! How you all worship them. No, respected madama, my papa, the Gonzaga himself, third Duke of Mantua, second Marquis of Monferrato, master of Castiglione, Marmirolo, Goito, Viadana, San Benedetto Po, Solferino and those-two-other-little-places-I-forget-the-names-of . . . has ruptured the negotiations for wedlock. I am still unbetrothed. And I want to make love to you.

Ippolita But what has happened?

Vincenzo And if I were betrothed to the pope's daughter herself, I would still want to make . . .

280

Ippolita (*protesting happily*) But, Vincenzo, please tell me . . .
Vincenzo Not . . . un . . . less.
Ippolita (*softer*) No, no . . .
Vincenzo (*softer*) Not unless . . .
Ippolita (*softer*) Not in the rose-gar . . .
Vincenzo (*barely audible*) Not unless.
　　　　　(*pause. The lark is faintly heard*)
Ippolita Contentment, rose-like, blooming through day and night, still
　　　　there tomorrow. Roses above me. Yellow un-nodding heads,
　　　　and golden beneath them his, bending to mine. Reprieve. Or red,
　　　　open roses, circling his head. Reprieve. The soft flesh of roses,
　　　　kissing me, caressed by the warmth of roses . . . And later, after,
　　　　he would tell me what had happened, there in the great palace
　　　　of Mantua, where I would never tread, he would tell me what
　　　　had happened, there in his father's palace.

　　　　(*a large room in the Reggia at Mantua. Vincenzo is wandering about
　　　　on the marble floor, so that we hear his voice from varying points,
　　　　occasionally with a slight echo*)
Vincenzo I am utterly at your command, father. I shall be quite happy.
　　　　I have told you so many times, father. And I have told *you* so,
　　　　mother. And I have told *you*, Counsellor Donati. I do not very
　　　　particularly mind whom I marry.
Duke That is no way in which to approach the sacrament, my son.
Vincenzo I shall approach the sacrament in the most reverent mood, father.
　　　　But it is not yet in sight, apparently. I merely meant it was a
　　　　matter of indifference to me whom I approached it with.
Duke Marriage is a sacred bond, Vincenzo. I did not approach marriage
　　　　lightly: did I, my dear?
Duchess (*an Austrian accent*) No. Neither of us did.
Duke Prayer, thought, consideration: those were my own preparatives.
　　　　In consequence, this house is almost three times as rich as when I
　　　　was a bachelor.
Vincenzo You were weighed in the balance and not found wanting, mother
　　　　dear.
Duchess Vincenzo, do not jest.
Vincenzo I am not jesting. Three times as rich, did you say, father?
Duke If not four.
Vincenzo One would hardly think so, would one, from the few signs we
　　　　show of it? If I am as lucky, I cannot promise to be so austere.

Duke I hate ostentation.

Vincenzo Yes, father. Even to the point of making your son and heir barely distinguishable from a stable-boy.

Duke It is your own base habits that make you like a stable-boy.

Vincenzo Well, if you will only enable me to take my place in better comp –

Duchess Come, come, you are exaggerating.

Vincenzo – any, perhaps my habits will change.

Duchess Let us be logical. You are speaking of a separate problem.

Vincenzo I hope my marriage may solve it. I would have thought that to break off negotiations with the Medici would be a way of delaying the solution.

Duke No, no. I should have thought more deeply. To marry with Florence would in the end be to throw the whole of North Italy into the hands of the Medici. I should have thought of it. But if you marry with Parma it will bring thirty years of quarrelling to an end.

Duchess Berhaps.

Vincenzo As mother so wisely says: Berhaps.

Duke And there are other reasons against Florence and the Medici.

Vincenzo Why? Are Parma and the Farnesi richer?

Duke You are being sordid and flippant, Vincenzo.

Vincenzo Not flippant, I hope, father.

Duke I have thought of this matter deeply. It is the question of your mother's feelings. Your . . . dear mother's feelings.

Vincenzo I shall be interested to know how you will make our delicate Mantuan sensibilities clear to Francesco de' Medici, Grand-Duke of Florence. Will you tell him that we like Parma better?

Duke I am not inexperienced in diplomacy, my son. Donati.

Donati Your Highness?

Duke Read out slowly and carefully the fourth paragraph of the letter to the Grand-Duke I dictated to you.

Donati Yes, your Highness. (*reads*) 'The monstrous and persistently scandalous intrigue you have maintained with one of the lowest women in the whole of Italy . . . '

Duke No, no. I meant paragraph three. (*to Vincenzo, who has giggled*) Will you be serious, sir!

Duchess Vincenzo . . .

Donati (*reads*) 'For many years, my lord, you, Francesco, though Grand-Duke of Florence and married to my wife's sister, a daughter of the Caesarean Emperor, saw no shame in discarding your wife's affection for that of a woman of Venice, to wit, Bianca Cappello, no less notorious then than now for the low insolence of her behaviour. After the death of your dear wife, my own wife's sister, you married your former concubine and again saw no shame in making your tender and innocent daughters sit beside her in places of worship and at public –'

(*Vincenzo is overcome by laughter. Donati breaks off*)

Duke (*angrily*) Well, sir, well?

Vincenzo You do not propose to say all this to the stupendous Bianca Cappello?

Duke I would not stoop to address her. My letter is directed to my brother-in-law, man to man. Not to his wife.

Duchess Zo-called.

Vincenzo You do not suppose that his wife, zo-called, will fail to see it, do you, father?

Duke That is of no moment. Let her see it, by all means.

Vincenzo (*laughs*) Take care, father – she will have her revenge on you.

Duke Revenge! What revenge can a common harlot of Venice take on me?

Vincenzo She is an *uncommon* one, father. Beware, oh Duke, beware.

Duke You trifle again. Continue, Donati . . .

Donati 'For which reason, we, Duke of Mantua, Marquis of Monferrato –'

Duchess Skib the titles.

Vincenzo (*laughs*) And skib the rest as well, Marcello. I can imagine. Oh, father, father, what a day's work you have done!

Duke Will you be silent, sir, will you be silent!

Vincenzo Yes, father, I will be silent. And I will marry whoever shall please you. I vow it, father.

(*he laughs again, his laugh mingling with that of Ippolita. Lark song again*)

And I vow it to you also, Andromeda: I do not care whom I marry. For there will always be you. Let them marry me to Parma. I do not care. There will always be you and I shall always come back to you, always. You are the love of my life, my own Andromeda, and I love you from here to Innsbruck.

Ippolita He had laughed at them, there in Mantua. We laughed at them again, in the rose-garden at Colorno. And through the laughter and the sense of reprieve, the further sense that from now on, this love was to be never other than a succession of reprieves; time gained, a little time gained, a little more time ... Oh, Vincenzo, Vincenzo. (*almost with anger*) Vincenzo.

(*dance-music up full. Then behind*)

I have forgotten how long after that it was, but one night during a ball, I suddenly became aware that Vincenzo was not in the line of dancers. I looked across the great hall to the doorway. He and Barbara were there, talking animatedly with Counsellor Donati. He had come unexpectedly on his way back from Parma to Mantua, and the new betrothal was already a fact.

Vincenzo Have you seen her, Marcello? Have you brought a picture of my betrothed?

Donati No, your Highness. No one in Parma has seen Princess Margherita for the last few years; she has been with her father in the Netherlands. A portrait is being copied and sent to Mantua.

Vincenzo You hear, Lanzoni?

Lanzoni (*approaching*) Hear what, Vincenzo?

Vincenzo I'm to be the husband of Margherita Farnese. That will shake the world, won't it, Barbara?

Barbara Let's hope it will stop this part of it from shaking.

Lanzoni Margherita Farnese! By God, Vincenzo, you always get the best of things. She's only twelve.

Donati No, sir. She is over fourteen.

Barbara Yes, she must be quite fourteen by now.

Lanzoni Ah, pity, pity! Still ...

Vincenzo (*takes him by the throat, but affectionately*) You are speaking of the future Princess of Mantua, Lanzoni; my bride-to-be.

Lanzoni Yes, I was saying: pity.

Vincenzo Go away. You do not understand these sacred matters. Go and get drunk.

Lanzoni Sir, I am drunk: I was saying ...

Barbara This is no time for coarseness, I think, Lanzoni.

Donati And ... your ladyship, I must ask that the news be not disclosed to your guests just yet.

Barbara No. I wonder if any of them fail to guess.

Vincenzo (*suddenly*) Donati.

Donati Your Highness?

Vincenzo My father doesn't know I'm here?

Donati One can never be quite sure, my lord.

Vincenzo No, one never can. Still, try to be evasive, will you?

Donati If the occasion arises I will try to indicate that I saw you not here, my lord, but at Viadana.

Vincenzo Perhaps I had better come back with you to Viadana tonight?

Donati It would make the position of all of us far nearer to comfort, your Highness.

Vincenzo I suppose so. Very well. Go and tell the men, Lanzoni. Ah ... Ippolita, my darling. Good news. I am to marry little Margherita Farnese.

Ippolita When?

Vincenzo Oh, soon, I expect ... Donati, you'd better go and keep an eye on Lanzoni. He's not in his most reticent mood.

Donati I will do my best, sir.

Barbara It is a wise match. It will heal a breach. Mantua and Parma have been at odds far too long.

Vincenzo For once you see eye to eye with my dear father, Barbara. It isn't often that happens.

  (they laugh)

  And of course you have your own interest in seeing us allied with Parma.

Barbara I? I don't know what you mean, Vincenzo. (archly) You know I don't.

Vincenzo Barbara, Barbara, may God forgive you ...

  (intimate laughter from both)

Ippolita She knew what he meant, and he knew that she knew. Vincenzo's father hated her; but Parma, not so: protected first by that little girl's grandfather, and now by her father ... mistress to both, perhaps ... or to neither. And her domains, precariously set on both their frontiers: roses of Colorno precariously blooming, trembling lest too violent a wind should leave them with only their thorns ...

Vincenzo And I suppose it is your ambition to entice the third generation of Farnesi into your brave bare arms, dear Barbara.

Barbara The third generation, dear Vincenzo, consists of little Ranuccio, the brother of your bride-to-be, and he is about eight years old.

Vincenzo Twelve, Barbara, twelve.

Barbara Well, what is the difference between eight and twelve? He is only a child. My own son is almost as old.

Vincenzo But, Barbara, I was highly accomplished at the age of twelve!

If Ranuccio's nurses are as able and as patient and as exacting as my own were, you need have nothing to fear in the way of dissatisfaction.

Barbara Go away, you disgusting creature. Go to Viadana. I hope little Margherita Farnese will reform you. Mantua must be like a sewer. I shall leave you to chastise him, Ippolita, my sweet.

Vincenzo (*caressively*) Ippolita, *my* sweet, let us go and say goodbye. A brief one: I shall be back the day after tomorrow.

(*fade music out*)

Ippolita But as we said goodbye, lying beside each other, it was not of him or of me that I thought. I thought of Margherita, unknown to both of us. That child, perhaps at this moment jolting asleep in the carriage that would bring her back through France, or waking and looking out at the sleeping villages, the miles of sleeping forest, and wondering about ... *him.* I loved him ... and yet felt pity for *her.* In arms better suited to caressing her dolls, she would hold him; and be a mother at the age of fifteen perhaps. She would know nothing of passion, as I had known nothing at her age. The two strange children: Margherita: Ranuccio, her brother. Their father, the duke Alessandro, had been Barbara's lover; their grandfather protected her in his absence. I was not of their high world. I had never set foot in the palace of the Gonzagas at Mantua, nor in the palace of the Farnesi at Parma ... where soon Margherita would be singing and dancing for the joy that was still, this moment, mine. And still I thought, poor child, poor little girl ...

(*rapid music on lute, very marked in rhythm. The hall in which the scene is played is large and echoing*)

Margherita (*singing to the tune*) La, la, la ... Louder, louder! Play louder. Why can't you play louder?

Musician I shall break the instrument, I fear, madamina.

Margherita Then break it! I am going to have a hundred lutes and a thousand fiddles, and a hundred thousand trumpets and a million drums. Play faster! (*singing*) La, la, la ... Stop!

(*music ceases*)

Ranuccio! Why are you looking so sulky? Answer me!

Ranuccio (*a boy*) I am not looking sulky.

Margherita Yes, you are. Look at yourself in the mirror behind you.

Ranuccio I won't. You are crazy and foolish, and you don't know what you are saying.

Margherita You are *not* sulking? Eh?

Ranuccio No! I never sulk.

Margherita Ha! I wish I could believe you!

Ranuccio I'm not sulking!

Margherita Do you swear it?

Ranuccio Yes, if you want me to, you silly creature.

Margherita You swear it?

Ranuccio *Yes!*

Margherita Very well, then. Take my hand and pretend to be my husband, the great prince Vincenzo. We shall hold a wedding-rehearsal. (*to the hall*) Pages! . . .

Ranuccio I won't!

Margherita Give me your hand. (*suddenly pleading*) Please, *please*. Ranuccio, we've played at husbands and wives before, and now I'm going to be really married, you won't.

Ranuccio (*fiercely whispering*) You're silly, Margherita, you're a fool; can't you see that they are all laughing at you?

Margherita Who?

Ranuccio The musicians. The pages. Everybody.

Margherita They're not laughing at me. Why should they laugh at me?

Ranuccio Because they know all about him.

Margherita And *I* know all about him too. He is a great prince, with beautiful blue eyes, and fair hair, almost golden. You know he is. You've seen the picture they sent of him.

Ranuccio He's the wickedest man in Italy, everyone knows he is. His father daren't even give him any money, he's so wicked; he would spend it on wicked things.

Margherita He would spend it on jewels, for me!

Ranuccio He wouldn't! He wouldn't! He's nasty and wicked.

Margherita He's not, he's not!

Ranuccio (*shouting*) He's nasty and wicked! He's dirty and horrible! And you will be the same! You'll be the –
　　　(*she smacks him across the mouth*)

Margherita How dare you? How dare you?
　　　(*pause*)

Ranuccio (*shouting*) You . . . filthy little whore!
　　　(*she smacks him again*)

Margherita (*shouting also*) You disgusting sinful boy! Go away!

287

Ranuccio I will! I'll never speak to you again as long as I live!
>   (*he is heard running across the marble floor. Then a great door is heard opening and banging to*)

Margherita Ranuccio! Ranuccio! Come back! (*weeping*) Fetch him back! Don't let him leave me! Ranuccio! Ranuccio! Don't leave me, Ranuccio ... !
>   (*this last cry is drowned in the loud music of the wedding. It drops down, but is still heard behind Ippolita*)

Ippolita (*harder-voiced*) And the wedding took place. Barbara went, an honoured, flattered guest, bright in her silks and jewels. I stayed behind, almost alone in her deserted palace, in her withered gardens. It was March. He had stayed with us, on his way to Margherita, braving scandal, braving his father's anger and the suspicions of Parma.
>   (*music out. Vincenzo's tones and words are exactly as on the earlier occasion in the garden*)

Vincenzo And I vow it to you also, Andromeda: I do not care whom I marry. For there will always be you. Let them marry me to Parma. I do not care. There will always be you and I shall always come back to you, always. You are the love of my life, and I love you from here to Innsbruck. You believe me?

Ippolita Yes, my love. Only go now. Go. Go to Parma, my own love. Go.
>   (*the wedding music is again faded in behind*)

Ippolita And I strode alone through the barren gardens of Colorno and thought of the revelry in Parma, nine miles away. And I thought of the wedding-coach, the shouting crowds, the trumpets. And I thought of her small hand lying in his, as they rode from the cathedral. And I thought, what have they found to say to each other? And I seemed to hear the bells of Parma from nine miles away ...
>   (*bells up, loudly. Shouts of the crowd and other festive noises behind Vincenzo and Margherita. He is kind and paternal in his manner to her, and, for the first time, very likeable. He is still only eighteen-and-a-half, but the difference in years between him and Margherita seems much greater*)

Vincenzo Well, we were very well-behaved in the cathedral, Margherita, weren't we? We ... went through with it finely, didn't you think?

Margherita (*splutters with amusement*)

Vincenzo You were splendid.

Margherita (*demurely reproachful*) I *wasn't*.

Vincenzo Oh, yes you were. So serious. And you looked *so beautiful*. You know, Margherita, I wanted to kiss you long before they let us.

Margherita Oh, my lord . . .

Vincenzo No, madama: you are to call me Vincenzo now.

Margherita Vin . . . (*she splutters again*) Vincenzo. Yes.

Vincenzo I . . . I was terribly frightened during the anointing, weren't you?

Margherita (*deeply*) No . . .

Vincenzo Weren't you?

Margherita (*much higher*) No. Of course not.

Vincenzo Well, you will have to be brave for both of us on these occasions in future. You'll hold my hand whenever you see me trembling, won't you?

Margherita Yes.

Vincenzo Because I love you very much, Margherita. Margherita *Gonzaga*.

Margherita Margherita Gonzaga. Yes.

Vincenzo And do you love me a little bit, Margherita?

Margherita (*ardently*) Yes. Oh, *yes*. I love you more than I have ever loved anyone in the world.

Vincenzo That's a good g –. That is wonderful, my darling . . . my . . . my own wife.

    (*they both giggle a little*)

Margherita Oh, I wish my mother were alive to see you. She would love you too.

Vincenzo Oh, I . . . I hope so. I don't think your brother Ranuccio loves me very much, does he? He looks very darkly at me.

Margherita Oh, but he will love you in time, I am sure he will. No one could wish for a better brother. He is at a difficult age.

Vincenzo Ah, yes. I'll send him a pair of our Mantuan horses, shall I? Perhaps that will cheer him up.

Margherita (*sagely*) T't. No, no, no, no, he has plenty of horses. What Ranuccio needs is a mistress. Oh, *look* at the crowds!

    (*bells and music up, and gradually out behind Ippolita*)

Ippolita And that day, as I wandered in the gardens of Colorno, and saw and felt the spring struggling against the winter, I determined that the child I was to bear him would not be born alive. And

without waiting for Barbara's return, I went back to Reggio;
to the solicitous gaze of my husband and the tender regard of our
children. And I lay ill; and no one came. Messages to *him* I dared
not send; and Barbara's letters were rare and uninforming. And
summer came and again it was Colorno and the banks of roses.
The lark sang. But there was no Vincenzo. Only rumours . . .
blossoming hideously under the blazing sun, rumours entwining
themselves round his name and Margherita's.

Barbara (*quietly*) Do you mean that you have heard nothing?

Ippolita No.

Barbara Well, that is what has happened.

Ippolita Perhaps it merely means that Margherita isn't fond enough of him.

Barbara It means nothing of the kind. It means what it *is*, and nothing else.
And in any case, Margherita worships him. I saw them at Ferrara.
You would think there was nothing wrong between them. And
in a sense there isn't. But everyone can see that they are not
husband and wife.

Ippolita How?

Barbara She will suddenly detach herself from her women, and . . . *trot* across
the floor, lifting up her skirts, and, if he is talking with other men,
she will gently take one of his hands in both of hers, and wait till
he turns to her. If he smiles at her, as he usually does, her eyes
shine. You see her ask her question, receive her answer, smile,
and . . . trot back again to her women. It is very pretty, and I
have seen people cry a little at the sight; but it is not the behaviour
of wife and husband.

Ippolita No.

Barbara And naturally, since people are whispering, they are often
whispering wrong.

Ippolita What are they saying?

Barbara The Farnesi are of course spreading rumours that the physical
disability lies not in Margherita but in Vincenzo.

Ippolita Every innkeeper's daughter between here and Mantua could
testify to the contrary.

Barbara Yes; in fact, some of them have obligingly done so. Unfortunately
the Farnesi adduce that as part of the trouble. I hope you won't
be tempted to step so nobly forward yourself, my sweet.

Ippolita I am not an heroic woman, my dear Barbara.

Barbara (*amused*) No. Few of us are.

(*very brief pause*)

Ippolita Well, poor Vincenzo. And poor Margherita. But I suppose it
will pass as she grows up.

Barbara It is not thought so.

Ippolita But . . . Barbara: what will happen to them?

Barbara The doctors are unable to discover any vocation for wifehood in
her: so the priests are now endeavouring to discover if she has a
vocation for another sort of life. So far, she screams as loudly
against the one as against the other. But the priests are more
hopeful than the doctors, and of course more persistent. The laws
of God are sometimes more flexible than the laws of nature.
And it seems that God is much concerned that Vincenzo shall
have an heir, so that Mantua will not lapse to the Gonzagas of
France . . . (*sighs*) I wish God were equally concerned with my
own fate.

Ippolita What do you mean?

Barbara You will imagine how . . . how interesting the position of
Colorno will become if Mantua and Parma are once more at
odds.

Ippolita But, Barbara dearest, you are assured of Parma's protection.

Barbara I wonder how long I shall be assured of it, if I continue to receive
Vincenzo here: that is all. And it is rather a large 'all'.

Ippolita What do you propose to do?

Barbara Nothing, my dear. Nothing at all.

      (*pause*)

Ippolita But I could not think of Barbara; only of Vincenzo. The whispering months dragged on; and I did not see him, and could scarcely
fashion his image in my mind, or recall his voice, even if I thought
of him all day long. And then, suddenly the image brightened:
and was a new image, sharp, large and painful. And I wondered
if this was the true one after all . . .

      (*suddenly and simultaneously, a loud piazza clock is heard striking
four: there is a pounding on a heavy door with the hilt of a dagger:
and Vincenzo is heard shouting*)

Vincenzo Castellan! Castellan! Open the gate at once! Castellan!
      (*he pauses while the final boom of the clock is heard*)
Castellan!

Guard (*inside*) Who is there?

Vincenzo Prince Vincenzo. Open at once. Let me in.

Guard Yes, my lord.
(*door*)

Vincenzo Close it, quickly. Where's the Castellan?

Guard He was just here, your Highness . . .

Olivo (*approaching slowly*) Good evening, your Highness.

Vincenzo Olivo, my dear man, forgive me for waking you, if I did.

Olivo I was not in bed, my lord. And a good deal of Mantua seems to be up tonight.

Vincenzo Send the man away.

Olivo (*to guard*) Go along, Gino.
(*pause*)

Vincenzo (*urgently*) Listen, Olivo, you must set guards along the waterside. At once. A murderer is trying to escape from the town. He may try to get across the lake.

Olivo A murderer, my lord? Indeed?

Vincenzo My friend Lanzoni has been killed.

Olivo (*not a question*) Lanzoni.

Vincenzo You know what he meant to me. He was the only friend I had.

Olivo Do you know who killed him, my lord?

Vincenzo Yes, I . . . I'm not sure. I . . . I feel certain it was that barbarian Scotchman, my father's favourite.

Olivo Crichton.

Vincenzo Yes, Crichton. I was there. I think I . . . I saw him fleeing. He will try to swim across the lake.

Olivo You *saw* him fleeing, my lord?

Vincenzo Yes, I . . . I'm not sure. Why do you keep asking questions? Isn't it a matter of urgency? He stabbed Lanzoni in the back. We were strolling towards San Silvestro; there was no one else in the piazza, and he . . . but for God's sake don't waste time, Olivo, send some men to the waterside; send all you can spare. There are many places where he could try to swim across. And three-quarters of the fools in the town are so bedazzled by him they'd be willing to help.

Olivo No, my lord. Crichton will not try to escape.

Vincenzo (*panicked*) They've caught him?

Olivo Yes, my lord.

Vincenzo (*afraid*) What did he say?

Olivo He is dead, my lord.

Vincenzo How . . . can he be?

Olivo Perhaps Lanzoni struck him first.

Vincenzo Nonsense: he just gave him a shove: almost a joke.

   Olivo Did you not strike him, my lord?

Vincenzo I ... no ... I may have aimed a blow at him ... with this thing, but I don't think so. I ... God in heaven (*intake of breath inadvertently*)
     (*pause*)

   Olivo It looks as though your dagger went in just over two inches, my lord.

Vincenzo Where is he?

   Olivo He crawled as far as the apothecary's. You say you saw him flee. Was he ... *able* to flee?

Vincenzo Well, I ... perhaps not flee, precisely, but ...

   Olivo Could he stand upright, my lord, when you last saw him?

Vincenzo I didn't ... yes, I think ... (*loudly*) God in heaven, man, how should I know!
     (*pause*)

  Duchess (*in great distress, but subdued in voice*) But my dear, dear boy, what you have done is a wicked thing, you must know in your heart it is.

Vincenzo (*wearily*) Very well, mother, I know it is. And I do not care.

  Duchess Your father is beside himself with rage. It is not as if this unfortunate Crichton had been a man of the people. He was descended from the kings of Scotland.

Vincenzo Have you ever met a Scotchman who wasn't? If he *had* been a man of the people I would be sorrier.

  Duchess Your father was so fond of him. He had just made him a counsellor.

Vincenzo He was fonder of him than of me, I suspect. And why the 'admirable' Crichton, for the love of God? Aren't any of the rest of us admirable?

  Duchess But you must know that people are suggesting that that is why you killed him. Because you were jealous of his gifts.

Vincenzo I can dance and argufy as well as he could, mother, given the chance.

  Duchess Nevertheless, they say you killed him deliberately, and from jealousy.

Vincenzo And you believe it.

  Duchess No. But it is said. Everywhere. Oh, my God, my God, how dreadful this place is ...

Vincenzo But whose fault is it that it is so dreadful, mother? (*suddenly*) Oh,

293

mother, mother, can't you imagine what my life has been this last year? All this weary, unceasing trouble about poor little Margherita, and my father against us all! What are we to do?

Duchess We must pray for peace and quiet, Vincenzo. And you must marry again, happily this time.

Vincenzo And who shall give us peace and quiet?

Duchess The good Cardinal Borromeo, your cousin Carlo, is doing his best. We must be patient. And pray.

Vincenzo Yes, good cousin Carlo. Yes. Do you know what I wish, mother?

Duchess What?

Vincenzo I half wish little Margherita would hold out against him. She may be no good as a wife, poor girl, but she's the only one of any of us who has ever known what joy there might be in life.

Duchess Vincenzo . . .

Vincenzo But the good Cardinal Carlo will deal with that.

(*pause*)

(*Borromeo is firm but kind, and is much troubled in conscience*)

Borromeo Now, my child.

Margherita Oh, don't, don't, don't, Uncle Carlo, don't make my life more miserable than it has been here all these months without him! Send him back to me, Uncle Carlo. I know he will come back if only you will tell him to. He is so good; and he will be patient if you explain to him. I shall be able to give him children one day, I know I shall. Only send him back. I don't care what he does, if only he won't leave me forever.

Borromeo Come, my dear dear child. You must not weep like that.

Margherita Have you seen him, Uncle Carlo?

Borromeo Yes, my child.

Margherita Did you talk with him?

Borromeo A little, yes.

Margherita What did he say? What messages did he send me?
(*pause*)

Borromeo Margherita, I want you to try to think for a moment of what . . .

Margherita What messages did he send me?

Borromeo He did not send you messages, my dear. It was . . .

Margherita He must have. He cannot have known you were coming here.

Borromeo Yes, my child, he did know.

Margherita He cannot have known. He wouldn't have let you come here and not bring me even his love.

294

Borromeo He did not think of me as a courier, Margherita. Nor must you.

Margherita But you have come to solve things for us, haven't you, uncle? You have come to make us happy again?

Borromeo I hope that in the end you will both be happy, my child. But I am sent by the Pope to try to discover the will of God for both of you.

Margherita But you love us both, don't you, uncle? You want to see us happy together, don't you? You'd like that?

Borromeo It would glad my heart to think you might be happy together, yes, my child, if God allows us to think of such happiness in this case. But you must know in your heart by now that it is very possible that He will not allow us to think so.

Margherita God is not so cruel as to wish us unhappy.

Borromeo He is never cruel, and He never wishes us unhappy. Of course He does not. But in order to light our way to the only true happiness, which consists in knowing and doing His will, sometimes He will send us a *little* unhappiness, which may for a time seem an intolerable one.

Margherita But He has done so already. I have been unhappy. I was unhappy because I could not please Vincenzo in the way they have told you of. But I knew that later, if ever I would be able to please him, I would be happy. Even when I was silly and frightened . . . even when . . . (*a sudden torrent of words*) Oh, uncle, dear uncle, all the while those terrible men and women were pawing me about, even when I lay for twenty-four hours shivering with fever because of what they had had to do to me, I knew I would be happy if I could make him happy, and I clung to that thought. Help me to believe it still, uncle Carlo, help me!

Borromeo (*after a pause*) You are feverish still, my child, a little, are you not?

Margherita No, I am not. Feel my forehead, feel my wrists.

Borromeo Do you feel capable of kneeling quietly beside me and praying for a while? Will you try?

Margherita (*remotely*) They say I mustn't pray. They say it is wrong to pray for what I want to pray for.

Borromeo Oh, child, dear erring daughter, they are right. I hope you have not framed your prayers in the way you make me fear you may have done?

Margherita Yes, yes, I have! Day after day, night after night . . . Oh, God, oh God, how wretched and miserable and cast away by all of you I am . . . No one will give me hope or aid. (*fade right out*)

> *(nuns chanting in background. During the following scene Margherita behaves bravely, but is often in tears. Ranuccio speaks almost without expression)*

Margherita This is almost goodbye, Ranuccio.

Ranuccio Yes.

Margherita You will come to see me?

Ranuccio Yes.

Margherita They are going to cut off my hair.

Ranuccio I will tear him limb from limb.

Margherita No, Ranuccio. Don't think ill of him.

Ranuccio He is the devil. He is Satan.

Margherita No, no, Ranuccio. You do not understand these things.

Ranuccio I understand everything.

Margherita *(weeping)* No.

Ranuccio I will kill him, when I am a man. As I shall be shortly.

Margherita No, no, Ranuccio. Try to love him. Try to be his friend. He needs friends.

Ranuccio He will never have any.

Margherita Nothing is anyone's fault, Ranuccio. It is God's will. Uncle Carlo Borromeo said so.

Ranuccio I despise Borromeo, and I do not believe it is God's will, and I hate the Gonzaga. And I will kill him.

Margherita No, no, Ranuccio. Oh, my God, my God! Can't you see, oh dear boy, dear dear dear brother, can't you see that I . . . I . . . *(she is unable to go on)*

Ranuccio *(impassively)* That you what?

Margherita That I love him. Beyond bearing and beyond belief. I would throw away the whole of the dreadful life before me for a single kiss or a single smile from him! I love him, Ranuccio . . .

Ranuccio *(suddenly shouts)* You don't, you don't, you don't! *(pause)* You don't, you don't!

Woman I think, my lady, we should leave your brother now.

Margherita Oh, Ranuccio! Kiss me. Hold me tight. Try to cry, dear dear one, try to cry.

Ranuccio *(almost in tears)* I cannot.

Margherita Come soon to see me.

Ranuccio Every week. Oftener, if you send for me.

Margherita Good-bye, Ranuccio . . . oh, try to love him. Try.

Woman Come, my lady.

> *(pause as she and the woman withdraw)*

Ranuccio (*simply*) The Gonzaga is Satan. I will stick my knife into the groin of the body that has defamed her and dishonoured my house. I will stick my knife into his groin and tear his body up to this gullet. And with my right hand I will stab his heart. I swear this before God Almighty. I will do it for God's sake, for hers, and for mine. I will be his death in his life and at the end of his life. I swear this before the Lord my God.

    (*pause*)

Barbara But these things pass, Vincenzo, my dear. These things pass. Do not mind so deeply. Nothing matters so much as that.

Ippolita I am sure Barbara is right, my darling. In a year's time it will seem as nothing.

Vincenzo In a year's time I shall have another wife. Donati is already in Florence trying to make the Medici forget we once rejected them, carefully removing the scabs from old sores. But poor little Margherita will have no other husband. I wish I could have seen her before she left Mantua.

Barbara I am sure it is better that you did not.

Vincenzo I hate to think of a child like that bearing rancour towards me: the monastery walls are blank places: what hideous fancies will her mind not sometimes paint on them? And the prayers: strange words can steal into the monotony of our prayers: 'I hate him, I hate him, I hate him.'

Ippolita I am sure she will not think that. She couldn't.

Vincenzo I wouldn't mind a grown woman hating me. I'm sure Margherita wouldn't have hated me, if only I could have spoken with her before they shut her away. I hope she finds peace there.

Barbara Borromeo says he is sure she has a genuine vocation.

Vincenzo Yes, they can find it anywhere, can't they, if they have to?

Ippolita It doesn't help to be satirical, dearest.

Vincenzo Doesn't it? Perhaps it does, just a little. But I see I am depressing you. I will leave you, and come back in a more cheerful mood.

Barbara Ask them to play you some music, if you would like it, my dear.

Vincenzo Thank you.

Ippolita And come back soon, my sweet.

Vincenzo (*sighs*) Yes, Andromeda, I will come back soon.

    (*pause as he goes*)

Ippolita It is a long while since he called me Andromeda.

Barbara There: you see? He will soon get over it. I hope *they* do.

Ippolita They?

Barbara The Farnesi. Not that Margherita's father greatly cares. He approves of the monastery; he wrote and told me so. But there are uncles and cousins and aunts.

Ippolita And Ranuccio.

Barbara Oh, he's only a child still. He'll forget, dull, silly little lump. But family feeling in Parma is a difficult thing.

Ippolita Most family feeling is.

Barbara Yes. (*amused*) And I wonder what family feeling in Florence is like at the moment.

(*they both laugh quietly*)

Poor Donati. He may have some difficult encounters.

Ippolita I suppose the Grand-Duke Francesco is still smarting under the previous insult.

Barbara It will not be the Grand-Duke himself. It will be the Grand-Duchess. The stupendous Bianca Cappello.

Ippolita But she has no say in the matter, surely?

Barbara No, perhaps not. You may be right. She may have no say in the matter. All the same I would rather like to be in Florence at the moment with Counsellor Donati. Though hidden, of course. Hidden.

(*the scene closes on a fade, as they laugh again*)

Francesco You must have seen many strange sights in your recent travels, Donati?

Donati Not a few, your Highness.

Francesco And his lordship of Mantua must have laid many strange undertakings on your shoulders.

Donati It is not for me to deny that, my Lord.

Bianca (*in slow teasing tones*) And this must be stranger than most, Doctor Donati? Wouldn't you say that? Stranger than most?

Francesco I have no doubt that my wife has in mind, Donati, ah, your previous advances to us of three years ago. And your curious retreat thereafter. I feel sure you would like to say a few words, my dear, yes?

Bianca You will have imagined, Doctor Donati, that we are a little disconcerted by these new overtures for the hand of my stepdaughter, the Princess Eleonora. Perhaps we are easily disconcerted.

Donati I fear my Lord Duke of Mantua may have expressed himself uncertainly when he broke off our earlier negotiations.

Bianca Your Lord Duke of Mantua did not *seem* uncertain at that time. The reasons he offered were impeccable in their clarity.

Donati I feel your Highness may have misunderstood the Duke's meaning.

Bianca Do you mean that he attaches different meanings to common words from the meanings normally accepted?

Donati That would sometimes be the implication, your Highness.

Bianca Do you yourself accept *his* meanings, or those of the outside world?

Donati I endeavour to effect a reconciliation between the two, when possible.

Bianca What meaning does your Duke attach to the word concubine?

Donati It might well depend on the character of the person of whom he used it, your Highness.

Francesco I think Donati makes a good point there, my dear.

Bianca Do you?

Francesco Yes . . . Yes, on the whole, I do. I think.

Bianca Would the Duke apply the word to a respectable person?

Donati It would not necessarily indicate *diminished* respect, your Highness.

Bianca Do you share your master's view of the meaning of that particular word?

Donati I can conceive of occasions when our selection of it might coincide.

Bianca And might it then have the same meaning as the word whore?

Donati By no means inevitably, your Highness.

Bianca But occasionally?

Donati Not . . . *un*occasionally, perhaps.

Bianca Would it have that meaning if you applied it to me?

Francesco My wife has a very logical mind, you know, Donati.

Donati I would not personally apply either word to a married lady such as yourself, madama.

Bianca I was not always married, Doctor Donati. Would you have applied that word to me when I was living as my present husband's mistress?

Donati No, your Highness.

Bianca Why not?

Donati I would have been dissuaded alike by civilised tolerance, by Christian charity, and by a considerable experience of the problems of married life in titled families, your Highness.

Bianca You think they are different from the problems of those of humbler conjugation?

Francesco Ah, now that *is* a question.

Donati I feel that they deserve – nay, madama, command – a different species of judgement.

Francesco Good. A good answer.

Bianca Do you think that God Almighty applies a different judgement to them?

Francesco (*attentively*) Ah?

Donati I devoutly hope so, madama.

Francesco Ah.

Bianca It is all one can hope, is it not?

Donati I . . .

> (*she disconcerts them both by a long warm satirical laugh, in which they hesitatingly join*)

Bianca Yes. Bless my soul. And his lordship of Mantua is now concerned for the succession of his family.

Donati As is natural, your Highness.

Bianca He can scarcely in that case deny us anxiety about ours.

Donati His hope was that they might be simultaneously assured.

Bianca And suppose they are simultaneously disappointed?

Donati I am sure the young princess is of the most capable disposition.

Bianca It is not of the young princess that we entertain question. It is of the young prince.

Donati I am sure your Highness need have no fear.

Bianca What makes you so sure?

Donati It . . . is a delicate question.

Bianca But susceptible, no doubt, of a delicate answer?

Donati I . . .

Bianca You . . . ?

Donati It has been thoughtfully computed that his Highness's women friends include fewer unpregnant ones than any similar group of women in a like position since the days of his great-great-grandfather.

> (*pause*)

Francesco (*mildly*) I think that was well put.

Bianca But you, as a physician, Doctor Donati, will be aware that unbridled excess may have peculiar consequences.

Donati It has been not unknown.

Bianca We are much perturbed by rumours of the young man's incapacity. It has been suggested that his unsuccessful union with
Margherita Farnese was due not to her but to him.

Donati I have heard the rumour, and am convinced of its mendacity.

Bianca Doctor Donati: you answered my own question delicately. I will
try to be as delicate myself. What we require of the young
prince's congressive ability is . . . quite simply . . . proof.

Donati (*after a pause: horrified*) Proof?

Bianca Proof. That was my word. I am glad you seem to be at one with
ourselves as to its meaning. Before a second innocent young
woman is beguiled into marriage, we would require a definite
physical proof of the young prince's capability of performing,
if only occasionally, the functions of a husband. Let me try to
put it in another way, Donati. We, the Medici of Florence, feel
a certain doubt at the back of our minds . . .

(*fade*)

Ippolita It was the scandal of the century. And it was the end of our love;
which matters less, perhaps. No one thought that he would ever
accept the Medici's conditions. But who could ever predict his
responses . . . to *anything*?

Vincenzo (*on a long delighted laugh*) And shall I conquer, sweet ladies, shall
I conquer? The eyes of Europe will be upon me! I *must* conquer.

Ippolita It is humiliating and disgusting, Vincenzo; you ought never to
have agreed to it.

Barbara Come, come, Ippolita, darling. Vincenzo is old enough to decide
these things for himself. Though at the same time I think that
perhaps a little more discretion might have been employed.

Ippolita It is outrageous.

Vincenzo I think it is the essence of Bianca's revenge that there shall be no
element of discretion. That is why she has insisted on Venice for
the . . . rendezvous.

Barbara (*amused*) She would naturally choose the scene of so many tender
exploits of her own early days.

Ippolita Tender exploits!

Vincenzo And I shall try to make this a tender one also. I hope the presence
of Donati and the Florentine agent outside the doors will not rob
the occasion of its natural glamour.

Ippolita (*angrily*) Doesn't your father object?

Vincenzo Strongly. Though I notice unwonted gleams of curiosity in his

eyes whenever the subject is mentioned. I think he would like
to come and watch.

Ippolita And doesn't the Church object?

Vincenzo Only formally. Provided the operation doesn't take place on a
Friday it thinks much good may come of it. (*he and Barbara laugh*)
And with God's help, I'll see that it does.

Ippolita I think it monstrous to take a poor simple girl like that and
coldly subject her to public humiliation.

Barbara (*protesting*) Oh, Ippolita, don't be foolish. The girl is to be splendidly remunerated; *and* found a husband too!

Ippolita And what of the poor girl's mother? Would you like such a
thing to happen to a daughter of yours, Barbara?

> (*Vincenzo and Barbara both laugh*)

You are disgusting and cynical, both of you. I won't stay and
listen to you.

Barbara Ippolita . . .

Ippolita No.

> (*she departs*)

Vincenzo Ah, well, life is never wholly merry, is it, Barbara dear? I somehow feel Perseus and Andromeda will not be together much
longer.

Barbara There are many other Andromedas in the world, my dear.

Vincenzo True, true . . . Still, she says very searching things at times,
doesn't she?

Barbara Such as what?

Vincenzo You see, Barbara, it's a curious thing, but I *do* feel a little despicable when I think of the girl's mother. It's strange, isn't it?

Barbara (*thinks*) Yes. Yes, I agree. It is hard on the poor woman. Very
hard.

> (*brief pause. Murmurs of talk*)

Girl's mother Oh, please, my lord Prince, may I just . . .

Donati (*sharply*) Hush, hush, my good woman, not now.

Mother Oh, but, *please* . . .

Vincenzo (*passing by*) What is it, Donati?

Mother My lord Prince . . .

Vincenzo (*not unkindly*) Who is this lady, Donati?

Donati (*embarrassed*) I . . . your Highness, I . . .

Mother I am the *girl's mother*, your Highness.

Vincenzo (*gulps*) Oh, I . . . good evening.

Donati (*inaudible*) I'm very sorry, my lord.

Mother I did so pray I might see you *beforehand*, your Highness. You see, I . . . (*she cannot continue*)

Vincenzo (*abashed*) Ah . . .

Mother Oh, my lord, I am so bad at expressing my feelings, but I did so greatly want to say . . . what a tremendous honour this is for my family and for my dear little girlie. I cannot tell you how proud we are. And she has always been such a good girlie, and I hope she always will be, I have always insisted on it, my lord. And at last she has her reward; I can hardly believe it. When she was a little tot, she was such a skimpy little thing we hardly expected her to survive, but she did, and she was always so delicate, and no one took much notice of her; but, oh my lord, to think that in spite of all that she should live to be . . .

> (*a pause: she is not so much seeking for a word as trying to avoid having found it*)

favoured by a gentleman prince. My little girlie. My own child. Oh, what a golden opportunity for her! I cannot tell you how grateful we all are, my lord.

Vincenzo (*terribly ashamed*) I . . . madama, I . . .

Mother Grateful, and honoured. I shall pray for you both, my lord, if you will forgive my mentioning you both in the same prayer. (*murmur from Vincenzo*) And I shall thank God that we have both, my little girlie and I, lived to see this night. (*steady accelerando*) The two kind gentlemen and myself have given her the most careful instructions, your Highness, and, my lord, and if there *should be* . . .

> (*a crescendo of dance music comes up behind the last lines of this. It continues through the next scene, which is a ball in Florence*)

Bianca (*ironically*) So, Prince Vincenzo.

Vincenzo So, your Serene Highness.

Bianca You have passed your examination. I must congratulate you, warmly.

Vincenzo I must congratulate you even more warmly, madama. The revenge you took was as admirable as any I have ever heard of. And as well-nourished.

Bianca It was not starved, I agree. And it gave more enjoyment than revenges usually do; and to a far greater number of people. Even to yourself, I hope . . . and imagine?

Vincenzo There were moments that were far from disagreeable. But even the strongest nerves might have quailed before a whole world's observation.

Bianca But I was informed that you welcomed the conditions?

Vincenzo Only because I at first misunderstood them, madama.

Bianca Were Donati's circumlocutions even more obscure than they usually are?

Vincenzo They were very misleading at first. Hence my early joy, so soon dashed from me.

Bianca What in heaven do you mean?

Vincenzo I must never say, madama.

Bianca Oh? Why?

Vincenzo I am young to lose my life. Which it might well cost.

Bianca Not if I am secret. As I can be.

Vincenzo You promise that?

Bianca I promise that.

Vincenzo Then, madama, let me say that I heard Donati's prefatory mumblings with rapture: for I was wholly at first – alas, for our ambitions! – under the impression that you were insisting on . . . testing me out yourself.

Bianca (*in amused outrage*) You scabrous imp! I will set the Grand-Duke to you!

Vincenzo I have your promise of secrecy.

Bianca (*a low laugh*) Yes. Yes, you have.
        (*they both laugh a little*)

Vincenzo I feel you have been easily satisfied.

Bianca Nevertheless, I *am* satisfied. You have your laureateship.

Vincenzo I feel it withered already.

Bianca Your future bride will refresh it . . . Eleonora has been looking at you for the last five minutes.

Vincenzo No. She is engaged with her waiting-women.
        (*fade Vincenzo's voice into the music, which itself ceases, not on a fade but on a diminuendo conclusion to the dance music*)

Eleonora (*slowly*) His eyes, which bore so lightly my fate within them, rested for a moment upon me. He smiled, and turned away, smiling differently upon her, upon Bianca, so long my father's whore that I could not think of her as stepmother. They laughed; and again laughed; together. How much of that laughter had my mother had to see and bear? How much would I have to?

Not from Bianca. She would not be in Mantua. But from others. No matter. (*creep in dance music*) Patience. Which means also to suffer. Or is that passion? He turned again and looked at me where I stood with my women and my sister.

Maria (*aged ten*) He is looking at you again, Eleonora.

Eleonora (*coldly*) Is he?

Maria Isn't he beautiful?

Eleonora Don't be foolish, Maria.

Maria What lovely golden hair – and such *blue* eyes. I would love such a husband.

Eleonora You are welcome to him.

Maria (*wistfully*) And they say he is terribly wicked.

Eleonora (*sharply*) Be quiet.

Maria (*excited*) He is coming over here! Oh, sister: the miracle of a young gentleman's thighs.

Eleonora Hush, Maria.

Maria (*fade*) Oh, shall I never be eleven?

Eleonora And he came towards us, smiling. And I saw in his eyes an estimate of my person, as though he had denuded me, there and then, as I stood, among my women. (*music out on last phrase*) I had rebelled against the thought of him. And I fell in love against my will, against every warning of my brain. But when? During the revels in Florence? Or after, when we had gone to Mantua? Was it perhaps at the moment when I learned that he would not enter his city with me on the anniversary of the day he had first brought Margherita there? Did it need jealousy to start a love? No matter. I had replaced her, in some sort. And I gave to the House of Gonzaga their long-required progeny. And they gave me, in return, their name ... I had never known so strange a family. I did not wonder at my husband's uncertainties of character. And I grew used to the unceasing family quarrels, and the affronts to his princehood and his greatness.

(*we are plunged into a family quarrel already well on its way*)

Vincenzo You have betrayed your promises to me, father: every one of them! You have humiliated me in the eyes of Mantua and in the eyes of Rome and Florence and Europe.

Duke When?

Vincenzo At every turn. You promise me things for the special pleasure of denying them to me later.

Duchess Do not accuse your father like this, Vincenzo: you know he *is* ill.

Vincenzo And am I not ill? Are we not all ill in this degraded city?

Duke (*furious*) Degraded! And who has degraded it? Never since it became a dukedom, never even before then, has my city trembled for its future as it does now.

Vincenzo Why should it tremble?

Duke Because it fears what awaits it when I shall be no more.

Vincenzo What awaits it is dignity, gaiety, pleasure, generosity!

Duke No! There will be only levity, waste, debauchery, and casual murder! It fears a tyrant.

Vincenzo (*astounded*) In *me*?

Duke What can it expect but tyranny and brutality from a prince who brawls in the streets at night? A riotous wastrel who sets hired mercenaries upon innocent men when they try to protect their decent womenfolk from him?

Vincenzo You speak as if one incident were a regular habit.

Duke Do you think my people don't note such deeds and multiply them in their fears?

Vincenzo (*wearily, after a pause*) Let them, then, if they will. When the time comes I will show them a reality they shall not need to fear. And they do not hate me. They know the cause of my wildness.

Duchess I wish I did.

Vincenzo How should a prince deprived of his just honours and benefits, denied his place in the council by the malevolent will of his father . . .

Duchess Vincenzo!

Duke By God, if I could rise from this bed . . . !

Vincenzo (*shouts*) For it *is* malevolence! You promise me estates for myself and my wife and children . . . promise me them, and then capriciously deny them!

Duke I did not promise you these things. I said I would consider them. I am still considering them.

Vincenzo You need consider them no longer. I have decided to rid you of my distressing presence in Mantua.

Duchess How? What do you mean? (*alarmed*) Vincenzo!

Duke (*furiously*) Answer! Answer!

Vincenzo I am going to the wars. My uncle in France will give me a commission, an army, a life of excitement, a life a prince should have: dignity; a dignified death!

Duchess You cannot! You cannot!

306

Duke You cannot leave Mantua when I am bedridden! When the cares of a state may fall on you at any moment.

Vincenzo Then why am I given no practice in the cares of the state? Am I to find them on my shoulders all unprepared, and despised by your antique counsellors? Is that what you wish?

Duke I have told you a thousand times...

Vincenzo No! Better the real death of a soldier than this death in life you choke me with in Mantua!

Duke I have told you a thousand times I am considering these matters; they are not to be decided in a day.

Vincenzo Or a week, or a month, or a year, or a lifetime! What corrosive monstrosity of an existence is this you make me labour under?
(*silence*)

Eleonora The revolving cycles of domestic damnation. And silences; and myself silent. Oh, the burning noons of Mantua, and the steep sun over the croaking marshes, the lake and the boatmen. The sluggish waters that stroked our isolation. All around us, stagnant waters, rendering us impregnable, it was said: but rendering us stagnant as themselves. Only to Vincenzo was Mantua not a prison. He could escape. I never knew where he went – frightened to ask, for fear I should be told. Did he go to the rose-gardens of Colorno, where Barbara Sanseverino still held her amorous court? Who were the women he met there? I had expected infidelity, though not so soon. Yet it meant much to Vincenzo to have a wife; and I taught myself that his defections, being inevitable, must not matter. We had coaxed an unpromising love into being, and even in him it endured a little, so that I could bear his waywardness, the changing loves of a season. So there was a kind of faithfulness between us. And other faiths I think he had. Did he think still of the child Margherita, who, in her monastery, was now a woman? Did she still think of him? Was it true that her brother Ranuccio, grown from a small harmless spider into a gross, ravenous and envenomed one, spinning from Parma his webs of accusation and menace... was it true Ranuccio took such care to keep Vincenzo's image sharp and clear before her, even in the monastery?

(*chanting in background*)
Ranuccio (*now a man*) Margherita! Margherita!

Margherita (subdued) I have that name no longer, dear brother. You know that.

Ranuccio You will always have that name. Did you know they have a fourth child now, dear sister? A fourth. The girl from Florence is doing her duty well.

Margherita I shall pray for your soul, Ranuccio.

Ranuccio And for his?

Margherita For his also. But yours is in greater need.

Ranuccio A fourth child. A daughter this time: his first daughter.

Margherita Let us rejoice that a child is born. May she be good and happy.

Ranuccio Can you guess what they have named her?

Margherita Dear brother, why do you seek to trouble me with things that are not my . . . *(breaks off in apprehension)*
　　　(music out)

Ranuccio (after a pause: smilingly) Yes, of course. They have named her Margherita.

Margherita It is the name of his sister.

Ranuccio It is the name of his real wife, falsely put off.

Margherita Leave me now, Ranuccio. Please leave me.

Ranuccio No, Margherita. Not yet; I have much to tell you.

Margherita I shall return to my prayers.

Ranuccio (angrily) Get up! Get up from your knees!
　　　(silence)

Eleonora Thus it was rumoured. And always bickering and snarling between Parma and Mantua: inquisition and torture of prisoners; confession, denial, and unenduring reconciliations. And Vincenzo restless. And so much silence between us. And his father the duke lumbering on through his baffled accusations. And lumbering finally into his grave, still protesting. And the awaited splendour of Vincenzo's accession.
　　　(coronation music)
And I lay ill, and heard only the splendid noises below me. And cared not for them, only that they made him happy. And thus he was Duke of Mantua.
　　　(hold coronation music, and then out)
And within a month came news that stirred us more; we heard of the end of a world. My father, the Grand-Duke of Tuscany and his wife Bianca were dying, dying mysteriously together, in Florence. End of a world . . .

308

VINCENZO

Francesco Bianca. Bianca, dear: is it you?

Bianca Yes, Francesco. Who else should it be?

Francesco No one. Only you.

Bianca Yes.

Francesco Have I slept?

Bianca A little.

Francesco Are you close to me?

Bianca Of course, my darling.

Francesco Can you put your hand in mine?

Bianca It's there, my dear; it's been there all along.

Francesco Oh. I can't feel it.

Bianca No matter.

Francesco I am dying, Bianca.

Bianca Yes. We are both dying, Francesco. Dying together.

Francesco As it should be. (*pause*) What are you thinking about, Bianca?

Bianca (*after a pause: in tears*) You. (*she controls them*) You, my love.

Francesco Bianca, Bianca.

Bianca What are *you* thinking about?

Francesco My sins.

Bianca We have shared many of them.

Francesco Yes. Yes, thank God. (*they both try to laugh*) Would you live it all again, Bianca?

Bianca Most of it. All of it, with you. Would you?

Francesco With you. It is my other sins I wish were not so many. I wish I hadn't let them kill my sister. Poor Isabella. A bad girl. But I wish I hadn't.

Bianca It doesn't matter now, dear. It was a long time ago.

Francesco And just for Bracciano. Silly fat devil.

Bianca Yes. He was.

Francesco Fattest man in Italy, they used to say. Did you know that?

Bianca I think so.

Francesco We've been together a long time, Bianca.

Bianca A long, long time.

Francesco You haven't often cried, Bianca.

Bianca I've had no reason to.

Francesco Crying now?

Bianca A little.

Francesco Are you in pain?

Bianca From time to time. Are you?

Francesco Yes.

Bianca Oh, my love.

Francesco It doesn't matter. We shall be together.

Bianca Yes. Wherever it is.

Francesco And we know where it will be.

Bianca Yes.

Francesco We could ... put each other aside. They keep telling me. Turn each other away. Renounce.

Bianca Yes.

Francesco But I couldn't.

Bianca Nor I.

Francesco I never could have.

Bianca Nor I.

Francesco You won't mind ... that place?

Bianca No.

Francesco Can you reach to kiss me, Bianca

Bianca I think so.

Francesco Please then. (*after a pause*) Please.

Bianca (*in tears*) I ... can't ... reach, my love. My love, my love, I can't.

Francesco Never mind, later. We'll kiss later. And we've had a good many, many kisses.

Bianca Many, many kisses. (*a slight wail*) Later.
(*silence*)

Eleonora They died so close together it was thought they were poisoned. I never believed it. And the image of them dying together there filled me with longing. Oh, not to die: but to die one day thus with *him*. My father and Bianca had been wicked; but something in them had endured to the end. It would be the end that would matter. Let Vincenzo wander from me; only, let him come back in the end.

Duchess (*grumbling*) I do not know why you are so silent with him and so unprotesting.

Eleonora Have I so much to complain of?

Duchess Well, if you are contented to be surrounded by your husband's mistresses as if the place were a barnyard ...

Eleonora You know it is not like that.

Duchess It is pity that Vincenzo is so beautiful still.

Eleonora His beauty comes from your side of the family, my dear.

Duchess It is pity he is not ugly like his father was. (*with gloomy pride*) My husband was the ugliest man I have ever seen, I am happy to say. No one would look at him much. It kept him from wandering. Most of the time.

Eleonora I prefer Vincenzo as he is.

Duchess Ah! you have no pride!

Eleonora Pride would hardly have helped me. And I have a kind of pride.

Duchess Yes. The pride of stupidity.

Eleonora I have what your own sister, my mother, had to have: patience.

Duchess It was never rewarded in her case. She had to watch your father courting Bianca Cappello half her life.

Eleonora It has been rewarded in mine.

Duchess I cannot see how.

Eleonora There is at least no Bianca in my life. I am used to Vincenzo's love-affairs by now. I can almost be thankful they are so many.

Duchess Why?

Eleonora Because they are so fleeting; and it means there is not *one*. If he had some woman in his life who occupied it all, as my father had Bianca, that indeed would be a final indignity, and more than I could bear. I would rather be the Bianca. But I thank heaven, however cynically, that there is not such a one.

Duchess (*quietly amazed*) Are you out of your senses? What do you mean: 'There is not such a one'?

Eleonora You know what I mean.

Duchess Yes, I know what you mean. But what reason, in God's name, have you for saying it: 'There is not such a one'?

(*pause*)

Eleonora And why had I said also, 'That would be a final indignity, and more than I could bear'? Indignity is never final; and we underestimate what we can bear ... One afternoon I heard a noise at the door of my apartments; turned, and saw Vincenzo. He was smiling encouragingly at his companion. Who ... was a small, exquisite child of five.

Vincenzo Come on, treasure: this is the way.

Eleonora (*on a sharp, terrified intake of breath*) Vincenzo!

Vincenzo Come on ... Ah, Eleonora, my dear, I know this is unexpected, but so are many good things in life ... This is a great day for this young man ...

Eleonora (*an undertone*) How dare you ... !

Vincenzo (*has not heard her*) Come, treasure. Tell the lady your name.

Silvio (*very distinctly*) Silvio del Carretto.

311

Vincenzo (*affectionately*) Oh, no–no–no, it's not. That was your name yesterday. You have a new name from today.

    Silvio Yes.

Eleonora (*again an undertone*) How dare you do this?

Vincenzo Now, come along: tell us what it is.

    Silvio Today I am Silvio Gonzaga.

Vincenzo Ah, but not only today!

    Silvio For always?

Vincenzo For always.

    Silvio (*absorbedly*) I am Silvio Gonzaga.

Eleonora (*sharply*) Take him away!

Vincenzo Eleo –!

Eleonora Take the child out of this room! Take him out of the palace!
At once. How dare you?

Vincenzo My dear, have you gone out of your mind? What are you saying?

    Silvio (*frightened a little*) I am Silvio Gonzaga.

Eleonora (*under her breath*) Take him away!

Vincenzo (*gently*) Look, treasure, I want you to wait in there for a moment.
I will soon join you. There is no need to be frightened.

        (*he ushers the child out, as he speaks, and gently closes the door*)

Vincenzo (*reproachfully*) Eleonora . . . !

Eleonora Why have you brought that child here?

Vincenzo But, my dear wife, he *ought* to be here by now. I want him here.
He is five years old. It is time he came here.

Eleonora You are outrageous! You cannot intend to keep him here!

Vincenzo This is senseless, Eleonora. He is my child, my own flesh and blood.

Eleonora Well?

Vincenzo Eleonora!

Eleonora If you insist on keeping one of your bastards here in the palace,
your own children become outcasts. You make them so.

Vincenzo Outcasts? Good God above! My own children, the flesh and
blood of both of us. Outcasts! Why, why, why, they bear my
name, they . . .

Eleonora They bear your name; they will inherit your titles, yes. And they
come from two great families, yours and mine. They will join
hands with other great families: in Austria or France or Savoy or
Germany or Spain or Rome! Yes, will they not! And their
children will have *their* hands joined again with Florence, Savoy,
France, Poland, Denmark, Naples, Spain; wherever it is thought
cunningest and most convenient.

312

Vincenzo Eleonora!

Eleonora A dozen famous names lovelessly multiplying across the length and breadth of Christendom. Begetting outcasts!

Vincenzo It's you, not I, that call them outcasts! I have always shown as much care and concern about our own children as I have for those less regularly . . . come by.

Eleonora Good God! How can you bear to say it so nakedly and shamelessly!

Vincenzo Is it shameful to be a devoted father? I have always loved my children, wherever they have been begotten.

Eleonora (*passionately*) Is adultery a sin, or is it not?

Vincenzo Of course it is a sin. I have sinned, and shall sin again, and shall hope to be forgiven. I am not a saint. But would you have me cast aside the honest wholesome fruit of sin? Silvio is the most beautiful child in the world. Would you have little children going about Mantua, growing up, recognisably mine, and rejected by me? What kind of figure do you think I should cut, if I let such things happen? (*with real solicitude*) I think you must be ill, Eleonora.

Eleonora (*after a pause*) Perhaps I am, then. Perhaps I am more than ill.

Vincenzo My darling, no.

Eleonora I feel as if I were treading a pathway towards insanity. If what you have said is right and what I have said is wrong, then I well may be.

Vincenzo No, no. You exaggerate. We all have these little obsessions; they may occupy our minds for days perhaps. (*reproachfully*) But we must be careful, Eleonora, not to hurt others by them.

Eleonora (*incredulously*) Have *I* hurt *you?*

Vincenzo I won't say . . . you've hurt me, my dear, but . . .

Eleonora But what?

Vincenzo (*with growing self-pity*) Yes! Yes! You *have* hurt me! Why should I try to hide it? You have hurt me! Why am I always subjected to disapprobation like this? It used to be my father; now it's you, my own wife. And all the time I have thought, and the whole of Mantua has said, that ours was a good marriage!

Eleonora Has it not been? Have I failed you in any way? Am I another Margherita Farnese?

Vincenzo You wicked woman! You wicked woman! To mention that girl's name!

Eleonora I am sorry. I didn't mean to.

313

Vincenzo All the things I hold most sacred are being destroyed!

Eleonora What are they?

Vincenzo I come back from the wars, from fighting the heathen Turk, travel-stained and weary . . .

Eleonora You have been back three months.

Vincenzo After exhausting and perilous journeys, I return to disputes and threats all around me, menaces from Savoy, intrigues in Parma, future wars oppressing my mind . . . I come back, not to the warrior's comfort and love; not, not to the things a husband has a holy right to expect . . .

Eleonora (*wearily*) I do love you . . .

Vincenzo Oh, no, Eleonora. You don't love me! God forbid that the things you say and think should be hallowed with the name of love.

Eleonora (*as before*) The things I say do not alter the love I bear you. I do love you.

Vincenzo Oh, no. (*pause: quieter*) I have tried my best. And I have failed.

Eleonora At what?

Vincenzo I am an affectionate man. I think I may say it, an affectionate man. I have always hoped I had the gift of winning affection from others.

Eleonora Have you any reason to doubt it?

Vincenzo Not until today. But I was fond enough to hope for more than that. I hoped to foster affection in others; I like people to help each other.

Eleonora I have, at one time and another, 'helped' a not inconsiderable number of your concubines.

Vincenzo Don't use that word! How can you?

Eleonora Two of them I have saved from being murdered by their brothers, as my aunt was murdered by my father.

Vincenzo Well, there is such a thing as family honour, is there not?

Eleonora (*a desperate whisper*) My God, my God!

Vincenzo I have thanked the Lord daily that our children are comely and well-contented; daily I have prayed Him to keep them so. I have prayed that there shall be, between my family children and my natural ones, that respect and affection, whose absence can place on a father's life the darkest incubus. I hoped to foster that respect and affection by tenderness to all of them, official child and bastard alike: for in that I deem true fatherhood to consist. But all my life I have been thwarted, a cruelly thwarted man! Thwarted by the avarice of my father, by the unremitting bigotry of my

dear mother, by cruel perversions in the laws of nature, by ungenerous foes, ungenerous emperors! I have asked for bread and
been given a stone. I have asked for the governorship of the
Netherlands, and been offered the command of a small squadron
of the Portuguese navy; ungenerous men, all about me! Never
has my life been allowed to blossom into fullness, never has the
great tree of my life been allowed to spread its branches to the
sun! I cannot bear the sight of you, Eleonora, at this moment!
You have wounded me more than I can find words to say.

    (*on the last sentence he rushes out*)

Eleonora (*calls after him*) Vincenzo! No . . . come back! Don't leave the
boy!

    (*brief pause*)

  Silvio (*some distance away*) Has father gone away?

Eleonora Yes.

  Silvio W-will he come back?

Eleonora Eventually.

  Silvio (*repeats, absently*) Eventually. Yes. (*pause*) I am Silvio Gonzaga
now.

Eleonora Yes.

  Silvio I saw some other children.

Eleonora Where?

  Silvio Through that window. Playing in the courtyard. Are they your
children?

Eleonora Yes.

  Silvio Shall I be allowed to play with them?

Eleonora I . . . don't know.

  Silvio Father said I was to love them with all the Power of my Very
Being.

Eleonora (*near to tears*) Did he?

  Silvio Yes. So I will, of course. (*he observes her*) My mother used to cry
sometimes, a little.

Eleonora Does she never cry now?

  Silvio No. My father says there is too much crying in the world. So she
has ceased. (*pause*) I never cry either. (*pause*) Do your children
cry?

Eleonora I will try to see that they don't do so in future.

  Silvio Yes . . . I expect my father has gone back to my mother. (*pause*)
What a very large tremendous place you have here, haven't you?

Eleonora Yes. Shall I show you to your room?

315

Silvio Yes, please. If it is not too much trouble.

    (*pause: then the opening of Monteverdi's 'Lament of Ariadne' is heard. Singer and orchestra are held behind Eleonora. They are brought full up after she finishes speaking*)

Eleonora And from then on, he was always there, Silvio, the child of Agnese del Carretto: till his presence at my husband's side, at every festival and celebration, became the accepted usage of Mantua. He had conquered all hearts, those of my children more powerfully than any. And he would sit at Vincenzo's right hand, watching the stage; both of them sharing, entranced, the joys and sufferings enacted there. It was not until after many years that I saw her, his mother, in the distance, watching them both. And by then Silvio was hers no longer.

Singer
> *Lasciatemi morire*
> *Lasciatemi morire,*
> *E che volete voi che mi conforte*
> *In così dura sorte,*
> *In così gran martire?*
> *Lasciatemi morire,*
> *Lasciatemi morire.*

Chorus
> *In van lingua mortale,*
> *In van porge conforto,*
> *Dove infinito è il male.*

(the singer is now heard clearly)

Singer
> *Dove, dove la fede,*
> *Che tanto mi giuravi?*
> *Così nell' alta sede*
> *Tu mi ripon degl' avi?*
> *Son queste le corone*
> *Onde m' adorn' il crine,*
> *Questi gli scettri sono,*
> *Queste le gemme e gl' ori?*
> *Lasciarmi in abbandono*
> *A fera che mi strazi e mi divori?*
> *Ahi Teseo, ahi Teseo mio,*
> *Lascerai tu morire,*
> *In van piangendo,*
> *In van gridando aita,*
> *La misera Arianna*

>
Che a te fidossi,
E ti diè gloria e vita?

Chorus   (*as before, but faded immediately behind speech*)

Silvio   Father.

Vincenzo Yes, Silvio?

Silvio   She is hurt, is she not, father, because the Prince has promised her a throne and jewels and to stay with her forever?

Vincenzo Yes, treasure.

Silvio   And because he has not done so?

Vincenzo Yes.

Silvio   How very, very sad, father. It *is* sad, is it not, father?

Vincenzo Yes, treasure.

Silvio   I am filled with grave distress. But I will not cry.

Singer

>
Ahi che non pur risponde!
Ahi che più d'aspr' e sord' ai miei lamenti!
O nembi, o turbini, o venti,
Sommergetelo voi dentro a quell' onde!
Correte, orche e balene,
E delle membra immonde
Empiete le voragini profonde!
>
Che parlo, ahi che vaneggio!
Misera ahimè! Che chieggio?
O Teseo, o Teseo mio,
Non son, non son quell'io,
Non son quell' io che i fera detti sciolse;
Parla l' affanno mio, parla il dolore,
Parla la lingua, si, ma non già il core.

Chorus   (*as before, faded behind speech*)

Silvio   She wished for a moment that the wild animals of the sea would tear him to pieces and swallow him, did she not, father?

Vincenzo Yes, Silvio.

Silvio   And then she was sorry she had wished it?

Vincenzo Yes, treasure.

Silvio   But it would have served him right, would it not, father?

Vincenzo Yes, in a sense it would.

Silvio   How sad and wicked.

Vincenzo But in the end you will see she is rescued and made happy by Bacchus, the god of wine.

Silvio Oh, father, I am so glad. Are unhappy ladies always rescued from their sorrow by the god of wine?

Vincenzo Very frequently, yes.

Silvio In life also, father?

Vincenzo Yes, my child. But we must not think that things on a stage are always quite like life.

Silvio No, father. But I am very glad poor Ariadne will be saved. As it would otherwise have been very sad and wicked.

Vincenzo Yes, treasure.

(*music out*)

Agnese Thus Silvio, my son, was removed from my care; and I, Agnese del Carretto, marchioness of Grana, lived without him. The pain of losing his daily presence about the Palace of the T almost made a great woman of me. How daring and imaginative of Vincenzo it had been! Perhaps it was the last imaginative gesture of his life. But at first our lives had been all daring and imagination. Ah, had they not! The world had been against us: his wife, his mother, his sister, the Cardinal of the Medici in Florence, the Pope in Rome. They were willing to tolerate his passing fancies; but when they failed to pass . . . ah me! To install me in the pleasure-palace on the very outskirts of his city asked courage of Vincenzo, and the courage was there. (*the slightest hint of mockery in her voice*) I *gave* him courage, he said. He said I gave him strength and determination.

Vincenzo Agnese, my light, my only one! What splendid things you will make of me! Art, war! Painting, that great art, war, that art no less: the things I love! What energy you could give me in my studies of both . . . ! You, Agnese, shall be the radiant image of the Madonna in every picture I shall commission, you shall shine on my shield and dazzle the eyes of my foe in my every encounter with him. It will be your hand I shall clasp when I seize my sword and brandish it aloft . . . !

Agnese At what point in the fifteen years of our love a slight note of absurdity began to creep in I never knew. Perhaps it was there unnoticed from the start, on the day I had first met him in the

318

palace of Barbara Sanseverino at Colorno. Perhaps, perhaps not...
And when has a man's absurdity ever prevented a woman from
falling in love with him? I gave him courage, he said. I gave him
energy and determination . . . War. Art.

Vincenzo (*weightily*) My dear Rubens. Rubens! (*he pauses: then rapidly and
lightly*) Rubens, I have no idea what sort of pictures you will
choose to paint in the course of the life that now spreads so
golden in promise before you. And I have no wish to influence
you, but if it ever *should* cross your mind, if you ever *should* – oh,
just once in a lifetime, let us say – have some incidental occasion
to paint that miracle of nature, a woman's behind, then let me
assure you you will never find any better guide to its execution
than our rough old Pippi, Giulio Romano, as we call him. Look
at that lovely nude Psyche over there, a friend of my dear grandfather's, as it happens. See how she turns in her embrace of Cupid
(oh, so lyrical, so lovely. Soldier as I am, I feel for these things
and recall them poignantly on the field of battle). And notice the
way old Giulio lifts the near buttock just slightly off the couch.
When it was first painted, so I'm told, if you climbed up on a
ladder and looked very closely, you could see the delicate impress
her seat had left on the cushion. The sincerity of it.

Rubens Yes.

Vincenzo (*with increasing energy*) But enough of soft idleness! War is our
theme. I want you to give your best attention to the decorations
for the festivities that shall celebrate my return. My executant
Follino will describe the scenic effects we hope you will aim at.
And if you have any time over, there are not a few themes from
my own military life that might inspire you. A curious thing
was observed during my last campaign. It was at Giavarrino; I
was rescuing a group of my men from the heathen foe (I had
to do it alone, there was no one else to help them) and it was
remarked that at the height of the fray an angel was seen hovering
over my head. It was identified as Saint Francis of Paolo. I've
often thought there might be something in that for a painter.
You . . . you . . . *feel* it, m'm? You . . . you . . . ?

Agnese (*entering at some distance*) Vincenzo, I think you should . . . oh,
I beg your pardon.

Vincenzo I am coming at once, my dear. Well, my dear Rubens, think
about it, will you? I must leave you to explore the rest of our

little palace yourself. Duty calls. A campaign, alas, is not all art. I wish you a good diversion. I am coming, my dear ...

    (*he joins Agnese*)

I was talking to my new painter, my dear.

Agnese Is he promising, do you think?

Vincenzo Oh yes. He seems to have very little to say, but I think he has the root of the matter in him.

Agnese Follino is here.

Vincenzo (*briskly*) Ah, yes, excellent, welcome, my dear Follino. You'll have had my note. Now, what we want for the days immediately after my return is a series of dramatic *intermezzi*, showing how we shall have besieged and taken Grosskirchen. As soon as the siege itself begins, I will arrange to keep you posted night and day with all news of the more spectacular exploits I perf ... p ... participate in. But there is no reason at all why the actual *scenario* for the thing should not be prepared immediately. After all, military valour, warrior-like ... ah, exploits, are of kindred cast throughout the centuries. We soldiers do but add our, aha, individual note. So ask my wife to give you access to the volumes of Plutarch in the library up at the palace. They will give you a general idea of what will be going on. Be careful to put them back the right way up. And if I can spare a moment I will give you a few further jottings before I to-horse.

Follino Yes, your Highness. And thank you, your Highness.

    (*he leaves*)

Vincenzo An excellent man.

Agnese And if you could spare *me* a few moments before you to-horse, my dearest, I would be –

Vincenzo (*warmly*) Ah, my Agnese! For you I would spare my life and being. It will be you that will shine on my shield, you that I shall brandish aloft over the heathen foe ...

    (*the last remarks are drowned in martial music. It is held in the background as Agnese speaks*)

Agnese I do not suppose Vincenzo is the only military leader who has given orders for the celebration of his return from the battlefield before departing for it. He merely went a little exuberantly further than others, that is all. It was his nature. And he was not the first artist to create his art before living it. Why the military life exercised so strong a spell over him is beyond my conjecture.

But thus splendidly he set out for his third . . . *visit* to the wars against the Turks.

(Vincenzo is dejected and ill)

Soldier Your Highness, there is Colonel Roswurm to see you.

Vincenzo Who?

Soldier Colonel Roswurm, sir.

Vincenzo Oh.

Soldier Shall I admit him to the tent, sir?

Vincenzo What? Yes. Couldn't it wait till tomorrow?

Soldier He spoke with great urgency, sir.

Vincenzo Well, let him come in.

Soldier Yes, your Highness.

(pause)

Roswurm *(a German commander)* Good evening, your Highness.

Vincenzo Good evening, Colonel.

(pause)

Roswurm I have come to receive your orders, your Highness.

Vincenzo *(vaguely)* Well, I've had terrible trouble with my knee.

Roswurm I am greatly distressed to hear it, sir. I trust it improves.

Vincenzo *(his voice goes, momentarily)* . . . . . . Urk. Urk.

Roswurm Sir?

Vincenzo *(clearing his throat)* Urk. My voice keeps going. I said, 'And the throat'. An inflammation. I've tried everything.

Roswurm The damps of the Hungarian plains are not easy on one from your own warm climate.

Vincenzo Well, it suited in the old days, God knows. Great times of warrioring we had, splendid. A man felt well and strong. You heard about Giavarrino, I suppose, three or four years ago?

Roswurm Yes, sir.

Vincenzo Splendid year for me, ninety-seven.

Roswurm Ninety-eight, sir.

Vincenzo M'm?

Roswurm The town was not taken till ninety-eight, sir.

Vincenzo No, I know. But . . . oh, I felt so healthy. I rescued a group of my own *mantovani* single-handed, you know?

Roswurm Indeed, your Highness?

Vincenzo Oh, it was nothing. Strange thing was that . . . Urk. Forgive me.

An angel. An angel was seen floating above my head in the height of the fray. Saint Francis of Paolo, everyone said.

Roswurm Did you see it yourself, sir?

Vincenzo ......

Roswurm I beg your pardon, sir?

Vincenzo I said, 'I couldn't look up'. It was the height of the fray. Janissaries, scimitars, the heathen foe, they gave me no ... Urk. No quarter. A splendid experience. It changes a man's whole life.

Roswurm What was the angel trying to do, sir?

Vincenzo (*disconcerted*) M'm? Oh. It was an angel. They ... appear, sometimes. At certain moments. (*vaguely*) Hovering.

Roswurm Sir?

Vincenzo It hovered.

Roswurm I understand, sir. And have you orders for me?

Vincenzo No. No, I don't think so.
> (*pause*)

Roswurm Then will you permit me to appreciate the situation, sir?

Vincenzo (*lost*) By all means.

Roswurm Well, sir, I have been asked to ascertain the following points, sir.

Vincenzo M'm?

Roswurm It is reported here, sir, that there are no ropes for dragging the heavy cannon in your sector. Is that true, sir?

Vincenzo (*dimly*) It may well be the case. I wouldn't like to swear to it, but ...

Roswurm And that three thousand loaves of bread have been allowed to go rotten for lack of fuel to cook them.

Vincenzo (*interested*) That I *hadn't* heard.

Roswurm And that two hundred cavalrymen were three days ago ordered on to the field unequipped with horses.

Vincenzo I ... I can't speak with any certainty on that point, Colonel Roswurm; as you will imagine, my knee has for some days completely incapacitated me ...
> (*the last remark drowned in music*)

Agnese The celebrations for Vincenzo's return to Mantua lasted twelve weeks and were of a magnificence hitherto unknown among us. Full news of the campaign did not arrive till later, and by that time Vincenzo had recovered from the ordeals of battle. They had aged him, and I observed in him what often goes with increasing age: a love of the company of people ever and ever younger, a proneness to ill-judged passion – though his desires were now not so clearly enunciated as in our earlier days together . . .

Vincenzo (*now forty-six, and approaching pathos*) But you see, Agnese, I *must* have her. She is said to be the best young singer in Italy.

Agnese So I have heard.

Vincenzo The fair Adriana. Adriana Basile. We cannot persuade her to leave Naples. I have written to her father, her mother, her husband. One feels so mistrusted. The greatest singers and actresses in Italy have performed here; it will be unendurable if we cannot have this girl. I must have her, Agnese, I must have her.

Agnese I am sure that she will be persuaded in the end.

Vincenzo My dear wife has at last consented to offer the girl her protection; in the old days such a thing would never have been dreamt of. Never.

Agnese Adriana appeared at last, after months of bargaining and procrastination. She was, like myself, a woman of Naples, and she brought with her the immense sweet mornings of my city. The fair Adriana; how exquisite in voice and person, like a high roseate cloud, an opening rosebud, a light sweet breeze of spring. Those were the things she brought so gracefully to mind. (*sincerely*) She was the silliest woman I ever met.

Adriana (*volubly cooing: full of herself*) Oh and oh and the day the news came that they wanted me, though I knew they didn't *all* want me at first till I made them, and the day the news came I had just gone out on to the balcony and oh it was a true Posillipo day and the sea was sparkling all the way up to the sky oh and the sky was shining all the way down over the water and it was all so beautiful-and-lovely that you felt all you could do was to take in a big-steady-breath-now of the beautiful big air and ever so beautifully and slowly just let yourself begin to *a-haaaa* . . .

(*she is heard singing a wordless melody, which continues to be heard behind her as she speaks*)

. . . and just float away high and lovely away with yourself and it makes you feel so beautiful-and-lovely just to do it and you feel it all over and through you as if you never wanted to stop and you go higher and higher . . . (*song alone briefly*) . . . and oh so lovely down again and you feel so *beautiful* and you float yourself

323

away (*long diminuendo as she speaks*) into almost nothing . . . and then really nothing. (*silence*) And suddenly you begin to begin all over again (*she has done so*) only better and better and it was just at that moment that they came in and told me. (*music out abruptly*)

Her mother (*approaching tearfully*) Oh, Adriana, my dear dear child, I dread to think what your husband and your father and your four poor brothers will say, but . . .

Adriana (*regardless of this memory*) And oh and the wonderful journey from Naples first to Rome and in Rome there was the Duke's son, little Cardinal Ferdinando Gonzaga so young and lovely to be a cardinal and the colour so suiting him and he so sweet-and-sweet and after a day or two we could both tell that we *both*; and whenever he came near me I felt I wanted to take a big-steady-breath-now and *a-haaa* . . . (*melody as before*) And oh and the joy and the light of it and when we came to Mantua (*song out*) I felt a little bit frightened because of the Duke and I'd never thought I would like him at all but oh I liked him almost as much as Ferdinando because he'd *been through so much*, and I like people who've done that, and his poor wife was so sweet to me and she'd been through even more, and so there were both dear Ferdinando my little little Cardinal, and dear Vincenzo, my big big Duke and all the way from Rome whenever Ferdinando had looked at me I'd felt I was taking a big-steady-breath-now and *a-haaa* . . . (*melody as before*) and oh and I always did and I *still* did and I went on but oh and when there were the two of them and *the two of them*, oh and I felt so happy and lovely and I felt I was singing a lovely duet with myself (*her voice is heard doing so*) and oh and oh and going up and down and up and beautiful little sounds bubbling out of both of me and oh and it was so beautiful-and-lovely! (*hold Adriana's duet a moment, then drop to solo, and hold as a long sustained shake behind Vincenzo*)

Vincenzo (*desperate but subdued*) But, you see, Agnese, my dearest friend . . . she never *ceases* . . . And after all, why should she, I ask myself? Why should she?

Agnese Are you not quite as fond of her as you expected to be?

Vincenzo I don't know, Agnese. (*Adriana out*) I sometimes wonder if I ought not to leave her to Ferdinando. And Eleonora is so ill, she cannot be expected to take her off my hands.

Agnese How ill is Eleonora?

Vincenzo I don't like to ask, I don't dare to. I'm full of fears, Agnese. Suppose I am left alone. (*pause*) Suppose I am left alone.

Agnese (*guilty of inattention*) I . . . you won't be left alone, my dear. There will always be myself, as there always has been.

Vincenzo What would there be for me without you?

Agnese You often are without me.

Vincenzo You spend so much time with Barbara at Colorno.

Agnese But Colorno is full of you, Vincenzo. Think how many times we were together there.

Vincenzo And now never together there.

Agnese It would be disastrous for Barbara if you appeared there now. She has the place on only the narrowest sufferance from Parma; Ranuccio will not rest till he has Colorno in his grip. It would only confirm his suspicions of plots against him if you came. Better to wait.

Vincenzo Ah, God, these eternal threats and menaces and fears. Ranuccio has always claimed Colorno, ever since he became Duke. But his father and grandfather confirmed Barbara's right in it. He can have no authority to move against her.

Agnese She knows that; but I cannot help feeling distressed for her.
  (*pause*)

Vincenzo Agnese.

Agnese Yes, my dear?

Vincenzo There . . . isn't anyone else, is there?

Agnese Anyone else? What do you mean?

Vincenzo A . . . younger man.

Agnese What foolish fancies you indulge yourself in lately, Vincenzo.

Vincenzo I . . . I've always hoped you and I might die together, Agnese. People do, sometimes. Like Bianca and old Francesco. A beautiful end to make. But perhaps that too is a foolish fancy.

Agnese Well, if God wills it, perhaps we *shall* die like that, Vincenzo.

Vincenzo (*happier*) Yes, yes: perhaps so. How beautiful. There is real art in such an end to two lives. I don't know why I thought you might have found another . . . But, of course, I would have known. In my heart I would have known if there was anyone else.
  (*pause*)

Agnese But, God willing, he would not know. There was no reason why I should not have gone on forever in the calm respected rôle of his favourite; I was the right person. We had our love of the arts in common, everyone said; our love of spectacular plays and ballets, everyone said; our passionate devotion to the Church, everyone said. And when Eleonora went her way into death, alone, it was natural that I should assume her place in the Palace itself. And Vincenzo had never once observed that the image engraved in my gaze was no longer his own. Colorno, Colorno: I had walked down the great stairway of Barbara's palace, and suddenly paused at the sound of a new voice expostulating with her; a voice free, clear, youthful and unabashed.

Sanvitale (*aged twenty*) But where is she, Aunt Barbara? Where is she? I want her, I want to see her!

Barbara (*now sixty*) I cannot quite see the aim of your curiosity, Gianfrancesco.

Sanvitale My aim is always a direct and simple one, like your own, dearest aunt.

Barbara You speak of days gone by, Gianfrancesco.

Sanvitale So you pretend. But Agnese's days won't have gone by just yet.

Barbara If you wish to refer to her in my presence, Gianfrancesco, you will kindly use her title, the Marchioness of Grana. You will also do so when you meet her.

Sanvitale And when I sleep with her?

Barbara That is not even a matter for speculation, my dear *little boy*.

Sanvitale (*laughing*) Are you daring me, Aunt Barbara? You are becoming staid before your time.

Barbara You will find the Marchioness of Grana also staid.

Sanvitale Not if what I have heard is true, aunt. It is said the horns grow round the Duke Vincenzo's head so densely that in certain lights they take on the aspect of a halo.

(*Barbara bursts out laughing*)

Shameful aunt! To laugh at your oldest friend.

Barbara There is no word of truth in it. And you will treat the Marchioness of Grana . . .

Sanvitale Agnese, Agnese!

Barbara You will treat the Marchioness of Grana as a lady. She is old enough to be your mother.

Sanvitale (*laughs*) But you know what rumours Ranuccio Farnese has spread about me and my mother, aunt.

Barbara Be quiet, you filthy reptile.

Sanvitale And I have no aversion from women old enough to be my mother. How old is she?

Barbara How old are *you*?

Sanvitale I am nearly twenty. Though when I am naked I would pass for a charming youth of sixteen, as you know.

Barbara As I don't know, Gianfrancesco!

Sanvitale Then we must remedy that, dear aunt.

     (*pause*)

Agnese I was old enough to be his mother, Barbara had said. We met that evening four hours later. I could not speak; and he chose not to. He had, it was said, a great variety of approaches to his women . . . There was no wooing. We learned to love thereafter; and it *was* love, even on Gianfrancesco's part. The one concession he made me was, at first, to keep it secret. But things are not kept secret.

Barbara (*mildly*) It is true, then, Agnese?

Agnese Yes, of course it's true.

Barbara A dangerous passion I would have thought it, my dear? If it is a passion?

Agnese (*sullenly*) I don't know what it is. Does it matter? I know what I am doing.

Barbara (*tiny pause*) You are old enough to know, certainly.

Agnese Barbara!

Barbara I am not being cruel. You are just over twice his age. I have seen this happen before, and always to a woman with brains.

Agnese You mean . . . Gianfrancesco . . . ?

Barbara Oh, no. You are probably the first woman with any brains he's ever met, apart from myself. (And indeed they may stand you in good stead with him for a time; he will enjoy the novelty.) No, I meant I had seen this little piece of machinery at work before. There is a demon in the blood that breaks upon our middle-age and suddenly flourishes a Gianfrancesco before us, and makes us feel that we may once again, for one more riotous epoch in our lives, be still young. But you will not manage Gianfrancesco as well as you manage Vincenzo.

Agnese (*wearily*) Vincenzo. I am tired of Vincenzo.

Barbara No. You will go back to him.

Agnese I have never left him.

Barbara Might you not have been with him now?

Agnese Why?

327

Barbara Gianfrancesco will not be back from Parma for three weeks. You might have spent some of that time consoling Vincenzo for the loss of Eleonora. Or so I would have thought. Or helping him to find a new wife. He is said to be looking for one.

Agnese (*almost absently*) He wants someone to die beside him in the dark like Bianca Cappello and Francesco de' Medici.

Barbara Ah, well, we all want that.

Agnese I shall be with him a week from today. We are standing as god-parents at a baptism.

Barbara Whose is the child?

Agnese Adriana's.

Barbara The girl who sings?

Agnese (*with meaning*) The girl who sings.

Barbara And who is the child's father?

Agnese She hopes to discover that later on.

(*church music, or Adriana's own, as before*)

Agnese 'A week from today.' Sunday to Sunday. Never did I think that in one week so much could happen.

Adriana A-haaa . . . ! Oh and it was the most beautiful-and-lovely day since the first beginning of the world and my husband was so sweet-and-pleased and everyone in the court wondered who had helped me to make the dear little thinging-thing but they all had too much breeding to ask me and oh it was so *moving* when my dear little Cardinal Ferdinando, looking *so* lovely, baptised the little thing and her godfather was my dear big Duke and her godmother was his other friend, Agnese, who was *going through so much* and we called the little thinging-thing E-le-o-no-ra, after the dear Duke's dear late dear wife and oh and it was all so lovely-and-beautiful and oh I *know* everyone – *everyone* was going through so much at that very time, and my heart bled for them but the choir was so beautiful and the trumpets I could hardly keep myself from *a-haaa* . . . !

(*she joins the choir. Fade music behind*)

Agnese Yes, everyone was going through so much! Was any of them going through so much as I, who dared not show my deepest dread? What we had feared for years had happened in a week. Ranuccio, in sudden frenzy, had shouted to the world that vast plots were in train against him. Within a week he had seized everyone on Parma's soil whom he suspected; among them Gianfrancesco ... Perhaps at this very moment confessions were being tortured out of him. And throughout the baptism the thought drummed through me, 'How can he be saved? How shall I save Gianfrancesco ... ?' At last I saw a possible way ...

Vincenzo Oh, my dear, thank God it's over. Do you think anyone noticed how distressed I was?

Agnese I think it probably escaped Adriana.

Vincenzo Oh, Agnese, the monstrosity of it! I solemnly declare that Ranuccio Farnese is the vilest man in Italy. To accuse me, me, me, Vincenzo Gonzaga, of plotting to do away with him. I don't even want him done away with, though of course I should be very very glad if it happened. (*brokenly*) And but to think of all those poor people, dear friends of ours many of them, pounced on, commonly pounced on by Ranuccio's spies and agents. Imprisoned. Put to the torture. It is a terrible thing. Have you had news from Barbara?

Agnese No. She is still at Colorno.

Vincenzo I don't know what I would do if anything happened to Barbara. She was the greatest woman of her day. I feel less concern about some of her relations, I'm bound to say. Prison is probably the best place for that dreadful young nephew of hers – what is his name, I forget?

Agnese ... Gianfrancesco?

Vincenzo Yes. Did you ever meet him?

Agnese (*after the briefest pause*) I can't remember.

Vincenzo Oh a villain, a young Satan.

Agnese In what way?

Vincenzo Why, he ... he goes after women. And some of the others are perhaps no better. But oh, let us hope poor Barbara is safe.

Agnese And the rest too.

Vincenzo The rest too. For twenty years Ranuccio has girded at me. I could have retaliated, but I never seriously took up arms against him, though with all my military experience behind me, I could have made short work of him. But I have always held back ... You know why, of course.

(*pause*)

Agnese Margherita?

Vincenzo Little Margherita, yes. For after all, whatever happened, she had once been my wife. And the memory of her always made me stay my hand against her brother. It was a way of being faithful to her. I've loved many women and always been faithful to all of them, though in ways I might find it difficult to explain very clearly. But it was a different kind of faith for Margherita. Perhaps because of the very fact that she could never be my wife in the proper way.

(*pause*)

Agnese You've been rather lonely, I'm afraid, these last months, Vincenzo.

Vincenzo Yes, I've missed you very much, Agnese.

Agnese No, my dear, it wasn't I you missed.

Vincenzo It was, my dear, who else?

Agnese It is Eleonora that you miss. Your true wife.

(*pause*)

Vincenzo (*near to tears*) True wife. Oh, Agnese, yes! Yes, yes!

Agnese The mature, sanctified companionship. The rest is smoke.

Vincenzo Yes. And oh, my dear, my children censure me whenever I speak of marrying again. They fear I might add to the number of my heirs, they say I'm old and would look foolish. (*with sudden indignation*) They say these things so *openly*, Agnese! You know how disrespectful young people are with their parents today. A terrible world we face. There was never so much as an angry word between my own dear parents and myself. Yes, my dear: Eleonora's death has tried me sorely. A wife. Sanctified companionship, as you say.

Agnese Vincenzo: may I speak to you very intimately, as an old and devoted friend rather than as a mistress?

Vincenzo Yes, of course you may.

Agnese You spoke of Margherita. (*pause*) Vincenzo, has it ever occurred to you that you might one day marry Margherita again?

Vincenzo Marry her again, my dear? How . . . No, I've never thought of such a thing. I . . . how could I?

Agnese It would be unusual, but not impossible. And rather wonderful, I think. I . . . I've thought a great deal about you lately, Vincenzo, though you may not believe me. And one day it occurred to me what a great thing, however strange, it would be for the world if you wished to and were allowed to marry Margherita again. I cannot help thinking it would make you happy. I know you have not seen her for thirty years, but I think she has inhabited your thoughts for more of that time than you will admit.

330

Vincenzo (*vaguely: preoccupied*) Yes. She has. She has. What an extraordinary idea, Agnese.

Agnese There is example for these remarriages.

Vincenzo Yes, perhaps so. But think of the state of affairs between Mantua and Parma. The idea would turn Ranuccio into a lunatic.

Agnese On the contrary, I think it might cure at least some of his lunacies. His voracious spying and seizing on innocent people is only the expression of his fear of being suddenly stabbed. If you married Margherita, at least his fears of Mantua would be allayed.

Vincenzo It might save Barbara and all those other poor devils, perhaps.

Agnese Yes, I dare say there is something in that too. Certainly there is no other hope for them. In any case, I wasn't thinking mainly of them. But I think after all these years I may claim to know you rather well, and . . . I know what you still feel for Margherita.

Vincenzo You . . . you make me realise that I *do* feel it, Agnese. (*brokenly*) Oh, yes, I do feel it, Agnese.

Agnese I think you should send messengers to Ranuccio and the Pope to sound their opinions.

Vincenzo Yes . . . yes, I might well do that. I must think, of course, first: I must think profoundly. But oh, Agnese . . . (*simply*) What a great woman you are.

Agnese Only devoted friend and old lover, my dear.

Vincenzo Yes. Yes, what days we have known.

Agnese Vincenzo.

Vincenzo Yes, my love?

Agnese Vincenzo; I trust that if you did marry Margherita Farnese again, it would not be with the thought of anything more than profound companionship between you.

Vincenzo Ah, you mustn't be jealous, Agnese. It's unworthy of you.

Agnese I will try not to be. But I was thinking more of her than of myself. And of Parma. Parma would not fancy the thought of insult yet again.

Vincenzo There would be no question.

Agnese Parma would, of course, have to understand that it was a marriage arranged deliberately and calmly to heal all wounds between Mantua and herself.

Vincenzo Yes, of course.

Agnese And above all, to bring companionship to you.

Vincenzo Ah, yes, Agnese! Companionship. Two old lovers in age. Do you remember how Bianca Cappello and old Francesco died together?

331

Like that: I've always thought how fine.

Agnese Yes, I have heard you say so before.

Vincenzo And Margherita . . . was such a child. Everyone loved her. What a hard, terrible fate, Agnese. I could make amends to her for all the world has done. You know, even during the very worst of the months we had together, she was so little and sweet and had such winning ways that you wanted to pick her up and hug her like a tiny child. She tried to be older than her years, of course, but you felt, 'Oh God: don't let anyone hurt this child.'

Agnese (*gently*) She will not be a child now: she will be forty-five.

Vincenzo Yes, yes. But it could make no difference to her. You could see she would always have the heart of a child. Oh, Agnese . . .

(*chanting of nuns heard. Margherita has developed in severity of manner*)

Ranuccio Sister Maura.

Margherita Good morning, Ranuccio. God bless you.

Ranuccio God bless you, dear sister.

Margherita I hope you come in a sober and gentle mood.

Ranuccio I am sorry you should doubt it.

Margherita I am afraid you have given me much reason this winter to fear your moods when you visit me.

Ranuccio That I must beg you to forgive me. These terrible plots against me are surely enough to excuse some distraughtness. I have much reason for exasperation.

Margherita But not for spite, malice or cruelty, Ranuccio.

Ranuccio I vow that I shall show none this morning, either towards you, or towards anyone else.

Margherita Thank you.

Ranuccio I have an important thing to say to you, Margherita.

Margherita It is when you say you have important things to say to me, that I have reason to fear you, Ranuccio. I warn you, with all the . . .

Ranuccio (*interrupts*) Margherita.
(*pause*)
Margherita. Please try to listen, with more charity than I perhaps deserve, to what I have to say.

Margherita Well, Ranuccio?

Ranuccio I have had a strange embassage this morning, Margherita. It concerns you, and you must therefore grant me permission to disclose it to you. I beg that of you.

Margherita (*after a pause*) Well.

   Ranuccio Vincenzo of Mantua has asked for your hand in marriage.

Margherita (*violently*) Ranuccio! God forgive you, and may He forgive me for reproaching you; but I swear to you that you will one day answer before the Lord for your wicked, insensate taunts to one who has never done you a moment of harm, and who has only asked to be left alone!

    (*silence*)

(*almost inaudibly*) Ranuccio . . .

   Ranuccio (*after another pause*) Vincenzo has asked for your hand in marriage, Margherita. I vow before the Cross that I am not jesting or lying. Forgive me my sins in the past, Margherita: let me speak now as Duke of Parma and your own true brother. I have always hated the man you married. He has always hated me. He has even conspired against me in the last twelve months. His underlings have confessed to that. But, for whatever reason, he has, in dignified and serious terms, sent to ask me if I would favour his approach to the Pope in this matter, in the hope that His Holiness would release you from your vows. I ask you to think long and seriously about this, Margherita. You are now too old for the former insults against you to be uttered. Your remarriage would perhaps end more than half a century of strife between Mantua and Parma. I can refuse Gonzaga's offer of my own accord, if I wish. And had I decided to do so, I would not be visiting you today. But it is in your authority, dear sister, to accept him or to reject him. You will have to consult your conscience and your heart, and to pray for guidance in this matter. I will only repeat: he has asked for your hand in marriage. I hope you will not long delay an answer.

    (*pause: change of acoustic. Bell*)

Margherita Oh, God, my Father in heaven, bless with Thy blessing my answer, for I know, now, oh Lord, what it will be; and let it not be base nor vile nor selfish in Thy sight. Thou knowest, oh Lord, how for thirty years I have lived within these walls, and that the wickedness of my will was slow to yield to Thy love and mercy. Thou seest also into the heart of him I loved, and was removed from, in the places of the worldly; and knowest that it was from the memory of his love and goodness to me in the world of men that I had my first glimpse of the love and goodness of Heaven.

And now that, after thirty years, Thou returnest us unto each other, oh Lord, let me prove worthy. Let not his glory dazzle me in an earthly way, but let all things be according to Thy will, and teach me to know Thy will, as surely as I know the reaches of Thy tenderness and love. (*with increasing ardour*) Oh Lord, those thirty years seem now but a moment of darkness with which Thou hast briefly shuttered my eyes. I shall open my eyes, oh God, and I shall see again the dear skies and the suns of my childhood. I shall feel upon my face Thy blessed rain again, and walk among Thy fields and gentle streams, shall relish again the sweet wind blowing the scent of rose and carnation into the hall. I shall press once more Thy winged birds to my cheek, and feel once more the sleek dogs' heads under my hand. I thank Thee, oh God, that Thou hast proved and pitied me, and returned to my heart in all its fullness and glory a love I thought I had forgotten. Oh God, bless my answer, for I know now what it will be. Amen.

(*pause: chanting again in distance*)

A nun (*gently*) Sister Maura.

Margherita (*affectionately*) God bless you, Sister Caterina.

Nun Good morning, Sister Maura, but we are all gravely concerned at your fasting and praying for so long in this cold weather.

Margherita Forgive me in turn for distressing you, dear Sister. I have come to no harm. It was an important prayer. I had to wait until God answered it.

Nun And you feel sure that He has answered it?

Margherita Yes, Sister. It is a happy answer. Oh, Sister Caterina, I have learned in these few nights and days of prayer more of the love of God than I have known in the whole of my life before. I seem to have seen God smiling.

Nun Sister Maura, I . . .

Margherita Sister Caterina, I have something to tell you. A thing at once sad and happy. I shall not be with you very much longer. If the Pope sees it as right, I am to leave you and to return to the world. Will you remember me in your prayers, as I shall . . .

Ranuccio (*from the door*) Margherita.

(*both sisters turn with a surprised murmur*)

Margherita (*with delight*) Ranuccio! Ah, dear brother, how glad I . . . (*she breaks off*)

Ranuccio (*clearly distressed*) Margherita. My dear, dear Margherita, I have

334

very difficult and painful news to break to you. May I speak to you alone?

Margherita (*frightened*) No. No. Sister Caterina must stay with us. (*breathless*) Ranuccio. (*pause*) Ranuccio! Say it. Tell me.

Ranuccio (*with difficulty*) This morning ... a messenger brought the ... painful news ...

Margherita (*whisper*) Ranuccio!

Ranuccio ... that Vincenzo Duke of Mantua ... died peacefully yesterday afternoon.

(*pause*)

Margherita No ... No ...

Ranuccio Margherita.

(*pause*)

Margherita (*whispers*) Hold me. Sister Caterina, hold me, don't let me fall.

Ranuccio Margherita, my ...

Margherita (*sharply*) No. Don't touch me, Ranuccio! Go away. (*whispers*) Go away.

Nun Sister Maura, let us ...

Margherita (*whispers*) Go away, Ranuccio.

Ranuccio I cannot say anything, Margherita.

Margherita (*with a low terrible insistence*) No ... No ...

Ranuccio I won't go away, Margherita. I will be here, outside the door. (*in tears*) God bless you, my dear one.

Margherita No ...

Nun (*pleading*) Sister, beloved ... Sister Maura ...

Margherita No ... No ... (*slowly, almost a whisper*) Sister Caterina. Hold me. I mustn't fall to the ground, must I? Hold me. (*almost inaudibly*) Thank you. Hold me ... (*her voice breaks with tears*) Love. (*pause*) Love ... (*wailing to herself*) Oh, love me, love me, love me, someone *please* love me, love me! Sister Caterina, love me a little, love me ... (*for a moment she cannot speak: then she wails*) ... lest for a moment I find the love of God prove not enough.